TEACHING
ENGLISH
BY DESIGN

PETER SMAGORINSKY

Second Edition

TEACHING ENGLISH BY DESIGN

How to Create and Carry Out
Instructional Units

Foreword by **Leila Christenbury**

HEINEMANN
Portsmouth, NH

Heinemann
145 Maplewood Ave., Suite 300
Portsmouth, NH 03801
www.heinemann.com

Offices and agents throughout the world

The author and publisher wish to thank those who have generously given permission to reprint borrowed material:

Excerpt from the Common Core State Standards. Copyright © 2010 by the National Governors Association Center for Best Practices and Council of Chief State School Officers. All rights reserved.

Library of Congress Cataloging-in-Publication Data
Name: Smagorinsky, Peter, author.
Title: Teaching English by design : how to create and carry out instructional
    units / Peter Smagorinsky.
Description: Second edition. | Portsmouth, New Hampshire : Heinemann, [2018]
    | First edition published: 2008. | Includes bibliographical references and
    index.
Identifiers: LCCN 2018023074 | ISBN 9780325108070
Subjects: LCSH: English language—Study and teaching (Secondary)—United
    States. | Lesson planning—United States. | Language arts—United States.
Classification: LCC LB1631 .S53 2018 | DDC 428.0071/2—dc23
LC record available at https://lccn.loc.gov/2018023074

Acquisitions Editor: Holly Kim Price
Production Editor: Sean Moreau
Cover and Interior Designer: Monica Ann Crigler
Typesetter: Valerie Levy, Drawing Board Studios
Manufacturing: Steve Bernier

Printed in the United States of America on acid-free paper
4 5 6 7   PAH   25 24 23
March 2023 Printing / PO 4500869231

Dedicated to those who've completed doctorates under my advisement, and who've taught me much about teaching: Deborah Brown, Pam Fly, Melissa Whiting, Patty Reed, Lynda Thompson, John Coppock, and Cindy O'Donnell-Allen from The University of Oklahoma; and Leslie Susan Cook, Steve Bickmore, Tara Star Johnson, Maria Winfield, Michelle Zoss, Elizabeth Daigle, Lindy Johnson, Chris Clayton, Stephanie Shelton, Meghan Barnes, Deavours Hall, Xiaodi Zhou, Joanna Anglin, and Darren Rhym from the University of Georgia.

CONTENTS

Darren Rhym is a high school English teacher in Greensboro, Georgia, and an adjunct instructor at the University of Georgia. He holds a Ph.D. in language and literacy education from the University of Georgia and has taught in several high schools along with Morehouse College and the University of North Georgia. Originally from Trenton, New Jersey, Darren earned degrees at Bucknell and Penn State before completing his doctorate under the advisement of Peter Smagorinsky.

FOREWORD   LEILA CHRISTENBURY

Will this unit solve all the world's problems? Hardly. But it will tie the curriculum to students' interests, give them tools to challenge inequity, and provide them with possible avenues for social action that they may not have seen as possible for them. From what we can tell, that's a lot more than they are getting out of school as presently conducted, and that's reason enough to give it a try.

—Chapter 15, *Teaching English by Design*

The vision of what a well-crafted unit can accomplish is a vision that is no less than the instructional gold standard. Like my friend and colleague Peter Smagorinsky, I believe that such units may well provide "a lot more than [what students] are getting out of school as presently conducted," a conclusion that is largely confirmed by my own recent observations of almost 120 English classrooms. Over three semesters of visits to both public middle and high schools, I saw English teachers who, when allowed to move away from the pacing guide and the scripted curriculum, could create and enact exciting, inventive, and authentic instruction that motivated students and inspired learning. When teachers were not so empowered, I saw little intellectual excitement, little creative thinking, and a whole lot of apathetic student—and teacher—compliance.

This is not where we want our twenty-first-century classrooms to be, and this second edition of *Teaching English by Design* shows the way to invigorating instruction and using, rather than stifling, the knowledge and creativity of our teachers.

When over a decade ago I had the good fortune to write the foreword to the first edition of this book, I concentrated on the role of the teacher and how *Teaching English by Design* made such a compelling case for unleashing the expertise of classroom instructors. At the time, the primacy of the classroom teacher, a factor that is most often ignored in educational research and in subsequent policy decisions, was on a national roll of sorts. Great teachers were being lauded and highlighted as the *most important factor* in student learning. What welcome news and how overdue! This recognition of the role of teachers thus seemed like an advance in our thinking, but as I noted in my foreword, it was quickly twisted to buttress the false assertion that an accomplished teacher could personally overcome any and all barriers to student learning. These barriers included, but were not limited to, student and family poverty and its concomitant stresses, inadequate student nutrition, community instability, insufficient school funding, and outdated or nonexistent classroom supplies.

But not to worry: The message of the times was that a great teacher remains undaunted and conquers such limitations. Let those teachers create fine instruction, and all will be well.

Obviously, all did not turn out well.

This unrealistic assessment of the influence of great instructors and of the power of their skills meant that most of the burden of student learning rested on individual teachers' shoulders, and therefore if there were blame to be apportioned regarding the extent and persistence of student learning and achievement (and in American education, isn't there always blame to be apportioned?), the fault lay with the teachers. Surely this rhetorical move absolved communities and their governments from repairing decrepit schools, ordering new laptops, and even assessing the safety and health of neighborhoods and factoring in their effect on student achievement. All of these societal ills were tangential: The teacher was all.

Now we are in a different political climate, and the heroic, all-conquering teacher is no longer the omnipresent meme.

But the message—and the centrality—of *Teaching English by Design* remains. Updated and highly contextual, this second edition adds to our understanding of targeted instructional expertise and how it enhances student learning and provides classroom work that is truly crafted "with students in mind." As so clearly articulated in the excerpt from Chapter 15 at the beginning of this foreword, teacher-created conceptual units—not scripted instruction or mandated curricula—can give students tools and avenues, approaches to issues of importance. No, the teacher is not the sole factor in student learning, but the teacher creation of instruction that is student-centered and student-oriented is a crucial component to student success and student achievement.

As I noted some years ago and is still true today, *Teaching English by Design* is a book with big ideas and bigger ambitions. This second edition once again honors the intelligence of students and the creativity and professionalism of teachers. The latter cannot conquer all, but given the freedom to enact rigorous instruction and innovative curricula, our students' learning—and their true intellectual engagement—is greatly enhanced.

Leila Christenbury is Commonwealth Professor Emerita at Virginia Commonwealth University, Richmond. She is a coeditor of Handbook on Adolescent Literacy Research *with Peter Smagorinsky and Randy Bomer, and a winner of the National Reading Conference Edward B. Fry Book Award.*

PREFACE

In this book I outline a way to plan a *conceptual unit of instruction*: a period of classroom time that you devote to a particular topic. Some possible categories for conceptual units are a *theme*, such as progress or coming of age; an *archetype* or culturally recurring character type or situation, such as the trickster or the journey; an *author*, such as Toni Morrison or Shakespeare; a *literary period*, such as the Harlem Renaissance or British Restoration; a *movement*, such as transcendentalism or postcolonialism; a *region*, such as the British Lake poets or Southern fiction; a *reading strategy*, such as understanding irony or identifying fake news; and a *genre*, such as the detective novel or science fiction.

If you learn how to plan in units, your teaching will have continuity and purpose for students. You will also relieve yourself of the burden of planning day to day. If your classes are well planned and interrelated, you will be able to focus on other aspects of teaching in your daily instruction. If you do not plan ahead, each night will require you to think of something new to do for each class the next day, perhaps till after midnight. Not my idea of a good time. To teach well and to stay healthy, after all, you'll need a good, restful night's sleep.

Central Metaphor

To talk about teaching and learning, I employ the metaphor of *construction*. This construction occurs concurrently at two levels. At the teaching level, you will be a builder of curriculum, of a classroom community, of conceptual units. Building requires tools, materials, plans, and methods of building. Your unit design, then, is described as a process of construction that engages you in purposeful, and at times collaborative, activity.

At the same time, your students will be builders. One of my premises about being a teacher is that *people learn by making, and reflecting on, things that they find useful and important*. Your unit design should involve students in the production of things called *texts* that matter to them. Texts are often written, but they can also be spoken or nonverbal (art, dance, computer-generated image, or spoken word performance, for instance). Like other kinds of builders, your students will work in a social environment where they'll get frequent feedback on their texts as they construct them.

Think of yourself, then, as a builder of curriculum and as one who helps students learn to build their own texts. This approach is known as *constructivist* teaching. As you might know from your experiences, schools are more likely to rely on what is known as *authoritative* teaching. In this approach, the teacher is presumed to be an expert who fills students with knowledge. In asking you to use a constructivist metaphor for teaching, then, I'm asking you to rethink what it means to be a teacher.

Constructivism is a theory; actually, there's more than one version, and for constructivists, each of us constructs our own version. So life in a constructivist world is very open-ended. The brand of constructivism that I embrace, however, is not strictly individualistic. Rather, it requires attention to the environment in which teaching and learning take place. This environment includes the social history of the school and all of the traditions and rituals provided by that history. A school in which English teachers have historically emphasized the cultural heritage of the West, imparted through the structure of the curriculum and the teachers' lectures and discussions (but mostly lectures), provides a set of routines and expectations that are difficult to teach within if you're working from a constructivist perspective.

Further, externally imposed testing mandates both occupy time and suggest a purpose for education that goes against the grain of a constructivist approach. When a set of practices and traditions collude to support authoritarian teaching, the constructivist teacher may take on a fairly lonely project within the confines of the school. Yet I believe that a constructivist approach provides opportunities for students to experience school far more richly than the conventional approach of sitting in class after class, listening to teachers talk, and then getting tested on what the teacher has said. Thoreau wrote in *Civil Disobedience* that "any man more right than his neighbors constitutes a majority of one already." While it is no doubt arrogant to assume that adopting one educational approach over another makes people "more right" than their colleagues, regardless of gender, I agree with Thoreau that there is honor in persisting if you believe that what you are doing is right, no matter how relentlessly others try to make you conform to their version of good and right teaching.

Many people believe that theories, including constructivism, have little to do with the classroom and its gritty realities. Applebee quotes one teacher who, when asked about contemporary literary theory, said that theories are "far removed from those of us who work the front lines!" (1993, 122). Yet I suspect that this teacher could not effectively work in the trenches or on "the front lines" without some theory of what she was doing. Regardless of which metaphor you use to characterize your classroom work (war, gardening, assembly-line production, incarceration, etc.), you have a set of beliefs about what you're working toward, how you should get there, which materials best enable a good trip, and so on. Indeed, the teacher quoted by Applebee conveys many of her beliefs about teaching simply by declaring that she's on the front line, presumably in a war against her students.

What I think that this teacher, and many others, reject is the way theory is presented. Typically, theorists present their ideas through an array of specialized, polysyllabic terms—*interiorization, heteroptia, interinanimation, phallologocentrism*, and other fine words bandied about in academic journals. These terms require the theorists to explicate extensive sets of formal rules and abstractions. I've done this myself when writing primarily for university researchers and theorists.

Teachers' interests are more pragmatic, and so wading through the technical language and abstract concepts of the theoretical specialist can be daunting and unproductive. As a result, many teachers say that theory is impractical and irrelevant. What I think they're really saying is that impenetrable theorists are impractical and irrelevant, at least to their needs.

In this book I try to present a theoretically grounded approach to teaching without getting bogged down in the task of the theoretician, which is to focus primarily on an elaboration of concepts through technical language. Instead, I present *theory as an extended metaphor*, much as the teacher does in locating herself on the battlefield of instruction. The essence of the theory I use in this book is that *people learn by making, and reflecting on, things that they find useful and important*. They do so through a process of composition in which they develop goals, locate appropriate tools and materials, develop plans, and construct a text. This text is always provisional; that is, it stands as a temporary statement of meaning that will later be revised—if not in this text itself, then in a new text that builds on the old. Throughout this process of composition, they revise their goals and plans to meet arising circumstances, use new tools and materials as needed, reflect on the emerging text, and reconsider how and why they're making it.

This process enables learners to construct new meaning as they work, both through emerging ideas and those that come through reflecting on the text during production. The learners I refer to include both those we call teachers and those we call students, although I think that their roles can merge in dynamic classrooms. While the texts constructed by learners may reach a point of temporary completion, they are part of an ongoing effort to construct meaning and so may serve as points of reflection for the development of new compositions. Texts, then, are occasions for learning through both the process of composition and reflection on the product: both on its provisional form during composition and on its equally provisional form when completed for school assessment.

All of this composing takes place in some kind of social, cultural context. The context of construction has a lot to do with the kinds of compositions and composition processes that are valued and encouraged. The context also includes the way in which you set up your classroom. If you place the seats in rows facing you at the front, you discourage the use of speech as a tool for exchanging and constructing ideas *among students*. If you allow for multimedia composing, then you open up students' tool kits for constructing meaningful texts.

An act or a text is never meaningful in and of itself. Rather, it takes on meaning through the validating effect of the environment. If a teacher values only five-paragraph themes and a student submits a statue to interpret a novel, then the statue will have no significance or worth in this context, regardless of what the student has learned or how the statue might be appreciated in another context.

For the construction metaphor to be useful, you need to get fulfillment from doing work. What I've outlined in this book will require a lot of work from you. You can't go on cruise control and let the teacher's manual or the curriculum do all of the thinking and teaching for you. Rather, you need to view instructional design as stimulating, intellectually challenging, important work that can potentially put you in the sort of "flow" described by Csikszentmihalyi (1990)—that is, an experience so engrossing that you lose track of time. You need to get satisfaction out of putting a lot of effort into something with the understanding that it will probably result in a provisional product that you'll need to revise—no yellowed lecture notes for you to trot out year after year. You need to enjoy the challenge of aligning goals and practices, of devising activities that students will find engaging and enlightening, of channeling your creativity into the production of the text that will serve as your unit of instruction.

You also need to be prepared to do work in response to what your students produce. Responding to students' papers takes a lot of time. But it's unlikely that students will learn to write unless they're writing, and it's unlikely that they'll grow as writers without your earnest response to their papers. There will be times when grading a volume of student writing (or other composing) will be a grind. But the overall satisfaction that you get from participating in your students' growth should overcome whatever time commitment is involved in evaluating their work.

You also need to be prepared to do work alongside your students. You might undertake a project of the same type that they are doing: writing with them during a writing workshop, keeping a portfolio about your teaching as they keep one about their learning, and otherwise learning in parallel with their learning. You might do a project to understand better how they are learning: studying the effects of your instruction, charting the development of relationships that follow from a change in your teaching, or otherwise systematically reflecting on your teaching. Sometimes it means trying to learn more about your students' lives outside school so that you can teach them in ways that build on their strengths.

Becoming an actively reflective practitioner will require an inquiring stance and the time that it takes to enact it. But doing so can make your work as a teacher much more stimulating than it would be if you were to simply pass around the handouts that accompany your commercial literature anthology and grade them with an electronic scanner, year after year, with the same emphasis and information taught and tested, regardless of how much the students themselves and the world that surrounds them have changed.

Your students also need to have some kind of work ethic. I think that most students do, but that much school instruction dulls it, at least with regard to schoolwork. I had a sobering experience about halfway through my fourteen years of teaching high school English. I was talking with a guidance counselor about one of my students and lamented that the student just didn't care about school because he wasn't responding well to my teaching. The counselor paused and then said, "You know, I've been a counselor here for twenty years, and I don't think I've ever worked with a student who doesn't care. *They all care.* Often, they're just fearful and don't do their assignments because they're afraid to fail at them."

This chance discussion provided me with one of the most important lessons I've learned about students' motivation. I had always taken an individualistic view of motivation: It's something that individuals have that propels them to success. The conversation with this counselor led me to take a more sympathetic view of young people and their motivations. First, I learned that young people's motivations are often intertwined with their adolescent angst and insecurity, often in ways that make them appear unmotivated to adults, including teachers. Second, I began to think about what my students might be motivated to do and to wonder if I were building their goals for learning into my teaching. Might the problem be with the context I was constructing and not with a lack of purpose in their lives?

Finally, I began to develop a much more social perspective on motivation, one in which the environment helps to provide motivating features. In doing so I was not relieving the students of personal responsibility or trying to inflate their self-esteem. Rather, I began to take some responsibility for setting up my classroom so that their motivations could be realized more easily, and for providing activities and goals that my students would be more likely to expend their motivations on. I found that when I involved my students in constructive, productive activity, they would work pretty hard and feel pretty good about what they produced. Of course, this engagement doesn't happen with everything you do. Some things you teach in the English curriculum are not going to light a fire under every student. But you can make an effort to teach so that it happens as often as possible.

My notion of work is not of the nose-to-the-grindstone variety, although there are times when that's what you need to do. Rather, it refers to the labor of love, the transforming potential of authentic, constructive, productive activity. I think that all great teachers love what they do and do it with passion. They follow the adage that you should "choose a job you love, and you will never have to work a day in your life." If they stay up till two in the morning, it's not because they don't know what to do the next day; it's because they're so involved with their work that they lose track of time. When you teach with this kind of engagement and passion, your students will know, and they will show their appreciation and respect in ways that surpass just about any sort of fulfillment that I can imagine.

ACKNOWLEDGMENTS

The impetus for this second edition of *Teaching English by Design* came when Connor Warner of the University of Missouri–Kansas City bumped into me at the NCTE convention in 2015 and said that his university was pressuring him to use more recent titles for their book adoptions. My 2008 publication date was looking a bit hoary to his administration, he said. (I don't think he said *hoary*.) I liked the idea of a new edition and asked Heinemann if they'd be interested, which they said was possible if I proposed something worthwhile.

I crowdsourced the field for suggestions on how to update and improve the book. Thanks to the following colleagues who provided feedback and helped to shape this revision: JuliAnna Avila, Christina Berchini, Megan Bonds, Bethany Corbett, Ashraf Elinbabi, Mary Hamner, Alexis James, Lindy Johnson, Monica Johnson, Tom McCann, Joseph Rodríguez, Shelbie Witte, and Bill Zimmerman. I'm sure that many, many others have influenced my thinking over time (the first edition had a couple of pages' worth of thanks), and I regret that I can't list everyone without burdening the reader with the cost of additional pages.

Later in the crowdsourcing process, a whole lot of people chimed in when I asked how I should organize certain parts of the book, and I appreciate everyone who contacted me with suggestions. Thanks as well to Mollie Blackburn and Adam Crawley for their help in shaping the section in Chapter 1 on LGBTQ+ issues in teaching. Tom McCann suggested that I include attention to performance assessments, which I've done in spite of protests from others who felt I was promoting them by attending to them, in spite of the imperatives they present to preservice teachers. I could not follow everyone's advice when it was contradictory, so hope I've found a happy medium with this revision, and others.

JuliAnna Avila and her students at UNC–Charlotte were especially helpful in recommending that I include a chapter on using these unit design principles in high-poverty schools. I enlisted the help of my friend, colleague, and (now former) doctoral student Darren Rhym, who is credited as coauthor of the new chapter (Chapter 15), and who helped me find resources for Chapter 14, which introduces the special circumstances of teaching where both the families and the schools have very little money. We coauthored the instruction with his wife and fellow teacher Melissa Perez Rhym's guidance. I think that this chapter helps to expand the possibilities for teaching through conceptual unit design to schools where students often have more on their minds than distinguishing present participles from gerunds.

Finally, thanks to Heinemann for allowing me the opportunity to update this book, to the people who've bought and assigned the book enough to merit a new edition, to those who encouraged its revision, to Sue Paro for ushering it through the approval process, and to Holly Kim Price and Sean Moreau, along with Pam Hunt and Val Levy, for helping to bring home the final version.

ABOUT THIS BOOK

Hello! And thanks for buying this book. I know how much these things cost. I hope that by the time you're done reading and thinking about teaching English by design, you'll feel that it was a few dollars well spent. You will probably want to run straight to your computer and bookmark a couple of web pages. First, there's the Virtual Library of Conceptual Units, located at http://www.petersmagorinsky.net/Units/index.html. This resource provides you with examples of the kinds of units I'm trying to teach you how to design in this book. Most of them are pretty good, and the best ones to use as models are the ones listed in red. You are welcome to use any ideas from these units in your teaching. Together, they provide a cornucopia of units and lessons within units that should make your teaching a lot more satisfying than it would be if you were simply to teach from the recipe provided in your anthology's teacher's manual.

A second web page to bookmark is the Outlines for Conceptual Units at http://www.petersmagorinsky.net/Units/Unit_Outlines.htm. This page will help you sketch out units on many, many topics. Many were road-tested in my own Illinois classrooms back in the day; others are still under development and awaiting your attention.

I wrote this book to help you learn how to design units of the sort you'll find in the Virtual Library. Designing a unit for the first time will be one of the most challenging things you've ever done. It's different from writing papers for English classes or other university courses. Designing a unit requires you to take into account a lot of things you might never have thought deeply about but that are essential to producing a unit that you and your students will experience in a positive way. You will need to consider who adolescents are generally, and what they can benefit from learning at the age at which you teach them. You'll also need to think about who the specific adolescents in each of your classes are: how they learn, which versions of English (if any) they speak, what their backgrounds are, and many other factors that are essential to understand in teaching and learning relationships.

You need to think about why you are teaching your particular unit topic and be able to defend that decision to your colleagues, your administrators, your students, your students' parents, and anybody else who takes an interest in your teaching. You need to identify a set of materials—literature, other writing, film, music, Internet resources—and decide how appropriate they are for your teaching situation. You need to identify how you'll assess your students and judge their performance so that you can distinguish between one grade and another when assigning grades to their work.

But that's the easy part. When learning to design units of instruction, most people struggle with teaching students how to do the tasks they are asking of them and designing lessons within the unit that lay out clear guidelines for students through the learning process. You may have never done anything like this before, and it can be daunting. I always have some students who find the task so overwhelming that they think that they'll never be able to complete a unit, but as the Virtual Library shows, almost all of them have.

I should confess that the first time I wrote a unit in my master's degree methods class with George Hillocks, from whom I learned these principles, I got a B– on it. But I stuck with it and eventually got the hang of it. So when you experience frustration, join the club; I ask you to accept it as part of the process of learning something new and difficult. Think of how your own students will struggle when you are trying to teach them a new task. You may be familiar with it, but they probably won't be. Work to understand their struggles as they go through the process, and support their learning by designing lessons that gradually move them into new competencies. I hope that this book provides just such a scaffold for you as you develop your skills as an instructional designer.

Performance Assessment in Teacher Education

I was urged in my crowdsourcing to give attention to the "performance assessments" that teacher candidates in university programs must now fulfill during their studies. Although I'm not a fan of these assessments, I recognized that realistically, addressing them in a book on how to teach lies somewhere between important and necessary, because these evaluation systems are required just about everywhere for certification.

But then I had another problem: Where do I put it? Because performance assessments—big, portfolio-like presentations of teaching knowledge and enactment—require continual attention, putting this chapter up front and then referring back to it seemed logical. But the idea of starting the book with a long chapter on performance assessment was met with resistance from my respondents, generally falling into two categories:

1. The book is about how to teach, not how to pass a performance assessment. Opening with a long chapter on how to satisfy assessment requirements would be an unpleasant labor for those wanting to know about teaching more than about getting assessed.

2. A whole lot of people, including teacher educators, really don't like these assessments, and giving them the book's most powerful rhetorical position—going first—would suggest an endorsement of these assessments and a belief in their primacy in teacher education.

Both concerns made good sense to me. But putting the chapter last would mean that you would learn about them at the end of the process, limiting the opportunity to produce the materials as you worked. And the last position in the book also provides rhetorical clout. My resolution was to provide a brief introduction to performance assessment at the beginning and then refer back to it throughout the book. A much longer, detailed, and critical look appears at the end if you want to know more about how they work, what they work for, and what difficulties may be encountered.

In the remainder of this preface is a general outline of what these assessments involve, without getting too elaborate. If you want to read out of order, you're welcome to jump to the end to see why these assessments are problematic, what they are really measuring, and how strategic you can be in preparing your dossier. My plan is to provide a fairly skeletal version here of what you'll be obligated to prepare in a typical assessment, refer back to it during the chapters where you'll learn how to design units, and then provide the more critical chapter to conclude.

I'll leave it up to you to decide how valuable the performance assessment process is, and whether my presentation makes sense in your classroom. The one inescapable fact about performance assessment is that if you're reading this book in a university certification program, you'll probably have to go through one of them, which means I've got to deal with it here. If you're reading this book at the beach or other pleasure venue, then as we say in the South, Bless your heart.[1] You're excused from paying attention to this part of the book.

Assessment *categories* tend to emphasize three areas: *instructional planning, instruction,* and *assessment.* This book is principally about the first area, although I

---

1. This phrase can mean many things. Here, I'm using one of the nice ones.

assume that it's difficult to plan well without knowing in advance what you'll assess, so where appropriate, I've included both. Documenting your actual teaching is a separate task that I'll entrust to your instructors in relation to the specific tasks of your state performance assessment.

This introduction is designed to acquaint you with what lies ahead, rather than to explain it in excruciating detail, which I save for the end. Part of the problem with a general book of this sort is that different U.S. states require different assessments. You might be using edTPA, which has national ambitions; or your state may have developed a vehicle of its own. As is always the case in teaching and learning, you'll need to adapt what I present to your own situations, so don't expect this book to speak directly to your personal circumstances at all times and in all ways.

But now, let's get down to what we're really here for: learning how to plan instruction and run classrooms that help advance your students toward greater understanding of themselves and others, enabling them to learn strategies for reading and producing texts in a classroom setting, and providing ways for them to connect their work in the classroom to the social worlds that matter to them.

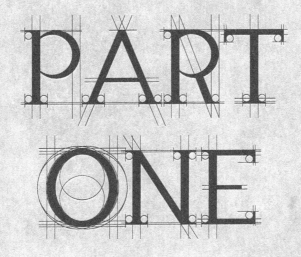

PART ONE

Teaching with Students in Mind

Students' Ways of Knowing

Something happened when I was teaching high school that I'll never forget, although to the other people involved it seemed to be a routine, passing moment that was entirely unremarkable. I was standing in the hallway between classes, talking to the English teacher who taught next door. We engaged in the typical brief banter that teachers exchange amid the currents of students going to class, talking, laughing, rummaging through their lockers, and catching their breath before the next class begins. Another English teacher walked by and, seeing my colleague, called across the clamor, "Hey, I'm just finishing up *Death of a Salesman*, and somebody told me that you have a really great test to use with it. Could you lend me a copy?"

"Sure!" she answered across the hallway's hustle and bustle, and then as the passing period came to an end, we scattered along with the students to start the next class.

The incident seemed so casual that I'm sure neither of the teachers thought anything odd about it at all. To me, though, the idea of teaching something for several weeks and then using an assessment developed by another teacher for other students is fundamentally at odds with everything I understand about evaluation. Testing students in this way involves the assumption that there is such thing as a good test that any students can take to demonstrate how well they've understood a work of literature. This belief in turn carries more assumptions:

✦ The text itself stands as a concrete work whose meaning is stable across readers and groups of readers, sometimes called its *official meaning*.

+ Anyone teaching the text will inevitably emphasize the official meaning.

+ The test itself stands as an objective measure of students' understanding of the official, invariant meaning.

+ Whatever knowledge students construct from the literature beyond the official interpretation is irrelevant in terms of their grade on the assessment.

+ It's fine to teach without any sense of how one will assess the students at the end.

+ Instruction is about the texts, which have a particular meaning, which can ultimately be assessed by an exam designed by someone who has never seen any of the teaching or learning.

+ Assessment does not necessarily need to be related to the unique exchanges that take place among particular groups of students and teachers when discussing texts or unit concepts.

Perhaps the utter casualness of the exchange I witnessed, its very mundane character, is what made it so striking to me. The assumptions behind it were so deeply embedded in my colleagues' conception of teaching that the loan of the exam could be uncritically secured through a chance meeting in the hallway. And so the test moved from one file cabinet to another, perhaps still being administered to this day, the meaning of the play remaining stable no matter who teaches the class or who enrolls in it.

My account of this exchange undoubtedly seems harsh. You might be surprised to learn that I liked both of these teachers a great deal and that both had extremely good reputations around the school. And perhaps that's what makes it all so remarkable: that two highly regarded teachers in a high school with a national reputation would view assessment in what struck me as a thoughtless and cavalier manner.

I tell this story to open this chapter because my focus here is on what students know and what teachers grade. Schools tend to have a well-established conception of what counts as knowledge. You will recognize this conception when I describe it, for you have undoubtedly been assessed according to it in most classes you have taken throughout your education.

I don't want to suggest that the dominant values of school are always off the mark or unimportant, even if in significant ways they often are. I do, however, hope to persuade you that you should also assess other ways that students have of knowing things. To do so, I review other ways that people can come to know something. You will probably recognize these other ways, too, although you may be less familiar with their role in formal education.

By designing assessments that take these other types of knowledge into account, you will be teaching in ways responsive to the range of diversity that your students bring to class. In some cases people's ways of knowing are inborn; some of us are genetically endowed with the capacity to configure space much better than others, although the rest of us can surely learn how to configure space better with the right strategies and knowledge. In some cases our ways of knowing come from our culture; some cultures promote collaboration whereas others promote competition, with competitive cultures governing how schools operate. In some cases the source of difference is not so clear; most people agree that heterosexual men and women tend to see the world differently, although it's never been firmly established whether they are born different or are socialized into different ways of knowing, or whether both factors combine to produce gender differences.

Regardless of the source of difference, your students will most likely exhibit quite a broad range of capacities. Throughout much of their schooling, these diverse students will be forced to fit the Procrustean bed of conventional assumptions about knowledge and assessment. Procrustes was an Attican thief who laid his victims on his iron bed. If a victim was shorter than the bed, he stretched the body to fit; if the victim was too long, he cut off the legs to make the body fit. In either case the victim died. Assessments can be deadly for students, too, when the same evaluation is viewed as a universal fit for all students, no matter what shape they are in relative to the test. If you instead allow for flexibility in the ways in which students can express themselves and come to know the discipline of English, you'll be assessing students on their own terms and through vehicles that suit their strengths. That sounds fair to me, unless the point is to create castes of winners and losers through your grading practices.

In school there are relatively few ways in which knowledge is assessed. Let's take something relatively simple—a bicycle—and see how you might know it.

- ✦ You might have memorized its different parts and be able to answer questions about these components.

- ✦ You might know how, from experience and perhaps some instruction, to ride the bicycle across a variety of terrains.

- ✦ You might associate the bicycle with your dear grandparent who bought it for you and fixed it when it broke, therefore knowing it through sentiment and love.

- ✦ You might know the history of bicycles and this particular type of bicycle's place in that history.

+ You may know the rhythms generated by riding it at different speeds and know its potential for producing percussive sounds, especially if you clip cards so that they strike the rotating spokes.

+ You may have had significant experiences while riding it and view those stories as central to your identity.

There are undoubtedly many other ways in which you could know a bicycle. If you were to study the bicycle in school, however, it's likely that you would be tested on your knowledge by your ability to identify its parts and their correct functions. It wouldn't matter much if you could actually ride a bicycle. You might know how to shift gears appropriately to ride the bike up particular inclines, but if you forgot the names of gear mechanisms you were asked to identify, you would be deemed unknowledgeable about bicycles.

I ask you to open your mind with regard to thinking about what it means to know something. This consideration should take into account a couple key points:

+ Achievement is a function of what you measure. Students are judged to be good or bad, knowledgeable or unknowledgeable, A students or D students, according to some means and focus of measurement. Far too often, those measurements are restricted to students' memory of official and/or factual knowledge. Any other knowledge they have, particularly when it departs from what has traditionally been considered "academic," is not considered noteworthy when their achievement is measured through a school assessment.

+ What you test is what you get. Assessment tends to set the terms for what teachers emphasize in instruction. And so when students will be assessed according to their memory of official knowledge, classes will likely be conducted to impress that knowledge on them, through lectures that impart the information or reinforce facts from the reading.

You must consider many factors when developing appropriate assessments. I present these factors in binary fashion; that is, I discuss each by outlining oppositional perspectives on it. I should caution that I often find binaries to be problematic because they involve a false dichotomy that masks everything in between. I use them more to outline firm positions on each topic that shed light on how schools work. Rather than viewing them as bipolar opposites with nothing between them, I see them as points on a continuum, with many possibilities between and outside the boundaries of their differences, even as they tend to set the terms for how schools operate.

Two Theories of Communication: Transmission and Constructivism

Two theories of communication, *transmission* and *constructivism*, will provide a vocabulary for further discussions of assessment. The argument I make here is not new, yet the problem I discuss is remarkably persistent. The most pervasive assumption about knowledge in schools is the *transmission* view, which conceives of knowledge and communication in superficial ways, while the relatively rich *constructivist* assumptions rarely influence curriculum, instruction, and assessment. This preference for the hard-and-fast over·the uncertain follows from the broader school need to sort and rank students into categories of "achievement." School is often a place for winners and losers. If everyone wins because each student solves problems uniquely, then the teacher must not be hard enough. Or so they say.

Transmission

As a student, you may have felt at times that what you knew was not measured by a school assessment. I still remember a college course I took in classical civilizations where, after reading all sorts of interesting history and literature from early Mediterranean culture and having a reasonable understanding of how these civilizations shaped subsequent history, I found a question on the final exam asking me to identify a classical figure named Bucephalus. Perhaps you don't recognize this character—I didn't while taking the test, and got the item wrong. Yet the professor believed that identifying Bucephalus was so significant that it should serve as a measure of my knowledge of classical history.

Bucephalus, it turned out, was Alexander the Great's horse. Fortunately we were not asked to identify his cat, or I might still be in college.[1]

Such, however, is the way that knowledge in school has typically been conceived and measured: Instead of focusing on important concepts, it fixates on labeling their parts, and sometimes it seems that the more obscure, the better. Another example: Not long ago, the certification exam for English teachers in one state asked candidates to identify the name of the frog in Mark Twain's "Celebrated Jumping Frog of Calaveras County." In case you've forgotten, it's Dan'l Webster. I suspect that if you taught the story, you could pick that up from the narration. In the isolated context of an exam, however, you might space out and be deemed an ignoramus.

---

1. My cat is named El Gato. There will be a quiz at the end.

When test makers pose questions of this sort, they assume that knowledge is objective and static, and capable of being handed down intact from one person to another, from text to student, from lecture to notebook and back again to the teacher on a test. When the questions concern the names of horses and frogs, rather than their significance, the test makers appear to believe that any detail will do for testing purposes. Or they might have something in mind that is simply indecipherable, such as when one high-stakes test included this true-or-false test item: "Huck Finn is a good boy."

This view of knowledge has been called the *transmission* view. Knowledge is thought to be a stable entity that can be transmitted like a baseball, thrown from one person to another, arriving in the same condition in which it began. And thus a teacher can say in a lecture that in Emily Dickinson's "A Narrow Fellow in the Grass," the narrow fellow is a snake, and students can write this fact down. Later, the students can prove they are knowledgeable readers by affirming the serpentine nature of the narrow fellow on a test. Woe unto the student who has constructed the narrow fellow as something else and has the poor judgment to say so on the official assessment.

Schools in general are conducted to support a transmission view of knowledge, because they tend to follow a top-down model of authority. Administrators make decisions that teachers put into practice. Teachers, though they usually lack schoolwide authority, are the authorities in their classrooms and so transmit their knowledge of facts to students. Students have the option of doing school in ways that lead to success or resisting those ways and being labeled as troublemakers or bad students, or even students of bad character.

To be a success, students show that they have mastered the knowledge that their teachers have provided for them, no matter how useful they find that knowledge or whether they even believe it. Indeed, Loewen (1995) argues that school textbooks frequently suppress historical facts in order to promote a sanitized, grand narrative of American history. It's also quite common for one commercial textbook to present facts that are different from the facts provided in another. The students' job is to memorize the particular version of history presented in the textbook they study— even though this version might be contradicted in a different textbook and be viewed with skepticism by many historians—and report it correctly on exams. Students have little say in deciding what is good or bad, right or wrong, meaningful or not meaningful. Their role is to show that they've received the information and can throw it back in the same form. Cynics have used such unseemly analogies as regurgitation, or mindless metaphors as parroting, to describe the expectations for students under a transmission pedagogy.

Constructivism

Even though schools are widely operated according to transmission assumptions, there are plenty of ways to know something other than to know it according to its official facts, right or wrong. Another view of knowledge falls under the umbrella term *constructivism*. As the word suggests, this idea refers to the notion that knowledge is built uniquely by each participant rather than received as a stable, unitary article of fact through a transmission. Learners draw on a variety of sources for the knowledge they create.

+ One is their reading of the codes provided by whatever text they are studying. If, for instance, a student reads or writes a science report on the dissection of a frog (not, presumably, Dan'l Webster), the expectation of the genre would suggest that a material frog existed and was duly parsed as described in the report. If, however, the same student were to read Swift's *Gulliver's Travels* and come across talking horses (not Bucephalus), the literary codes would suggest that the animals not be viewed literally. If a student included an account of a talking frog in a lab report for a science class, the teacher would likely assume it was either an unfaithful science report, one unusual frog, or a work of fiction; and would likely assign it a low grade because it did not include the proper codes for science reports.

+ A second source of constructed knowledge is the learner's personal experiences. While reading *Gulliver's Travels*, someone with personal experience in human avarice might imagine greedy people of prior acquaintance. Doing so would infuse the literary characters with a particular and probably idiosyncratic meaning. In contrast, a transmission view would frown on an idiosyncratic reading of literature as a departure from the official meaning and in all likelihood would dismiss the interpretation as irrelevant, unnecessarily personal, or incorrect. These frowns might become even frownier if a student reader infuses a literary scene with emotion, the bane of what transmissionists view as the proper, detached method of reading. The Common Core State Standards, for instance, require students to *read like a detective within the four corners of the text* (Coleman and Pimentel 2012) without the corrupting influence of emotions. That assumption about reading might be common, but it runs counter to how actual people, outside the bounds of educational policy, actually read, making it a very poor "core" upon which to found a curriculum.

✦ A learner's attributions of meaning can also be a function of the social context of reading. If, for instance, a class were reading *Gulliver's Travels* in preparation for the Advanced Placement exam, then the teacher's instruction might focus students' readings on AP values. The AP scoring rubrics would provide the guidelines for learning how to read and think about the novel. In contrast, if adult members of a book club were reading it, the reading might be accompanied by wine and snacks, the conversation might include much laughter, the discussion might digress to consider personal experiences with avaricious people or talking horses, and open emotions such as crying would be viewed as appropriate responses. There would be little attention to how to write a high-scoring essay that would please AP judges and more attention to what the readers did and didn't get from the book. The conversation might include a lot of storytelling, rather than a lot of analysis. Similarly, it would be highly inappropriate to respond to Swift's satire in an AP class by bursting into tears except, perhaps, upon receiving a test score. In both cases, the social context helps to determine appropriate responses.

✦ Finally, the cultural backgrounds of the learners can influence their construction of meaning. Margaret Mitchell's *Gone with the Wind*, for instance, for many years was among the twentieth century's most beloved novels, at least among white readers. Toward the end of the century, however, its depiction of Southern gentility came under criticism because of its unproblematic view of slaves. In both novel and film, the slaves are devotedly subservient and regret the fall of the South. This portrayal was accepted for many years by the novel's and film's devoted admirers. The current climate has fostered more critical views of this depiction of the contented slave. *Gone with the Wind* is now read as racist by readers who view its representation of Southern gentility as a valorization of oppression. Different worldviews can provide the framework for a different kind of meaning.

Any assessment ought to provide the occasion for new learning. It is possible that transmission-oriented assessments can allow for new learning, although most such assessments I've seen do not (my enduring knowledge of Bucephalus' identity notwithstanding). Rather, many assessments of this type reduce some pretty splendid literature to a tedious job of memorizing information that's forgotten before long. Most taxonomies of cognition place simple memorization fairly low on the hierarchy and rank inference and generating new knowledge fairly high. Yet school assessment concentrates on rote memorization and location of facts, even in the decidedly ambiguous and symbolic world of literature.

Two Views of Speech and Writing: Final Draft and Exploratory

Related to the transmission and constructivist views of communication are Barnes' (1992) descriptions of the two kinds of classroom speech.

1. *Final-draft* speech, which often occurs in conjunction with transmission pedagogies
2. *Exploratory* speech, which can serve to achieve constructivist ends

Final-Draft Speech

In his studies of classroom interactions, Barnes found that assumptions about knowledge affect the ways in which students speak and write in school. Most readers of this book will understand Barnes' metaphor of final-draft speech. A final draft is the one in which all of the kinks have been worked out, all of the bad ideas rejected, all of the language smoothed over. It has a certainty about it that reflects an authoritative view of the topic. The product is complete and presented for the teacher's approval, although often the teacher does most of the talking in classrooms where the value is on final-draft speech.

Barnes argues that in too many classrooms, discussions are conducted so that only final-draft speech is rewarded. That is, students are encouraged to participate only when they have arrived at a fairly well-thought-out idea that they can present to the teacher for approval. Under these circumstances, a lot of students don't say much at all because they are thinking through their ideas and never quite reach that finalized state where their thoughts can be offered for the teacher to approve. By the time they've articulated their thoughts in their head, the discussion has moved along, and the contribution is no longer relevant. Rather, the teacher—who has often taught the book or the class a number of times and can provide an authoritative interpretation in reasonably polished form—occupies much of the floor.

This conception of speech is compatible with a transmission view of communication because only finished, authoritative ideas are considered legitimate, and for the most part the teacher is the one who has them. The teacher's role, then, is to provide official knowledge for the students, who demonstrate their expertise by repeating it back as faithfully as possible on assessments.

Exploratory Talk

Barnes argues that classrooms ought to encourage more exploratory talk, in which students—and teachers—think aloud as they work through their ideas. Such talk is tentative, spontaneous, provisional, half-baked, and constructive as students discover what they have to say by voicing their emerging thoughts.

Allowing such talk changes much about classrooms. First of all, it changes the purpose of discussion from transmitting official knowledge to constructing new knowledge. This shift in turn alters the dynamics of discussions. The teacher no longer exclusively holds the floor but instead orchestrates students' efforts to realize new ideas through exploratory talk. The contributions of speakers needn't be formal and authoritative but can be partial, playful, and experimental. Because ideas are not being offered as finished products for final approval, the discussion allows its participants to inquire and grope toward meaning. These conditions apply not only to the students but to the teacher as well, who also has the opportunity to realize new thoughts and insights through the process of discussion.

The idea of exploratory talk also extends to writing. Writing is rarely viewed as an opportunity to discover ideas through exploratory, tentative expression. A constructivist approach includes informal opportunities for students to write freely as a way to find what they have to say without concern for submitting the finished product for approval. Used in this way, writing serves as a tool for learning, part of the student's tool kit for constructivist thinking.

This conception of writing and speech contributes to what some have called a *growth model* of education (Dixon 1975). In this view, the emphasis of school is on students as well as, and perhaps more than, on subjects. The purpose of the class then shifts from teaching the subject—lecturing on the Victorians, explaining the significance of literary symbols, and so on—to considering how engagement with a domain will contribute to the personal growth of learners. Such an emphasis relies on language as a tool for exploring ideas and creating new knowledge and is less concerned with the knowledge displays inherent to transmission pedagogies that rely on final-draft speech.

Paradigmatic and Narrative Ways of Knowing

Bruner (1986) has argued that there are primarily two ways of knowing, paradigmatic and narrative. Schools tend to rely on paradigmatic knowledge more than narrative. These ways of knowing are not necessarily tied to transmission and constructivist assumptions about learning. That is, either paradigmatic or narrative knowledge can be constructed or it can rely on presumably transmitted facts. Unfortunately, paradigmatic knowledge is often reduced to knowledge displays for teachers, robbing students of the opportunity to construct new knowledge through analytic thinking. But it needn't be that way.

Paradigmatic Knowledge

Paradigmatic knowledge is the most widely emphasized way of knowing in American schools. It is concerned with rational problem-solving and scientific procedures of investigation involving formal verification and empirical proof. The scientific report is an obvious example of how a paradigmatic approach is used in schools.

English classes, however, also include an emphasis on paradigmatic knowledge. The approach to literary criticism known as New Criticism (not so new anymore—it was introduced in the 1930s) was founded on principles of scientific analysis. New Criticism has become well engrained in American schools and the textbook industry, and is central to how literature is taught and assessed in both AP Literature and the Common Core State Standards. Paradigmatic approaches to literature involve any of the kinds of analytic essays typically required in English classes.

+ *Comparison-contrast* papers, which involve a comparison of one author with another, one period with another, one novel with another, and so on.

+ *Extended-definition* essays, which involve the generation of a set of criteria that define a term and the effort to classify various items according to that definition. Examples might include defining realistic literature and determining if a particular author's work meets the definition, or defining an abstract term such as *progress* and judging various actions or conditions (e.g., the frontier society in Thomas Berger's *Little Big Man*) in terms of the criteria of the definition.

+ *Analytic* essays, which require the analysis of some aspect of a literary work that follows the conventions of argumentation. Such essays usually involve a major thesis, a set of claims (in school, usually three), and supporting evidence for each claim, often adding up to what is known as the five-paragraph theme—one of those school assignments that is reviled by writing theorists yet ubiquitous in US classrooms. An example might be to analyze Twain's *Adventures of Huckleberry Finn* and identify the (three) human vices that are exposed through the action in the novel.

The paradigmatic mode accounts for the bulk of writing done in American secondary schools. Because of the emphasis placed on paradigmatic thinking throughout school, it is not surprising or inappropriate that students get considerable experience with paradigmatic writing about literature. Argumentation and analysis are skills that I would expect someone to learn in school, although African American scholars like Majors (2015) argue that the forms of argumentation emphasized in schools are not attentive to the ways in which many non-White people learn to make points in homes and community settings.

But conventional academic argumentation and analysis are not the only forms of expression students should acquire in English classes. People also think in storied ways, as I review next.

Narrative Knowledge

Bruner argues that the *narrative* mode of thought, which gets surprisingly less attention in a field so heavily concerned with stories, is a common and important medium through which people think. Narrative knowledge refers to peoples' effort to make sense of things by rendering them in story. Narrative does not rely on the paradigmatic elements of logic, verification, and rational proof. Rather, it is concerned with *verisimilitude*—the likeness of truth—and with the creation of characters and events that represent emotional and social truths but need not replicate them. Authenticity is the hallmark of well-formed narratives, even while they may contain falsehoods.

Narratives might be evaluated according to the degree of emotional resonance they prompt in readers. It would be plausible, for instance, for a student to write a narrative about a talking frog in a dissection tray, although probably not for a science class. The evaluation of its quality would be based not on whether such a thing was really possible but instead on the extent to which the frog was able to articulate or represent some truth about the human, or perhaps ranine, condition and its spiritual, affective dimensions.

My goal in justifying narrative thinking is to argue for an increased role for other ways of thinking and making sense of the world, ways that have been central to sense making throughout history, according to psychologists. Even in a discipline as devoted to stories as English, narrative ways of knowing are rarely allowed as ways *for students* to express themselves, especially for assessment.

Gendered Ways of Knowing

Women vs. Men, or Connected vs. Authoritative Knowing

Do traditional school practices favor boys, girls, both, other gendered identities, or none of the above? It depends on whom you ask. Some observers of schools have argued that, as the American Association of University Women (1995) claims, schools shortchange girls. As evidence, they point to the ways in which schools operate according to masculine conceptions of knowledge. Feminist critics point out that the predominant emphasis in school is on paradigmatic knowledge taught primarily through transmission assumptions involving final-draft uses of language. Girls, according to this argument, benefit more from constructivist knowledge facilitated by exploratory speech and narrative ways of knowing. Boys, because of their more aggressive and competitive behavior, are more likely to get noticed and called on and are treated more favorably.

On the other hand, there's much evidence to support the view that girls do better in schools than boys. Sommers (2000), for instance, reports that in comparison with boys, girls get higher grades, are more likely to go to college, take more rigorous academic programs, enroll in AP classes at higher rates, enroll in more high-level math and science courses, read more books, score higher on tests for artistic and musical ability, are more engaged academically, do more homework, and participate more frequently in student government, honor societies, debate clubs, and school newspapers. More frequently than girls, boys get suspended from school, get held back, drop out, get diagnosed as having attention deficit hyperactivity disorder, commit crimes, get involved with drugs and alcohol, and commit suicide. (Girls attempt suicide more often, but boys succeed more often.) At my university, women students comprise 57 percent of the enrollment, men 43 percent. Undoubtedly they enroll in greater numbers because in high school they were the better students.

There appears to be no easy resolution to the disagreement over whether school benefits one sex or the other. There does seem to be some agreement, however, that heterosexual boys and girls experience school differently. I think it's worthwhile, then, to think about gendered ways of knowing to bring an informed perspective to the discussion.

In much of the literature, ways of knowing are distinguished as either masculine or feminine, as the province of men/boys or women/girls. Although I agree that women and men are often different from one another in consistent ways, I hesitate to apply these terms so that they suggest absolute differences between the two (or, for that matter, that gender is neatly divided into only two types, as I will review shortly).

I therefore use the terms *authoritative* and *connected* in place of men's and women's psychological makeups. These terms allow for a discussion of the issues without so strictly dividing the world into two distinct, gender-based groups. I'm sure you can think of plenty of examples of people who do not act in accordance with their gender profiles, while at the same time seeing that these two ways of relating exist, even if they don't always coexist so well. These two types are points on a continuum rather than absolute categories. Most people, I suspect, fall somewhere in between these two extremes.

LGBTQ+ Ways of Knowing

My summary of connected or relational and authoritative or detached ways of knowing, often tied to feminine and masculine orientations to the world, is designed to account for how people engage with one another. I have taken pains to disassociate them to an extent from sexual orientation and gender identity and expression.

But the world is a mighty messy place. The old male and female binary just doesn't account for how all people are put together or how they identify. Although people from outside this binary have always been around, their needs, and indeed, their very existence, have been poorly recognized.

LGBTQ stands for lesbian, gay, bisexual, transgender, and queer or questioning. Even this bundle of terms is problematic and insufficient to many, however. Some institutions now have expanded the list to the more inclusive yet cumbersome LGBT-TQQFAIGGQHDSGAPBDSM, for lesbian, gay, bisexual, transgender, transsexual, queer, questioning, flexual, asexual, intersex, genderf**k, gender queer, hyposexual, demisexual, semisexual, grey ace, polyamorous, bondage/discipline, dominance/submission, and sadism/masochism. Expect this list to expand as other orientations and identities are added. It's complicated out there. I use LGBTQ+ to account for the full range of sexualities outside the historical male/female binary.

I believe strongly in civil rights, and if you do as well, you must eventually address the fact that you will have kids who don't have a heterosexual or cisgender orientation. Conducting class to provide them with a fair education might concern you as much as does equity for any other historically marginalized social, racial, religious, or ethnic group.

I assume that populations from outside the heterosexual and cisgender majority will exhibit authoritative (often masculine) and connected (often feminine) ways of relating, although I don't think I could predict who would perform how. The presence of this population and the abusive treatment to which they have been historically subjected in society suggest that they merit your attention.

If you wish to explore the pedagogical issues involved in teaching LGBTQ+ issues, then there is much available online to inform your thinking. The website of GLSEN (http://www.glsen.org/), for Gay, Lesbian & Straight Education Network, provides abundant resources for teaching about bullying, school climate, civil rights, mutual respect, and other issues that often follow from having an LGBTQ+ identity. TSER (Trans Student Educational Resources, http://www.transstudent.org) provides resources as well. The goal of these lessons is to help LGBTQ+ students see themselves reflected in the curriculum and instruction in positive ways, to help all students reach more complex and informed understandings of the world, and to encourage respectful thinking and actions, critical thinking, and social justice.

It's perhaps too early to say if different "ways of knowing" will emerge through the increased visibility of the LGBTQ+ population in the social mainstream, a process that is now underway. When I asked field leader Mollie Blackburn if such "ways of knowing" have been identified, she said, "I don't know of any 'ways of knowing,' beyond the notion that people from marginalized groups know those margins better than those who don't live in them, but also know the center from a sort of etic perspective."

By *etic* she means outsider's view; the view from the inside is known as *emic*. I think that this perspective is important to keep in mind: that LGBTQ+ people know how the social mainstream looks from the margins, like others who find themselves on the outside looking in. Instruction can deny their visibility and legitimacy by omission. If you see your teaching role as advancing civil rights, you might investigate more inclusive ways of teaching to provide a more equitable environment for marginalized students in general.

Inevitably, I think, teachers will need to address issues following from the emerging visibility of LGBTQ+ people and perspectives in society and in schools. How they will do so is one of the most compelling questions facing educators as this societal recognition becomes more taken for granted and normalized in classroom life.

Authoritative Ways of Relating

People who take an authoritative view of the world tend to take a competitive and aggressive stance toward other people. In a discussion their goal is to win and so assert their greater authority, rather than to compromise, co-construct new knowledge, or learn more about the other people involved. Their competitive stance suggests a need for autonomy, therefore making collaboration both unnecessary and perhaps even counterproductive. Some people might even consider it un-American, because the nation is founded on competitiveness and enlightened self-interest. The need for autonomy reduces attention to other people and their needs and feelings, resulting in a lack of connection to others, who, after all, are competitors.

This de-emphasis on personal connections leads away from empathic and emotional language and toward the language of analysis and abstraction. The point of schooling then becomes to work toward the creation of taxonomies and hierarchies that establish rules that resist contextual considerations. Classroom time is devoted to analysis of literature, emotional responses are discouraged, and the strongest arguments prevail (with strength at times determined by force as much as logic).

Connected Ways of Relating

Connected knowing refers to ways of relating to other people and constructing knowledge that are more collaborative, less competitive, and more likely concerned with the personal relationships of the people involved. Talk that characterizes connected knowing is often

- *Tentative*, indicated by hesitations, false starts, qualifiers, politeness, intensifiers, repetition, slow rate of speech, deferential remarks, and tag questions;

- *Nurturing*, indicated by efforts to encourage the contributions of other speakers and be attentive to how they feel about the process;

- *Connected* with other speakers, indicated by the way in which discussions are cohesive and collaborative; and

- *Indirect*, allowing speakers to establish a rapport and requiring listeners to make inferences.

Because of concern for the emotional well-being of others, connected knowers are less aggressive in group discussions and are more likely to support others or co-construct knowledge with them. Because they are less concerned with autonomy, they are less emphatic about developing universal rules and more interested in understanding how situational factors affect behavior. The acceptance of the tentative possibilities for language is consistent with Barnes' characterization of exploratory speech.

Multiliteracies, New Literacies, Multimedia Composing, Semiotics, and Twenty-First-Century Literacies

Humans have always expressed themselves symbolically. Words themselves serve as symbols for referents. Drawings on cave walls have been found that are 40,000 years old, typically depicting what was important to societies: human activities, local creatures, and so on. For that reason I refer to these most ancient of textual forms, those that are material and have a sense of permanence and substance, as *First Literacies*, including when they occur in our contemporary society (Smagorinsky 2018a).

For many years, words provided the principal medium for education in US schools, in spite of the availability of other sign systems. Students were taught reading and writing, and were mostly instructed and assessed through verbal means no matter what other means they could employ: art, dance, performance, material production, and much else. But "book learnin'" provided the coin within the academic realm.

More recently, with the advent of personal computers and online capabilities, other symbol systems have grabbed the attention of educators. No matter which name you call it by—multiliteracies, New Literacies, multimedia composing, semiotics, twenty-first-century literacies, or something else—you might consider that

- ✦ Many kids engage with digital technologies more than with conventional print literacy outside school;

- ✦ Other sign systems have played distinctive roles in the development of human cultures;

- ✦ Kids' futures are probably better aligned with understanding multiple sign systems than with just words; and

- ✦ School might have greater appeal to kids if they found it more relevant to their contemporary worlds.

What acts of composition might students participate in to make sense of your curriculum and instruction? Digital literacies have seized the attention of many educators. Yet as I've argued, multimodality is not confined to technological tools. Students can still paint, draw, act, dance, sculpt, design, and engage in many other sorts of material practices. Don't forget, then, that computers aren't the only way into the future. Some of us still like to get dirty when we work.

Second, technology is not a solution to all matters. Indeed, it can be a distraction. Give kids Internet access, and your class will become background noise to a lot of them. Your school also might have limitations: old computers and software, limited bandwidth for whole-school access, demands on available computers for standardized testing, and no doubt many more obstacles to your foresight and planning. And although kids today might be considered "digital natives" who don't need instruction in how to compute, they don't necessarily know how to channel that knowledge academically. When her school provided each student with a tablet for their academic work, for instance, one teacher I know passed them out and was then treated to a mass "twerking" performance in which the kids used the tablets in a lascivious manner. Oops.

Like many plans for educational improvement, then, technological panaceas should be treated with both enthusiasm and caution. Consider the consequences—all of them—when you incorporate technology use into your instruction. And don't forget to bring along the butcher paper and paint, some clay, a batch of *papier-mâché*, a guitar, and other real stuff for kids to make meaning with.

Summary

In general, school assessment misses the point by ignoring many ways of knowing. A transmission approach is largely predicated on ill-founded assumptions about the nature of learning. Schools valorize abstract, static, logical, analytical knowledge at the expense of idiosyncratic, dynamic, protean knowledge. Emergent understandings through exploratory uses of speech are discouraged in favor of neatly packaged, final-draft speech that is typically borrowed from elsewhere rather than generated by students. For the most part, students work at the lowest end of the cognitive ladder, foregoing synthesis and synergy in favor of rote memorization and mimicry. In following such an approach, teachers underestimate what young people are capable of and limit students' school learning to its most reductive, least interesting parts. In place of this method, I urge you to consider the possibilities of teaching students in ways that challenge them to draw on a wide range of their intellectual resources to construct new knowledge and meaning in relation to the English curriculum.

Performance Assessment Prep

Many beginning teacher performance assessments include a section on "Knowledge of Students to Inform Teaching," which this chapter can help you prepare for. Learning about your students, without being invasive, is a good idea whether or not you're being assessed, because as I've argued throughout this chapter, you should always plan your teaching around who your students are.

This chapter has outlined some key areas on which to focus, without covering all territory. For instance, you might be required to explain how many students are on IEPs (individualized education programs) due to a special classification such as having a diagnosis of a "learning disability." Or you might be expected to say how you will address the needs of immigrant, racially minoritized,[2] or other sort of student often classified as "at risk." Just be aware that it can be dangerous to assume that all members of nonwhite races are automatically at risk, and that white students are not (Smagorinsky 2014a). There is no all-purpose answer to these questions; your personal attention to the specifics of your class enrollments will provide the material for your instructional planning and how you present it for assessment purposes.

---

2. I use "minoritized" rather than "minority" to signal that even when in the majority, people of nonwhite racial groups tend to be diminished by others, such that they are treated in ways that make them of lesser importance.

Nonetheless, this chapter provides you with scholarship to generally help you frame how you present your teaching and its sensitivity to your students' characteristics. When you create exhibits from your teaching plans, you might be asked to relate your teaching focus to

+ Evidence of what your student know, can do, and need to learn how to do;

+ What you know about your students' everyday lives, their cultural and language backgrounds and practices, and their personal interests;

+ What you understand about the needs of English language learners (ELLs), primarily students whose families do not speak English at home;

+ What you know about students with IEPs and how to individualize their instruction;

+ What you know about your students' cognitive, physical, and socio-emotional development;

+ How this knowledge is informed by your understanding of theories of human development; and

+ How you will teach specific genres of social engagement (analysis, argumentation, evaluation, interpretation, narrative, and others) in relation to the specific characteristics of your students.

During your field experiences, pay careful attention to the students, taking notes that can both inform your instructional planning and eventually provide material for your responses to assessment prompts about student characteristics. You could also begin to observe carefully how field-based mentor teachers work with diverse populations of students, whether they standardize or differentiate instruction, how they manage students with IEPs, whether they teach the subject or the students, how they respond to students with different learning needs, and other facets of classroom life that follow from your knowledge of your students and how it informs your teaching.

2

Providing Scaffolds for Student Learning

The notion of an *instructional scaffold* (Bruner 1975) refers to the way in which experienced and capable people assist others in learning new knowledge and skills. Bruner grounds this metaphor in an early, questionable translation of Vygotsky (1962). I have argued that scaffolding is not a very Vygotskian idea because it is oriented to immediate teaching and learning effects rather than long-term human development (Smagorinsky 2018b).

For our current purposes, it doesn't matter whether scaffolding follows from Vygotsky's "zone of proximal development." (I think it doesn't and is a misinterpretation.) What matters is that scaffolding can provide a strong instructional support for people learning to do new things. An example would be the way in which an experienced carpenter teaches a novice how to build a cabinet. The carpenter might use a variety of methods to teach the skills of cabinet making: providing information verbally (e.g., explaining why it's important to use safety goggles), modeling (e.g., demonstrating how to strike a nail without bending it), showing how to find resources (e.g., doing comparative shopping by phone), and so on.

As the learner grasps the concepts and learns to use the tools properly, the carpenter begins handing over responsibilities to the novice. This transfer might involve providing feedback and support while the novice begins to apply the concepts (corners should be square) and use the tools (a T-square helps to make a right-angle cut precise). As the novice demonstrates increasing competency, the carpenter allows more autonomy and intervenes only as needed. Ultimately, the novice grasps how to build a cabinet and can work independently.

In learning complex, new knowledge, a person benefits from an extended process of using concepts and tools across a variety of contexts: building a china cabinet with glass doors, making built-in kitchen cabinets, making cabinets from different materials, and so on. The novice described previously might learn from the initial building experience how to build a level freestanding cabinet from oak but might struggle with how to use the softer maple in a confined kitchen space without denting it. Knowledge learned from the first experience might require modification and refinement when applied to the next. Multiple experiences would be necessary for the novice to be considered a skilled builder of cabinets. When encountering new circumstances, the novice would benefit from additional support from the carpenter to recognize how to adjust knowledge of concepts and tools to new circumstances.

The scaffolding metaphor has its critics, and their reservations are worth noting. Searle (1984) posed the important question: *Who's building whose building?* In other words, the scaffolding metaphor suggests that the person providing the support will lead the learner toward the best possible construction. Searle raises questions about the extent to which a teacher's decisions are always in the students' best interests. He suggests that it's possible that students have entirely different needs and purposes from those served by the kinds of constructions that the teacher has in mind. He also critiques the conventional notion of the teacher as someone who teaches rather than learns. Critics of authoritarian approaches to schooling maintain that teachers ought to learn through the process of teaching. Teachers' notion of a building, then, can potentially change through their engagement with learners and their ideas about what needs to be constructed.

This criticism is important to keep in mind when teaching. You should always ask yourself, Whose building is being constructed here? Whose needs will it serve? Who is learning what through this kind of construction? Are there other possible ways to envision and build this text?

Dyson (1990) finds the scaffolding metaphor to be overly rigid and too focused on the teacher as expert. She suggests the metaphor of *weaving* instead, which she finds more flexible and democratic. A literal scaffold on a building provides a supporting, inert, immobile framework for the structure and the builders who work on it. Teachers and learners, however, are alive and animated. They are responsive to one another and so need to be both sensitive and adaptable. They mutually influence one another, which Dyson sees as a central reason for adopting the weaving metaphor, in which a common product emerges from integrated, joint activity. Although teachers often lead, they do so with careful attention to the child's progress, remaining open to the idea that the student may come up with an approach to learning to which a more impervious scaffold might be insensitive.

A final concern about the scaffolding metaphor is that it suggests, if we apply the analogy strictly, that one scaffold is enough: A single scaffold serves to support the building, the building goes up, the scaffold comes down, and everyone goes home. If teaching and learning were so easy, we wouldn't need all these books about education. When people learn through guided activity, scaffolds are continually being built, modified, adapted to the learner's growing understandings, or cast aside and replaced with something more appropriate in relation to the learner's conceptual and practical progress.

An instructional scaffold therefore needs to be more organic, more protean, and more supple than a building scaffold. Scaffolds must be amenable to change as the learner grows. Teachers, then, must also be learners as part of this process, in terms of what they discover about the students and their learning, about their own teaching, and about the possibilities for ways to manipulate the material that is the subject of the learning. The scaffolding metaphor needs to be reimagined to serve as the kind of learning support available in the constructivist classroom.

Learning Procedures for Learning

Since the 1970s (see, e.g., Bransford 1979) many educators have emphasized the importance of teaching *procedural knowledge*—that is, knowledge of how to do things. To return to the example of learning about bicycles: I would need strategies for remaining balanced, attuning my legwork to the speed I desired, applying the brakes without flying over the handlebars, and otherwise knowing how to operate the bike safely and efficiently.

As noted in my review of transmission approaches to education, however, much school instruction is centered on students' learning of *declarative knowledge*: the ability to repeat information provided by someone else. For bike riders, declarative knowledge would consist of knowledge of the names of each part of the bicycle, even if they did not know which way to push the pedals. In English class, instruction based on declarative knowledge is evident in grammar lessons in which students identify parts of speech in someone else's sentences, in writing instruction in which students label and then try to imitate the parts of model essays such as the five-para-graph theme, and in literature instruction in which students are assessed according to their recall of facts that the teacher believes are important.

An emphasis on procedures is focused more on *ways to do things*. It is thus more generative and constructive. A generative approach to learning grammar might come through sentence combining, in which students join given clauses and phrases into new sentences that are syntactically complex (see, e.g., Strong 1994). A writing teacher, instead of focusing on the traits of finished products, would focus more on how to render ideas and content knowledge into a given kind of text. Teachers of literature would concentrate on strategies such as how to generate images for reading, how to interpret a symbol, and how to recognize and interpret irony.

These efforts are consistent with the idea that for assessment purposes, students should have the opportunity to interpret or produce something new, rather than be tested on what they have already covered. And so, instead of reading *Animal Farm* as part of a unit on animals as symbols and then being tested on their recall of the teacher's explanation of which pig represents Trotsky and which represents Stalin, the students would use their knowledge of how to interpret an animal as a symbol by reading a fresh literary work, such as Walt Whitman's "Noiseless Patient Spider" or Daphne du Maurier's *The Birds*, and writing an interpretation of how the animals function symbolically.

A Process for Instructional Scaffolding

There are many constructions of what an instructional scaffold is and is not. One teacher's scaffold might be another teacher's wrecking ball. I don't pretend to have *the* definitive idea of how to go about supporting students' learning. I do offer one general approach that is compatible with the idea of designing conceptual units and that is attentive to students' need for procedural knowledge. This approach relies on instruction that begins with a teacher's introduction of a concept or procedure through accessible materials, has the students work initially on learning the concept or procedure in small groups that enable exploration and error without penalty, and ultimately has the students working independently as they are weaned away from the teacher's and fellow students' support.

Let's look at examples of instructional scaffolding of students' learning in two areas. In the first scenario, the teacher shows students how to use an all-purpose tool, the double-column response journal, to promote literary understanding. In the second, the teacher instructs students in procedures for writing comparison-contrast essays. Both involve a sequence in which the students move from

+ learning procedures through teacher-supported activity using familiar or accessible materials, to

+ applying the procedures to new materials with peer feedback in small groups, to

+ performing independently with unfamiliar materials of appropriate complexity for the students at this point in their development.

Double-Column Response Log

I am indebted to Cindy O'Donnell-Allen, whose senior English class I observed for a year, for this approach to using response logs. Although Cindy didn't invent response logs, she developed a way of teaching students how to use them that was very effective. Cindy wanted to promote students' sense of agency. She felt that one way to help students achieve it was to use response logs as a tool for learning different ways of thinking about literature. She did not want them to rely on her for their interpretations, which she felt would do them little good once they passed her tests and left her class.

Rather, she wanted them to develop both a stance that they were competent and insightful readers, and a set of strategies for pursuing their insights and questions. Based on her years of teaching, however, she found that her students had been conditioned to answer their teachers' questions rather than pose inquiries themselves. They therefore needed to be taught different kinds of questions to ask, particularly the sort of open-ended questions rarely posed to them in school. They also needed to be taught the specific format of the response log, which was used infrequently in her school district.

Ultimately, she wanted to have the students produce a reading log according to an assignment like the following; in a school with advanced technology, this task might be carried out through an app on a device rather than with paper and pen.

Keep a reading log in response to the literature we are studying during this unit. To keep your log

 ▷ Divide each page with a vertical line down the center.
 ▷ On the left side of each page, record significant passages from the literature you read.
 ▷ On the right side, across from each passage, include at least one question of each type for each work of literature studied.
   ▷ Ask *open-ended questions* that would help you understand the passage better.
   ▷ Give your personal response to the passage (i.e., any thoughts you have in connection with it).
   ▷ Give your personal *evaluation* of the passage.
   ▷ Think through a possible *interpretation* of the passage.

Three rules:

1. Remember that your journal does not need to follow the conventions of textbook English. Rather, the purpose is to think about the literature without worrying about the form your thoughts take.
2. Turn in your response log every two weeks. I will read your log and respond to your comments. If you make an entry that you do not want me to read, place an X at the top of the page, and I'll skip it. Really.
3. Keep in mind that *I am required to share any thoughts or suggestions of violence, suicide, substance abuse, family abuse, or other harmful behavior with the school counselors.*

A lot of teachers stop at this point. That is, they think of a good assignment, present it to students, and then wait for the results. Cindy was very careful, in contrast, to support the students' initial efforts at maintaining their reading response logs, which was a new genre of writing for them. She assumed that simply making the assignment and collecting the logs was insufficient. She needed to think about how to structure and sequence the students' experiences so that they would learn how to keep them as she intended.

The first consideration in providing learning scaffolds is to think about what is involved in using them, in this case, what it takes to keep a reading log. For many students, writing in a double-entry response log requires them to reorient themselves both to reading and to writing. As school readers they are not accustomed to being asked what they think about the material. If generating their own ideas matters, however, they would benefit from learning how to take an inquiring stance, use writing for exploratory purposes, understand the importance of taking risks, and realize that some schoolwork will not be penalized for being incorrect.

Given that students are likely unaccustomed to responding to literature in generative and constructive ways—by posing questions, responding according to their personal experiences and dispositions, evaluating the work according to their own criteria, and constructing an interpretation—they also need to learn how to generate these responses in the context of the double-entry log.

Cindy thus set for herself the responsibility to help students reposition themselves in relation to their school reading and teach them how to respond in these personal, idiosyncratic, open-ended, generative ways. The sequence that she developed involved the following general stages, which I illustrate with examples from her double-entry reading log instruction:

+ The teacher introduces a skill, strategy, or procedure to the whole class. This introduction includes:

  + A clear explanation of the nature of the task (e.g., what a reading log is and why they're keeping it);

  + Explicit information about the expectations for what the students will do (e.g., using the log to pose particular kinds of questions and try to answer them); and

  + Modeling how to make reading log entries, using accessible materials so that the students can clearly follow the explanation (e.g., taking a literary selection and thinking out loud while formulating reading log entries).

+ The teacher then asks students to work collaboratively on a similar kind of problem, using accessible materials so that they can succeed in their initial learning (e.g., they are provided with an accessible work of literature and, in small groups, pose a set of reading log questions about it).

+ Students get feedback on these initial efforts. This feedback can come from peers (e.g., groups exchange and critique one another's efforts) and/or the teacher. Teachers who provide the response need to collect the work and respond to it by the next class session.

+ Students get the critiques back. If the class is ready to move forward, they can then begin with a reading log entry that they keep individually, which in turn gets some kind of feedback from peers or the teacher. If the initial log entries do not come close to expectations, the small-group stage might be repeated with new materials.

The sequence Cindy used went from *teacher modeling* in a *whole-group* setting, to *small-group practice* with immediate *feedback*, to *individual application* of the procedure. This sequence is a good example of one kind of instructional scaffold. If applied rigidly, a teacher might move along before students are ready, so one characteristic of a flexible scaffold is that you are attentive and sensitive to how the students are performing and adjust your teaching according to what they need. A second characteristic of a flexible scaffold is that the teacher does not simply expect students to do things as modeled but encourages them to generate new ideas about how to do the task. The purpose, then, is not to get students to mimic the teacher faithfully, but to use the teacher's modeling as an opportunity to learn a new way of thinking about something.

When I saw Cindy go through this sequence of teaching students *how* to engage in response, I was impressed with her understanding that students would have difficulty inventing their own procedures for asking questions. Her insight was especially keen and important in a school in which most of the Department of English faculty emphasized US cultural heritage as a body of knowledge to be learned intact rather than reconstructed or reconsidered. She assumed that they would benefit from being taught some ways of generating open-ended questions to provide themselves with richer reading experiences.

It's true that she decided whose building would get built. But I'm convinced that, for too many students, the lot might still be vacant if she hadn't.

There are occasions, then, when it's beneficial for you to impose an agenda on students and teach them how to do a particular thing in a particular way. Primarily, it's important to do so when there's a good way to do something that they would be unlikely to think up on their own.

Comparison-Contrast Essay

The comparison-contrast essay is a staple of secondary school writing instruction. People voting for one candidate against another, deciding which Harry Potter novel they like best, selecting where to go on a first date, or engaging in countless other kinds of decisions go through a process of comparing (finding similarities) and contrasting (outlining differences) to make the best choices for themselves.

A common method for teaching the comparison-contrast essay is to provide students with a model essay and have them label its parts. This approach does not, however, teach inexperienced writers *how* to produce these parts of the structure. Following is one way to strengthen students' understanding of how to generate ideas for the purposes of comparison and contrast and ultimately write comparison-contrast essays on their own.

In this approach, which I learned from George Hillocks (Hillocks 1995, 2007; Hillocks, McCabe, and McCampbell 1971), the teacher designs activities through which students work initially in small groups on a task-oriented problem. Their activity in solving the problem leads them to develop procedures inductively for how to solve subsequent problems of a similar type. They then use these procedures to work through increasingly complex problems of a similar nature, beginning in small groups and gradually weaning themselves toward independent performance.

Ultimately, I'd like my students to be able to compare and/or contrast two things of a fairly complex nature. In literature units, the culminating task might be to write an essay comparing and/or contrasting two constructs or characters central to the unit concepts: two utopias in a unit on utopias and dystopias; two movements such as realism and naturalism; two writers within a genre, such as Wordsworth and Keats among the British Lake poets; and so on. I would not want my students to write their first comparison essay at such a formidable level, however. Rather, I'd want them to learn procedures for comparing and contrasting by working initially with familiar, accessible materials.

I would begin, then, by having the students do the following:

+ Get in a group of three to five, and identify two familiar, accessible things to compare and contrast. Following are some possibilities:

  ♦ Two restaurants. Pick two of the same type, for example, two Mexican restaurants or two pizza parlors

  ♦ Two social groups in your school

  ♦ Two musical groups of relatively similar types, such as two gospel choirs or two calypso bands

  ♦ Two TV shows or movies of the same type, such as two "odd couple" stories or two police dramas

  ♦ Other comparison of your choice

+ Think of areas in which you can compare and contrast the two items. For instance, let's say that you have listened to both the Beatles and the Rolling Stones, and wonder which is the better band. What *categories* might you use for points of comparison? These categories should be aspects of musicianship that are important to you. You might, then, rule out eye color because no matter what color their eyes are, their music still sounds the same. Categories that matter could include songwriting ability, singing ability, virtuosity on their instruments, influence on other musicians, and longevity in the music business. What areas of comparison can you think of for the two items that you are focusing on?

+ Think about how your two items measure up in each of the areas of comparison you have identified. For the Beatles–Rolling Stones comparison, the groups might be evaluated as follows in each of the five areas outlined above.

Songwriting Ability

Beatles: Lennon and McCartney the primary songwriters; early in career, recorded rhythm and blues songs by other writers; toward the end of the band's life, often the songs had nonsensical lyrics; wrote many classics

Rolling Stones: Jagger and Richards the primary songwriters; early in career, recorded rhythm and blues songs by other writers; wrote songs that generally made sense; wrote many classics

Singing Ability

Beatles: All four members sang; Starr rarely sang lead and had a not unpleasant voice; Harrison sang more often and was OK but too nasal; Lennon or McCartney sang most leads and had strong voices; McCartney best on "pretty" songs; great harmonies

Rolling Stones: Jagger sang lead on all songs; sassy, edgy voice; not always quite in tune; decent harmonies

Virtuosity on Their Instruments

Beatles: McCartney had to overdub Starr's drumming on later, more complex material; McCartney played multiple instruments; great ensemble sound; few long guitar or keyboard solos; great rhythm

Rolling Stones: strong musicianship across the board; Jagger played some percussion but mostly sang; changed personnel following death and other turnover so musicianship varied

Influence on Other Musicians

Beatles: Often thought to be the world's most influential rock group; pioneered theme albums copied by the Who, Jethro Tull, and so on; early leaders in incorporating Eastern music; leaders in psychedelic rock

Rolling Stones: Known to many as the world's greatest rock and roll band; mostly a rhythm and blues band who borrowed from black US performers; sexuality mimicked by other bands; among the first to use elaborate showmanship in their live acts (makeup, lights, smoke, etc.)

Longevity in the Music Business

> Beatles: The group disbanded within ten years, but its music is still popular; Lennon was murdered at age forty; Harrison died at age fifty-eight of cancer; McCartney still recording; Starr still recording (as of 2018)

> Rolling Stones: Still together after over fifty years; Brian Jones died a "death by misadventure" at age twenty-seven shortly after quitting the band; Jagger and Richard were constants, with periodic turnover at other positions in the band; drug addiction affected the band's durability; individuals took leave from the band for solo projects and substance abuse rehabilitation.

+ For the two comparison items you have selected, think of examples you can give for each in all of the categories you have identified. Then, begin to assemble this information into a written comparison. After looking over your notes, you might discuss them with your group or freewrite about the similarities and differences between the two things you are comparing and contrasting. You should also begin to think about the conclusions you could draw from your inquiry. For instance, for the Beatles–Rolling Stones comparison, you might develop the thesis that the two groups are both highly influential and talented but that you prefer the Beatles because they were more innovative in developing new directions for rock and roll music, while the Rolling Stones mainly stayed within the rhythm and blues genre for more than fifty years.

This sequence should help the students to learn *how* to conduct a comparison-contrast inquiry: selecting well-aligned items for comparison and contrast, identifying categories for comparison, and thinking of examples for each item in each category. As a result of this process, they will develop procedures for conducting similar inquiries in other areas. Note that the instruction begins with attention to *content* rather than attention to *form*, with particular focus on *how to manipulate and think about the content*.

Next, students can begin drafting essays based on the information that they have assembled. They might work in relation to the following guidelines:

+ The thesis you developed previously—for example, that the Beatles and Rolling Stones were both popular, influential bands but that the Beatles were more innovative because their music grew beyond their rhythm and blues roots—could provide the basis for an introductory paragraph to an essay comparing and contrasting two items.

✦ Next, try to develop a paragraph for each area of comparison. For example, if you were comparing the Beatles and the Rolling Stones, you might start by comparing and contrasting them according to their singing ability. However, instead of just listing the illustrations from your notes, think of examples that would support the major points you are trying to make. You might say that because all four Beatles could sing, they were able to produce better harmonies than the Rolling Stones and so had more flexibility with their song arrangements, which allowed them to develop more complex songs. By doing so, you are providing data in support of your thesis that the Beatles were a better band because their sound took new directions over time. When possible, give specific evidence to support your claims, such as that the Beatles' harmonies and multiple singers gave their albums a divergent sound, while the Rolling Stones' reliance solely on Jagger gave all of their music a similar sound. Further, provide a *warrant*—that is, an explanation (often beginning with "Because . . .") of why the example supports the claim and thus serves as evidence.

✦ Finally, draw some sort of conclusion based on your comparison and contrast, possibly developing the ideas you stated in your thesis. You might conclude, for instance, that songs recorded by the Rolling Stones across five decades all have a very similar sound, while songs recorded by the Beatles during the 1960s show a radical change from derivative rhythm and blues to highly sophisticated acid rock, incorporating influences from multiple cultures and sources.

The task focuses on content. Issues of form are treated as ways to present and make sense of the content. At this point, each student proceeds to write an essay based on the information assembled and organized. You might want to adjust this plan and have the students write this initial essay on familiar material in the small groups as a way to provide immediate feedback as the students discuss how to present the information and evaluations in essay form. The choice you make reveals your sensitivity to the students' need for scaffolding at this point in their writing development.

The process of thinking about and organizing this comparison actually helped me to refine my previous thinking and to generate new ideas about these two groups. I had always liked the Beatles better than the Stones, but here, because I was forced to articulate my ideas for this comparison, I pushed myself to explain why and in the process generated new thinking. This process is central to the idea of *writing to learn*: People often use writing as a way to discover what they have to say. This idea is very compatible with the emphasis on *exploratory speech and writing* in the classroom, and it supports the belief that writing consists of more than simply transferring ideas from the head to the page. Rather, writing—and the talking that accompanies writing in this teaching approach—may also serve as a way to generate new ideas through the process of articulating one's thoughts.

After writing their drafts, students should have opportunities for formal feedback from their peers. A small-group feedback session can provide them with both response to their writing and an opportunity to develop their critical reading skills by critiquing their peers. To set up this stage of the scaffold, you might give instructions of the following sort:

After you have written a draft of your essay, get back in your small group to share your writing.

+ Proofread the essays of your groupmates, pointing out passages that you feel are strong and suggesting ways to improve the writing, particularly with regard to the writer's use of evidence to support each comparison and contrast. One way to evaluate the writer's use of evidence is to see if there is a warrant in which the author explains why the evidence supports the claim.

+ Pay careful attention to the writer's conclusions and how well they are supported by the evidence in the presentation.

+ Make comments in the margins of the draft wherever you feel they would be helpful, and write a summary evaluation at the end of each draft you read. Feel free to discuss the essay with the writer and other members of the group.

Following this feedback session, each student should have received a critique from several classmates. Based on their suggestions, the author then produces a draft to be submitted to the teacher, or perhaps to a reader from outside class who would find it interesting.

This sequence should prepare the students for a more sophisticated comparison-contrast essay. It's possible that they would benefit from exploring an intermediate topic before taking on the task of comparing and contrasting such complex constructs as naturalism and realism; perhaps they might compare and contrast two writers within one movement, such as Stephen Crane and Jack London within the naturalism genre.

Perhaps you will have all or some of the preparation done in small groups; perhaps you will go straight to an individual assignment. It really depends on how much support you believe that your students need to stretch their thinking and abilities without overwhelming them with too great a leap. As you can see, instructional scaffolds require a great deal of judgment and decision-making on the teacher's part.

You can't simply go through a lockstep set of activities without evaluating students' response and progress and making adjustments in your plans. You thus provide the support that proponents of scaffolding advocate for, without the rigidity that concerns its critics.

Summary

Ideally, you would provide instructional scaffolding any time you taught students how to do a new task: read ironic literature, write a narrative, produce compound and complex sentences, and any other process that requires new kinds of complex thinking. Unfortunately, the overall school culture works against such process-oriented teaching and learning: Anthologies must be read in their entirety and possibly in order, tests must be taken, skills must be explained (if not learned). But consider the long-term effects of simply giving and grading assignments, as opposed to giving assignments and taking responsibility yourself for how well students complete them. Personally, I would rather have students really learn how to do a few things in school than cover many things superficially and with little lasting effect. The task for teachers, then, is to balance what the school absolutely requires that they do with what they can create time for and accomplish. This effort takes more time for sure. But I think it's time well spent.

Performance Assessment Prep

The performance assessment tasks typically require you to promote a positive learning environment that engages students in learning that deepens during instruction. You would be on safe ground to position your teaching as involving instructional scaffolding, which eases students through increasingly complex learning experiences and ultimately allows them to work independently on problems similar to those they've been taught to engage with.

As you begin to design you lessons, consider how your instructional sequence enables increasingly deep engagement with what the assessment calls "complex texts," a term that concerns me and that I critique in this book's final chapter. However, the assessors won't care what I think, so on the assessment, make sure you know who's grading your work.

Many performance assessments will require you to videotape your teaching and provide a commentary on it. I can't help you with the videotaping, but the commentary could draw on this chapter's attention to scaffolding, which can conceivably help your students grow toward the independent application of learning procedures and strategies and thus satisfy the demands of this sort of task. During planning, you can only anticipate what will and won't happen; on your commentary following teaching, you will likely be prompted to explain how your reflection on your practice could produce tweaks and improvements. This chapter may help you account for your teaching in ways that fit with the assessment criteria.

3

Planning the Whole Course

The end is where we start from.

—T. S. Eliot

Recall the story with which I opened Chapter 1: After several weeks of discussing a play, one teacher borrowed another teacher's exam to administer. This chapter explains how to plan your assessment *before* teaching rather than after, to reduce the likelihood of disjunctures between what your students learn and what you grade. You will establish a clear, tangible goal for your teaching and for students' learning and in the process will identify what you need to be responsible for in your teaching.

In a sense, then, you'll be *planning backward*—that is, you'll think about the end point first and then use that goal to plan the path of instruction. To me, this approach provides an excellent way to ensure that your teaching and assessment will be well aligned, and that students will find your classes purposeful and helpful in accomplishing the unit goals.

I approach instructional design by focusing first on the whole year. By thinking of the whole year before I design individual units in detail, I am searching for overall coherence in the students' experiences in my class. I hope to plan so that our discussions and inquiries over the course of the year involve what Applebee (1996) calls *curricular conversations*: integrating units through overarching concepts that allow for extended explorations of key ideas and that provide continuity across the various units. By mapping out my master plan for the year at the outset, I hope to establish a sense of unity for the more particular decisions I make during the planning and teaching of the individual conceptual units.

Sophomore-Year English Curriculum

For the purposes of illustrating curriculum development, I have designed a hypothetical curriculum for the sophomore year in high school. *The culminating projects can be produced by any student, regardless of perceived ability*, because the students are using prior knowledge as the basis for constructing new knowledge.

The projects allow students to reconstruct the material they engage with in class so that they learn something new. All students, except perhaps those with severe impediments to learning and expression, are capable of producing such texts in some fashion.

The Yearlong Curriculum: Overarching Concepts and Assessments

We will first consider what might serve as overarching concepts for the whole year. These themes are often suggested by the title of the course you are teaching. If you teach British literature to high school seniors or American literature to juniors, for instance, your identification of an overarching concept will be limited by the range of literature afforded by the curriculum. Often the overarching purpose for English classes in grades 7–10 is less clearly specified than it is in grades 11 and 12. In grades 7–10, the curriculum often consists of a set of skills to be learned, or perhaps a set of literary forms, sometimes called "genres," such as short stories, poems, novels, and other textual clusters.

To identify themes, consider the following: After a year of engaging with literature and related arts, producing writing and other texts, and learning about uses of language and other forms of communication, what kinds of culminating texts can my students produce to show what they've learned? How is this learning related to a set of concepts that have recurred in our engagement with the year's materials? How can I ensure that new learning takes place through the process of constructing these culminating texts?

Many schools now use a common district-wide end-of-course exam that might displace the possibility of producing such a text for your class. Any ideas that you take from this book will ultimately have to be adapted to your particular teaching environment.

In thinking about what your students will produce for this culminating assessment, you might also think about what *you* could produce as a way of helping you understand your own learning during the year. Some teachers produce their own version of the texts required of students, in order to synthesize their own learning during the year. You might want to demonstrate to your students that you, too, are in the process of learning, and create a culminating text to share with them.

Such a stance would reinforce a constructivist perspective because it would mean that texts are continually open to reinterpretation and do not have a static, official meaning. You would also show that your engagement with the kids and the material has caused you to change and learn, reinforcing the idea that educational processes should promote the construction of new meaning for both teachers and students.

Considerations in Curriculum Planning

If the sophomore year does not have an official guiding theme, I suggest that you establish one, possibly through negotiation with students and/or colleagues. For the sophomore curriculum, the literature anthology—in conjunction with whatever mandates are issued by the state, country, district, school, and department—will constrain your choices. Your anthology may be organized according to literary forms: poems, short stories, drama, a Shakespeare play, nonfiction prose, and possibly a short novel. Often these texts have little thematic relation to one another and simply embody the designated form. If you wish to teach so that your instruction is responsive to overarching concepts, these forms are insufficient as guiding principles. With a more conceptual focus, you'll need to teach the selections in an order quite different from the way in which the anthology presents them.

Types of Overarching Concepts

Overarching concepts are the related sets of ideas that unify a whole curriculum. Overarching concepts may include, but are not limited to, the following types:

+ *Theme*: A theme provides a recurring idea, question, or topic that is developed across a series of units. An example for an American literature curriculum would be *Whose perspective provides the American outlook?* For the British literature curriculum, a theme could be *How is the evolution of British literature a reflection of the social worlds in which authors from different eras lived?*

+ *Strategy*: A strategy reinforces a particular way of approaching reading and/or writing. Broadly speaking, a strategy could encompass *attention to learning processes*. More specifically, it could focus on a particular skill such as *understanding narrative perspective* in texts that students both read and produce (Smith 1991). Tenth-grade students' experiences with literature, then, might be guided by the questions, *Who is the speaker in each text, and how does the speaker's perspective contribute to the way in which the story is told? To what extent is the speaker trustworthy and reliable?* and *How would a different speaker tell the same story?*

✦ *Stance*: A stance is a perspective taken toward living and learning. Some educators view schooling as an arena in which to foster a stance toward life, such as being imaginative, caring, thoughtful, inquiring, critical, or inclusive. An overarching concept for the tenth-grade curriculum might be *How do I position myself in a school with so many different social groups?*

✦ *Aesthetic awareness*: Aesthetic awareness turns students' attention to questions of how to evaluate the quality of experience and of artistic forms. An overarching concept for the sophomore curriculum could be one they answer inductively rather than through the received wisdom of professional literary critics: *What criteria help me distinguish quality literature from literature of lesser quality?*

Each of these questions is open-ended and amenable to idiosyncratic interpretation and construction by the unique students in your pluralistic class, and thus each is open to a constructivist approach to teaching. Let's look at one type of overarching concept that could serve to unify the sophomore curriculum, and then consider a set of other overarching concepts that could provide other conversational threads for the course. Students might find it tiresome to have a single emphasis for a whole course, so it's wise to provide a set of overarching concepts rather than just one.

One Possible Theme: Negotiating Thresholds

When you look at what high school sophomores tend to read, you'll notice that much of the literature concerns some kind of transforming experience, often emerging from a conflict. This emphasis can serve as the basis for an overarching theme such as *negotiating thresholds*. This theme concerns the manner in which tenth graders are on the border between adolescence and adulthood, peer-group values and home values, and other critical junctures in their lives that require a decision about which direction to take.

A rationale for this overarching theme could come from the findings of developmental psychology, which sees this age as one of identity formation. If the school or community is experiencing problems with inappropriate negotiations of these thresholds—bullying, discrimination, harassment, fighting, gang involvement, and so on—then these factors could also figure into the rationale.

The theme of negotiating thresholds could suggest a series of units through which students would read and produce texts dealing with some of the key conflicts they'll face in their mid-teen years. For our hypothetical curriculum, the following thematic units would serve this purpose well:

+ Coming of age

+ Conflict with authority

+ Gangs, cliques, and peer pressure

+ Discrimination

Keep in mind that thematic units are only one of several types of units you can develop. For my hypothetical curriculum, I designed four other units for the year's activities. They represent some of the other types of conceptual units I outlined previously and additionally include the open-ended approach to instruction known as a workshop:

+ Heroic journey (genre)

+ Shakespeare: *Julius Caesar* (works of single author, or themes such as loyalty, power, ambition, and others)

+ Writing workshop

+ Reading workshop

A Shakespeare unit is often required in the sophomore curriculum, with *Julius Caesar* typically included in the literature anthology. The Shakespeare unit is therefore a somewhat pragmatic choice, though it is also highly defensible from other perspectives. Thematically, its attention to loyalty would fit well with the overarching theme of negotiating thresholds, in that early adolescence is a time of shifting loyalties as youth locate themselves socially. The unit on the heroic journey is compatible with the theme of negotiating thresholds because the genre involves the hero's overcoming of a series of obstacles in the course of the quest.

A writing or reading workshop is an open-ended block of time in which students have the opportunity to write or read on topics and in genres of their choice, with the teacher serving as resource. The teacher also writes or reads along with the students. Because they involve a complex set of managerial skills, I do not devote extensive space to workshops in this book. Rather, I recommend you consult other books that explain their operation in detail (e.g., Bomer and Bomer 2001). Workshops can fit well with other overarching concepts you might identify for your whole course and can be appropriate when emphasizing the stance of *self-determination*.

To provide students with varied formats and focuses, it would make sense to distribute and sequence the units across the year as follows:

FIRST SEMESTER

Coming of age

Writing workshop

Discrimination

Heroic journey

SECOND SEMESTER

Gangs, cliques, and peer pressure

Conflict with authority

Reading workshop

Shakespeare: *Julius Caesar*

This distribution places one workshop, two units on negotiating thresholds, and one unit from a different type of concept in each semester. It places Shakespeare at the end of the year, a good location given the play's likely difficulty for many students and their maturation as readers over the course of the year. This variation in focus and format should help keep students as stimulated as students can be, even while they explore recurring ideas.

Possibilities for Overarching Concepts

Following are overarching concepts of three types—strategy, stance, and aesthetic awareness—that could conceivably complement the negotiating thresholds theme. You would never use all of these focuses for a single course. Rather, you would identify a few to provide conversational continuity for your class across the various units.

Strategy

Understanding narrative perspective. When he taught high school English, Michael W. Smith (1991) made narrative perspective a recurring issue in students' engagement with literature. He believed that understanding literature was dependent on understanding who told the story. Central to this knowledge was the ability to recognize a narrator's limitations and how those limitations affect the narrator's reliability. Holden Caulfield in *The Catcher in the Rye*, for instance, has a uniquely jaundiced view of his world that prevents him from seeing many of his own flaws.

Smith identified a set of questions that recurred in each unit of instruction, providing his classes with an overarching strategic approach, regardless of the topics covered in the units.

Cultural modeling. Lee (2000) has argued that teachers can build on students' cultural resources when teaching them to become literate in a particular domain. For many students, school is already well aligned with their cultural resources. School, as many critics have pointed out, is conducted according to the norms of the white middle class (Smagorinsky 2017). As a result, white middle-class students tend to be well matched to the expectations that schools have for successful performance.

Lee has argued that students from other backgrounds also bring plentiful cultural resources to school. Because the curriculum focuses on Western history and literature, and on middle-class speech patterns, these resources often go untapped. Her primary interest is in African American students and their rich uses of figurative language in their daily speech. Lee has argued that teachers can do two things to help African American students have more fulfilling experiences in school:

- ✦ Include more literature by African American writers to allow for clearer connections to the speech and experiences of African American students
- ✦ Explicitly draw attention to figurative properties of African American English to help provide students with strategies for understanding literature, not just by African American writers but by any writers who use figurative devices

A teacher who uses cultural modeling as an overarching strategy routinely finds ways for students to reflect on and analyze their own cultural practices, particularly their uses of language. Formal knowledge of these language practices then serves as essential knowledge in students' experiences with literature that employs similar devices.

Dramatic images. Another strategic approach that could govern a whole course would be to teach students a range of strategies for helping them visualize literature. Images can be created in a variety of ways to help students visualize how characters might interact. Others have identified various approaches to using art and drama in ways that help students both represent their understanding of literature and develop new understandings through the process of interpretation (Cahnmann-Taylor and Souto-Manning 2010). Wilhelm (1997), drawing on ideas developed by Enciso (1992), argues that these approaches are particularly helpful for students who resist reading and are frustrated over how to make sense of texts; among their chief problems is a difficulty evoking those texts through images.

Stance

Critical literacy. Some observers of school advocate what they call critical literacy taught through *critical pedagogy*. Critical literacy aims to teach students about power relationships, particularly when one group or class of people has advantages over another; I illustrate one such approach in Chapter 15 of this book. Critical pedagogues try to get their students to examine their own class status and to see how their communities and nation privilege some groups of people over others. Teachers who emphasize critical literacy as an overarching stance routinely have students ask questions about who has power and why. This question can be directed to virtually any kind of human relationship, including

+ The school (e.g., which kind of people make decisions, which are in subservient positions, etc.)

+ The classroom (e.g., who speaks about what, whose opinions are likely to be favorably rewarded, etc.)

+ The characters in the literature (e.g., how characters of different class, gender, and race are portrayed by writers of different class, gender, and race)

+ The traditional literary canon (e.g., authors of which class, gender, and race get privileged status; which topics and themes get privileged status)

+ Society as a whole (e.g., how class, gender, and race are implicated in power relationships in society)

Self-determination. Some teachers believe that education should be geared toward helping students determine who they are and what their purposes are. The role of the teacher is to provide the environment in which students work, without overly specifying what that work is or which standards it should meet. Teachers who embrace this belief would employ the most student-oriented approaches described in this book: negotiating the curriculum with students, establishing writing workshops, and so on.

Multicultural awareness. A traditionalist would wish to preserve the literary canon. A multiculturalist would wish to diversify it to include more women, authors of color, LGBTQ+ authors, and authors from traditionally underrepresented nations and cultures. Multicultural concerns would perhaps include a heavy dose of critical literacy, critiquing established norms and questioning why things are as they are. There would be a strong effort to read authors from diverse backgrounds and to consider the ways in which different cultural practices contribute to different worldviews.

Summary

A number of other worthwhile goals for schooling have been identified by others that could serve as overarching concepts. The goals that you identify for a whole course will be determined by a variety of factors. I encourage you to think about the importance of having a limited set of overarching concepts to serve as the conversational thread across a whole course of study and to think about how you will assess your students' learning at the end of the course.

Assessing Students for a Whole Course

For the sophomore course, we'll use the overarching theme of *negotiating thresholds*. I have already provided a brief rationale for this theme. With an overarching concept serving to provide continuity across the units, you must next consider what students will do at the end of the course to synthesize their understanding of the year's work. Although end-of-course exams might preempt this project as a high-stakes assessment, it provides a more student-centered culmination to the year's learning than such externally developed exams typically allow for.

You may need to think in terms of semesters rather than years, depending on how your curriculum is set up and on how many students transfer classes at the semester break. My reference to a year's final exam, then, might need adjustment depending on how your school is organized and conducted.

I have identified a set of possible culminating texts for a whole course of study. It is not likely that you would use all of them for a single course; my goal instead is to identify a *possible range of assessments*. The following assessments help students *synthesize their knowledge* from the year and *construct new knowledge* through their process of producing them:

- Assessment of the students' own learning about learning through a *portfolio*. This kind of assessment would fit well with an overarching stance of *self-determination*, with the portfolio helping students determine what they have learned and what they have learned it from.

- Assessment of the students' understanding and evaluation of literary form through their writing of an *extended definition of good literature*. Students would detail what counts as quality literature, and for that matter, what counts as literature.

- Assessment of the students' learning about the year's overarching concept through a *multimedia project* synthesizing knowledge gained from the year's engagement with texts and classroom activities. This assessment would combine the course's attention to *negotiating thresholds* with a course-long emphasis on the strategy of *generating dramatic images*.

✦ Assessment of the students' understanding of the literary texts through an *essay analyzing literary characters' changes* in relation to the overarching concept. This assessment would take a *paradigmatic* approach to understanding the theme of negotiating thresholds.

✦ *Assessment developed by students* based on their own construction of the purpose of the course. This assessment would fit with the *stance* of *self-determination*.

Each of these assessments provides an opportunity for students to learn something new. Doing *all* or even *most* of these projects for a single course would probably be more than they could manage. Rather, these assessment types illustrate possible ways in which you can use a final exam to enable students to construct new meaning through engagement with the course's overarching concepts and the materials and activities through which they have explored them.

Portfolio

One kind of culminating project that serves any curriculum well is the portfolio. Portfolio assessment is borrowed from the world of the arts. Rather than having each and every effort evaluated, an artist (or student) works at a variety of projects and then chooses the best products for evaluation. This conception of assessment assumes that not all work is intended to be graded and that evaluation should focus on the work that best represents the artist's ability.

In education, the idea of a portfolio has been adapted rather than adopted wholesale. For the culminating project for the sophomore curriculum, I focus on a kind of portfolio called the *process portfolio*, which encourages students to reflect on their learning processes, rather than to feature their best work (a *showcase portfolio*). A process portfolio gives students the opportunity to go through their year's work and select artifacts that demonstrate key learning experiences. A key learning experience is not necessarily reflected in a polished, final product. In a process portfolio, the *exhibits* may include

✦ Something that received a poor grade, yet through which the student learned something about the topic, the importance of good work habits, and so on

+ A rough draft for a piece of writing, rather than the final draft, if the rough draft served as an occasion for significant learning or if the rough draft received feedback that contributed to new understanding

+ An abandoned effort, if the abandonment came about through an important realization

+ A text produced by someone else, if through reading that text the student gained critical new insights

A process portfolio enables reflection on significant learning through the exhibition of key learning experiences, even if those experiences produce rough or unfinished texts. The process portfolio assignment might look like this:

Throughout the year you have had a lot of experiences with literature and other art forms. In response to these texts, you have produced a variety of pieces of writing, art, and other forms of expression. Presumably you have learned something about yourself, the literature, how to write, how to read, and other things.

Your culminating project for the year is to prepare a portfolio in which you present things you've produced that have resulted in your most valuable learning. These are called exhibits. The exhibits you present do not need to be your best work. Often we learn the most from our rough drafts, our frustrated efforts, and other experiences that do not yield our best products. You will not be graded on the quality of the exhibits that you include. Rather, you will be graded on how carefully you reflect on what you learned from producing them.

Your portfolio should include the following:

▷ Title page with name and date.

▷ A minimum of eight items that serve as your exhibits. You must include a minimum of one exhibit for each of the eight units we studied. Your portfolio may include additional exhibits if you wish.

▷ A written statement that identifies and discusses significant learning based on each exhibit, consisting of a minimum of two hundred words.

▷ A longer synthesis paper in which you discuss how these artifacts as a whole reveal what you've learned this year about both yourself and the material we have studied, consisting of a minimum of one thousand words.

These word minimums are somewhat arbitrary and would need adjustment for different groups of students. If you plan to use a portfolio assessment of any kind, students need to know at the beginning of the year, so that they can save their work. You might weave instruction in reflective thinking into each unit, stressing to students that they need to save at least one exhibit from each unit for their portfolios. You might want to provide models of successful portfolios, particularly if students are not required to produce them elsewhere in your school. But models are not enough; they will need procedural knowledge of how to prepare and write about the exhibits.

Extended Definition of Good Literature

Eisner (1985) has argued that one way to know something is through an understanding and appreciation of its form, what he calls *aesthetic knowledge*. To a transmission-oriented teacher, this emphasis might imply a duty to explain to students the aesthetic aspects of literature—Shakespeare's metaphors, the rhyme scheme he employs in particular kinds of verse, and other aspects of form—and then assess students' knowledge of them on a test.

A constructivist would make aesthetic knowledge an overarching concept for a course of study. Instead of taking the typical textbook approach of memorizing technical vocabulary and adopting the values of literary critics in evaluating literature, students would develop criteria for evaluating the quality of literature. If constructing this definition became a goal of instruction, then you would need to devote classroom time to discussing the relative merits of different literary works. Students are rather quick to express their opinions on whether or not they like a text. Such comments are seldom treated as legitimate in classrooms, where the typical response from the teacher is to ignore or suppress negative evaluations of a piece of literature and discuss it anyway.

Yet such comments could serve as the starting point for helping students articulate what they see as qualities in literature (and the lack thereof). Why is a story boring? What makes literature interesting? Is it possible for a boring story to be a good work of literature? Can literature that someone finds personally offensive still be quality literature? Is it possible for different people to have different conceptions of what counts as good literature?

If these questions are routinely asked during literary discussions, and if you consistently help students formulate their opinions into criteria for a definition of quality literature, then you are helping them to develop a formal understanding of what they think good literature is. You will need to provide instruction in how to write extended definitions as part of your writing instruction as well. If you are effective in both of these areas, then you might be able to ask students to do the following on a final exam:

> Throughout the year you have read a variety of texts: poems, short stories, plays, novels, essays, songs, and more. You have undoubtedly liked some of these better than others. For your final exam, write an essay in which you explain what distinguishes quality literature (broadly defined) from literature of lesser quality. To do so, provide the following:
>
> ▷ A set of criteria or rules that state clearly what each literary quality is
> ▷ For each criterion, an example from literature we have read this year (including literature you have read on your own) that illustrates the rule at work
> ▷ For each criterion, a *counterexample* from literature we have read this year (including literature you have read on your own) that comes close to meeting the conditions of the rule but falls short in some way
> ▷ For each example and counterexample, a *warrant* that clearly explains why the criterion is or is not being met
> ▷ For your whole argument, a *counterargument* expressing the viewpoint of someone who might disagree with you
> ▷ For the counterargument, a *rebuttal* in which you defend your position

The purpose of the class is established from the outset, allowing students to work confidently toward a worthwhile goal. They are engaging in a practice central to their domain: the construction of criteria for evaluating literature. Those criteria might vary from student to student. The assessment of their knowledge will be based on how effectively they construct their argument, rather than on how close their opinion is to the teacher's or to that of professional literary critics. If they argue that Justin Bieber is the greatest literary artist of all time, then suck it up and try to understand why. The Nobel Prize for Literature committee that honored Bob Dylan had to defend their decision, too.

Multimedia Project

A third kind of culminating project enables students to reflect on how they have changed personally through their engagement with the year's reading and activities, with special attention to the overarching concept (e.g., negotiating thresholds). The year's activities have presumably included considerable reflection on the themes of the individual units that have contributed to the development of the conversation surrounding this theme. If this theme has consistently served as the conversational thread running through all of the units, then students should be conversant in thinking about how their own lives have changed in relation to the changes they have seen in literary characters.

These reflections can be brought together in a multimedia project, produced in a form of the students' choice. Such an assignment might look like this:

> Throughout the year we have read a series of texts that concerned the theme of *negotiating thresholds*. Undoubtedly, like the literary characters, you have negotiated thresholds yourself in the last year or so. For your culminating project for the year, your assignment is to produce a text that in some way depicts how you have personally negotiated significant thresholds during the year. Select one significant experience, or one set of related experiences, and use your project to depict how you have changed. Your project can take any form you choose. Some possibilities include:
>
> ▷ A written narrative about a significant experience or set of experiences
> ▷ A narrative about a significant experience or set of experiences, produced in a different form (song, computer graphics, cartoon series, drama, or other medium)
> ▷ A work of art that depicts the experience and how you have changed; be prepared to explain how the work of art accomplishes your goals
> ▷ A text that combines any of these forms and others to depict your changes

This type of project enables students to reflect on how their schooling has helped them realize personal growth. Many teachers avoid projects of this sort because they feel it's hard to grade them "objectively." I recommend grading it as you would a portfolio, focusing on the extent to which the student has accounted for change (or lack thereof). Some teachers find that in order to assess these projects fairly, they need to ask that some products (e.g., a sculpture) be accompanied by an oral or written explanation.

Analytic Essay

The assessments thus far have focused on the students and how they have learned about their own learning, their development of aesthetic criteria, and their personal changes in relation to the year's overarching concept. Teachers may also feel the need to assess students on their understanding of or response to the literature studied. Often these assessments require students to answer questions about their memory of facts from the literature: whether Ponyboy was a Greaser or a Soc, whether Dan'l Webster was a frog or a toad, whether Huck Finn was a good boy or a bad one.

Such assessments, while being easy to grade and "objective," are questionable because they require the repetition of superficial knowledge and do not enable students to construct any new meaning during the process of assessment. I advocate instead some kind of extended writing, which is more likely to encourage complex thinking through which students can synthesize and extend their knowledge (Langer and Applebee 1987). To write an extended essay on the year's literature centered on the theme of negotiating thresholds, students might respond to the following:

During the year you have read about a great many characters negotiating a variety of thresholds, some successfully, some not. For your final exam, your task is to write an essay in which you select three literary protagonists from our year's reading and explain how effectively each one negotiated a significant threshold in the literature. Each protagonist should come from a different unit of study. To do so, you will need to:

▷ Describe the threshold being negotiated (e.g., a conflict between two social groups, a conflict between two sets of goals, a change between two stages of maturity, etc.)
▷ Describe the conflicts involved and why the situation is problematic for the protagonist
▷ Describe how the threshold is negotiated
▷ Evaluate whether or not the threshold is well negotiated

From your description of these three protagonists' experiences, draw a conclusion about how to negotiate a threshold. In doing so, make sure to refer to all three protagonists and contrast their negotiations.

Evaluating this kind of final exam will take you much longer than it takes to grade an "objective" test. You can't take these essays and run them through a scanner, then compute the grade by adding up the number of correct answers. Rather, you have to read them carefully and apply some kind of evaluative criteria, likely involving a complex set of factors: the detail of the reviews of the protagonists' experiences, the fidelity to some kind of language standard, the insight of the synthesis at the end, and so on.

Assessment Developed by Students

Another way to approach a final assessment is to dedicate class time toward the end of the course to having students generate tasks and questions through which their engagement with the course can be evaluated. This kind of assessment fits well with a teaching approach in which students help to plan the curriculum, with any approach that falls within a constructivist perspective, and with the overarching concept of self-determination. It relies on students to reveal what they have learned through their identification of authentic tasks and projects that will demonstrate how they have constructed the purpose of the class. Students could either generate a menu of tasks, projects, or questions; or negotiate a class-wide project. You could then ask them to develop a scoring rubric through which their work would be evaluated and possibly allow them to participate in the evaluation themselves.

Taking this approach requires a key role for the teacher—ensuring that students generate tasks that meet both their own sense of authenticity and the school's notion of rigorous and appropriate assessment. Students need to know that if they design a frivolous assessment, then you have a responsibility to the community to replace it with something more fitting. You might need to identify a set of guidelines for student-designed assessments. You might specify, for instance, that the culminating text must:

+ Account for material from each individual unit of study from the course

+ Synthesize knowledge across the various units

+ Meet the expectations of some literate community

+ Reveal a construction of new knowledge

+ Communicate effectively with the specified audience

If your overarching concept is designed to address a community-wide problem such as environmental contamination, students might submit their final exams to the city mayor or other official. Doing so would both provide them with an opportunity for social action and give them an audience for their exams beyond the teacher. Most writing-process stage theories begin with something like "brainstorming" or "drafting," and end with "publishing." In this approach, the final stage is *social action* that goes beyond the completion of the text (Johnson and Smagorinsky in press).

Students could follow any one of a number of processes to design this assessment. They might start by generating possible tasks in small groups and then explain them to the whole class, with the teacher serving to orchestrate the discussion. After each group has presented its ideas, the class as a whole can negotiate some kind of agreement on which one would serve as the most fruitful opportunity for a final assessment. Another possibility would be for the class to generate a menu of projects from which individual students or collaborative groups could choose.

This activity is a departure from the other assessments reviewed in this chapter in that the specific mode of assessment is developed at the end, rather than the beginning, of the course. It does meet the spirit of the general approach, however, in that it is responsive to the content and process of the instruction that have led to it. What distinguishes this method is that the students determine what is significant about the class and identify assessment vehicles through which they can synthesize their understanding and create new knowledge.

Culminating Texts for Teachers

I have referred to the ways in which teachers can produce texts during the year to construct meaning from their teaching. Following are some possible ways in which you can compose a text that contributes to your own learning and shows others how you have changed through your teaching.

Work That Parallels Student Work

One way to reflect on your teaching is to produce the same kind of culminating text that your students are working on. This approach would work best, I think, on open-ended projects such as keeping a portfolio, producing a multimedia text that synthesizes your experiences and understandings, or maintaining a journal or log in which you reflect on your own teaching in relation to your students' learning, development of relationships, personal growth, and other consequences of being in your class.

Portfolio

If you were to keep a process portfolio, your exhibits could include student work that taught you something about your teaching (with confidentiality protected), feedback on unit evaluations, excerpts from a log you've kept on your teaching, articles or books that you read that changed your teaching, or other artifacts through which you learned how to be a better teacher. As with students' process portfolios, the purpose would be to reflect on what you've learned, rather than to showcase your best work. Students will undoubtedly be interested in knowing what you learned from teaching them and how you will teach differently as a result of their experiences in your class.

Multimedia Project

You could also produce some kind of creative or multimedia project that represents what you've experienced and learned through your teaching. Producing some kind of creative work that represents your teaching experiences might fascinate your students and help them view artistic composing as more legitimate in school.

Teaching Log

If your students are keeping journals or reading logs, you could also maintain a teaching log in which you reflect on your teaching. Through a teaching log you can identify problems with your instruction and think about how to make appropriate changes. You can think about how a unit is working and whether it works better for some students than others. You can think about classroom dynamics, school politics, curriculum debates, media views of education, or other issues that affect how you contemplate your work.

Systematic Reflection on Teaching and Learning

Ethnographic Experiments

Moll (2000) has recommended that teachers conduct inquiries into what he calls the *cultural resources* of students by getting to know students and their families outside school. His work in the Tucson area is designed to bridge the cultural gap between middle-class white teachers and the working-class Mexican American students they teach. These students often do poorly in school yet engage in sophisticated cognitive and social lives at home and in the community. Moll's idea is for teachers to get a better understanding of students' competencies outside school and adjust instruction so that the students can build on these strengths and resources in their classroom work. This approach entails getting out into the community and observing students and their families at work.

Moll also believes that communities will develop greater respect and trust for teachers if they cultivate these sorts of relationships. Students will then be more likely to trust that a teacher's decisions are in their interests and be less likely to resist both the system and its individual teachers. Community studies of this sort work best, he finds, when they are conducted by teams of teachers to allow for the sharing of ideas and impressions, collaboration in the development of new teaching approaches, and support for one another's efforts.

Frame Experiments

Hillocks (1995) argues that teachers can learn a great deal about their teaching by conducting frame experiments, that is, by experiments that inquire into the consequences of teaching methods. These investigations might involve comparative studies, such as teaching two classes differently and contrasting student work produced in response to the two approaches. They might involve experimenting with new methods—using more drama, using small groups in different ways, trying writing workshops—and taking careful notes on the changes that result in your classroom. The idea is to make a systematic effort to study the effects of your teaching methods on students, using whatever means of inquiry are at your disposal.

Studies of Classroom Relationships

Freedman and colleagues (1999) report on a project in which a group of teachers studied the ways in which relationships played out in the classrooms in response to changes they made in their teaching. Unlike Hillocks, who was interested in how teaching affects students' schoolwork, the teachers working with Freedman were concerned with how to set up strong classroom communities. In a typical study, a teacher in an urban, multiracial school would assign literature that focused on racial conflict and observe how relationships among students changed as a consequence of classroom discussions and activities. For teachers interested in the relational aspects of schooling, this approach can reveal the kinds of feelings that often simmer beneath the surface of classroom order.

Summary

The first step in designing a cohesive constructive curriculum is to think about the big picture—your approach to the course as a whole—and about how students can demonstrate their learning in relation to that theme at the end of the course. If you conceive of the purpose of a whole course, the individual sections—the units that you design—will make more sense to students both in and of themselves and as they provide continuity across the school year.

Performance Assessment Prep

This chapter is about the big picture, and performance assessments are more focused on short-term teaching practices and goals. You won't be required to demonstrate that you are a curriculum specialist, only a classroom teacher of impact. So this chapter may help you contextualize the lessons you feature in your dossier at the broadest levels, without necessarily figuring into your evidence or commentary.

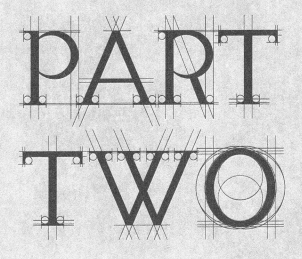

PART TWO

Teaching Composition Within a Unit Design

4

Goals for Conventional Assessments

The next step in designing your curriculum is to set goals for the individual units that contribute to the course-long conversation about the overarching theme. Once again, I plan backward in thinking about assessment—that is, I think first about what kinds of culminating texts students could ultimately produce from engagement with the material in each unit. These texts will then serve as goals when planning the path of instruction. They also serve as the texts that I will assess in order to give students grades for the class.

Constructing Units, Constructing Texts

I encourage you to think of your classroom as a *construction zone,* to borrow an analogy suggested by Newman, Griffin, and Cole (1989). To work within this zone, you should begin with some kind of plan. If you were building a house, you would undoubtedly begin by envisioning what the house would look like when you were finished. You might even draw or build a small model of that final product to help you see your ultimate goal during the process of construction. You would also prepare a blueprint, a detailed set of plans that would help you build the house according to a set of specifications.

Having this model and blueprint provides you with a goal and a plan for realizing it. It does allow for flexibility, however, depending on circumstances that arise. If your plans call for a skylight, yet you learn during construction that softwood trees drop debris on the house, you might abandon the skylight idea. If you are building the foundation and unearth a subterranean spring, you will probably move the house to a different site on the lot or change the blueprint to include a creek running through the living room. If your circumstances and goals change, then you will adjust the blueprint and model accordingly. One school I taught in outside Chicago had been designed by a California architect, whose plans included separate buildings joined by open-air walkways. The architect must never have visited the site during the winter, because nobody wanted to walk between those buildings from November to March; and ultimately they were enclosed. If you don't adjust to emerging conditions now, you'll probably end up doing it later, and you'll pay a price for your lack of foresight and flexibility.

Beginning with a sense of your outcome, and with a design for realizing it, does not lock you into a rigid plan. Rather, it provides you with a goal and a pathway that you can adjust in response to changing conditions. Following your plan regardless of intervening events can cause your house to slide into a sinkhole, or your walkways to be unwalkable. However, if you try to build a house without any idea of what it's supposed to look like, your stairway to the second floor might let out in the middle of the bathroom. Planning ahead might take time, but it can help everyone arrive in what they mostly agree to be a good spot.

My task, then, is to envision what students will be working toward as a consequence of their engagement with the unit texts and activities. These goals will come in the form of culminating texts that I will assess. The construction metaphor applies simultaneously to two things. One is the design of the unit itself. The other is the texts that students will build in relation to the unit. Both of these are goal-directed acts that require the use of tools and materials.

Conceptualizing Your Unit Focus

You will need to consider the questions, Whose unit of study is this, and who gets to decide what it is about? Conventionally, a teacher is the primary decision maker in the classroom. In this tradition, the teacher picks the unit topic and decides what's important for students to learn about it. The teacher then fashions goals, assessments, lessons, activities, and so on so that students can make progress toward grasping the unit concepts. Taking this approach, the teacher needs to think through the concept under study and plan carefully so that students can explore the key issues in a detailed and connected way.

For instance, in a unit on discrimination, you might think through what it means to discriminate, perhaps starting with examples from your own experiences or from the media. When a parent prohibits a seven-year-old from watching a PG-13 movie, is this discrimination? When a teacher tends not to call on a student who earnestly makes embarrassing statements, is this discrimination? When people who get swindled out of money say they have been "gypped," are they throwing shade at Gypsies? Your consideration of a broad series of examples will help you identify what you think is important to understand about discrimination and plan instruction appropriately.

Setting Goals

In Chapter 1 I reviewed a great range of ways in which students could know something. It would be very difficult to provide opportunities for assessing all kinds of knowing in every unit. Rather, you should try to provide diverse assessments over the course of the whole year. For any individual unit, you should provide a more limited set of major assessments, such as culminating texts through which the kids will undertake significant construction of new and important texts, knowledge, and meaning.

This chapter and the next focus on identifying the major graded texts that students produce during a unit. As a teacher you will be responsible for grading both major assessments and the smaller ones that lead up to them. To return to the construction metaphor, you will evaluate not only the finished house but also some (not all) stages of building. For now we will concentrate solely on planning the major texts that students will work toward. In so doing, we are thinking about what the house as a whole will ultimately look like.

Conventions and Alternatives

Buildings, like academic knowledge, tend to be constructed through the use of conventional tools. To drive a nail, most carpenters use a hammer. To divide a board in two, most use a saw. School, too, has its conventional tools. Students are likely to write with a pen, pencil, or keyboard and to write on paper or electronic files or web boards. In school they most typically use these tools to take notes and write correct answers on exams or to write analytically.

But in constructing buildings and doing school, you don't always follow the established conventions. There are certain established ways of doing things that often make alternatives hard to see. These well-established methods are deeply ingrained in our ways of conceiving of school, because school was that way when we were kids and has been that way for generations. If things were different, then it just wouldn't be school. Yet these ways of schooling were developed in response to a different set of circumstances than what exists today and might not fit today's conditions so well.

I used the ways of knowing outlined previously to think of culminating texts that students might produce for different units in the sophomore curriculum. Different students have different needs that can be met through studying English in your class, which suggests the need to plan assessment that allows students of different makeup and background to have the same opportunities for success.

Unit Goals as Unit Assessments

In making a distinction between conventional and alternative assessments, I am not saying that an analytic paper is never creative, exploratory, and so on. My distinction is based on the findings of recent research in human development, cultural psychology, rhetoric, intelligence, semiotics, gender, and other fields. This research has provided legitimacy, if not widespread acceptance, for considering a broader range of texts and learning processes than English classes customarily provide.

I focus primarily on the final form that their texts will take. Traditionally, teaching has focused on the proper look of a final product, without teaching students procedures for creating them. Here, we will first consider what we are working toward and then think about how to teach students how to get there.

Even though I am beginning by describing the ultimate form, it's important to understand that, as they say in architecture, *form follows function*. In other words, the form is not simply a set of things to produce. Rather, the component parts of something like an argument serve the social purpose of persuasion. And so it's important to stress during instruction that the production of a *claim* in an argument is not just something to do so that an essay will get a good mark from a teacher. Rather, it's one part of what people do when trying to convince other people of a point they want to make. I'm asking you to shift attention from the product's form to the social purposes for writing or other composition.

Not every context calls for the same approach to argumentation. A serious scholar writing for other serious scholars, for instance, usually takes a relatively dry, unemotional approach, elaborating on each point in excruciating, at times tedious, detail. Some might find it so laboriously meticulous that it ends up being unpersuasive, in part because they dismiss the scholar as a pedantic drone. In contrast, arguing on a TV talk show usually requires a participant to outshout opponents, listen as little as possible, and employ whatever tactics it takes to claim victory. When you think about unit goals, you need to keep in mind both the final form and the social action that produces it. It's vital, then, to stress the social purposes of any texts that you evaluate, particularly the ways in which they enable writers to communicate with particular groups of readers.

Each assessment discussed here includes a set of elements. First, students are presented with a description of the general task (to write a personal narrative, to write a literary analysis, etc.). Beneath the statement of the general task is a set of items separated by pearls.[1] These items serve five primary purposes:

+ Providing students with a clear set of parameters for producing their texts

+ Providing students with an understanding of how their work will be evaluated

+ Providing the teacher with a set of goals to guide instruction

+ Identifying for the teacher what students need to learn and know how to do

+ Providing the teacher with criteria to guide assessment

The assignments do more than simply tell students what to do. They also outline responsibilities for you in your teaching.

The following assessments fit within the overriding values of school yet can be produced in ways that students find meaningful and that enable them to engage in significant social action. Thinking analytically is a key skill not only for school success but for participating in many of society's activities and professions. It ought to be central to any language arts program offered in school, although it should not be the only kind of thinking and writing evaluated in school. Writing of this sort is widely assigned in school and used on high-stakes assessments, often reduced to five-paragraph themes (see Hillocks 2002; Johnson, Smagorinsky, Thompson, and Fry 2003) oriented to form over content. *Engagement with content* should be the primary consideration in writing instruction, with attention to form coming later. Form should follow function, yet function should have a form in mind.

---

1. The old term, "bullet points," seems inappropriate in an era of school shootings.

Extended Definition

One kind of conventional form that students can learn to produce is the extended definition. Extended definitions serve as the basis for most laws and governing rules, as well as for any kind of scientific classification. Consider, for instance, someone proposing a law to control sexual harassment in the workplace. In order to enforce such a law, you would need to define what it means to harass someone, what it means for that harassment to be of a sexual nature, and what it means to do this in a workplace. You would need to define these terms so that, as clearly as possible, a set of independent observers (e.g., a jury) could say with some certainty whether a particular action was or was not an act of sexual harassment in the workplace. Having a carefully worded, specific, and well-illustrated definition is particularly important in potentially ambiguous cases. Such a definition could be adapted to schools to help administrators deal with such problems as sexual cyber-bullying taking place between students, but off school grounds.

Thematic literature units can provide opportunities to work at developing extended definitions. Often they center on topics such as progress, loyalty, success, justice, courageous action, and other aspects of culture and character that require definition in order to be understood. In our sophomore curriculum, the unit on discrimination would be a good place to include instruction in writing extended definitions. Writing an extended definition of discrimination could help students think through what it means to act in discriminatory ways.

Some literature might present blatant cases of discrimination, such as the legally instituted racism described by Richard Wright in his oft-assigned autobiography *Black Boy*. Other cases are less clear and are constructed differently by people of competing ideologies. Through the process of defining and illustrating discrimination, students can help clarify for themselves how to evaluate social interactions they personally engage in and those they observe in their day-to-day lives, the news media, and other sources.

A unit on discrimination could feature sustained attention to the question of how discrimination is defined and illustrated, with classroom activities including personal writing or other composing, discussions of literature, and efforts to consider the two in terms of one another. You would also need to provide formal instruction in how to define abstract concepts. I briefly reviewed one approach when talking about criteria for comparing and contrasting the Beatles and Rolling Stones. You could provide the following prompt for a culminating text in which students would define and illustrate what it means to discriminate:

These pearls serve a variety of purposes, most obviously to inform students of what they are responsible for and what you will grade. They also specify a set of

Throughout the unit we have considered the effects of discrimination on both the person who discriminates and the person who is discriminated against. We have looked at questions of discrimination in a variety of situations, using examples from current events, from your personal experiences and observations, and from literature. In some cases, there has been disagreement on what counts as discrimination. Your task is to write an essay in which you provide an extended definition of discrimination. To do so, include the following:

▷ A general introduction in which you provide an overview for your definition
▷ A set of *criteria* or rules that state clearly what discrimination is and is not
▷ For each criterion, an *example* from literature, current events, or your personal experiences that illustrates the rule at work; at least half of your examples must come from the literature studied in class
▷ For each criterion, a *counterexample* from literature, current events, or your personal experiences that appears to meet the conditions of the rule yet that lacks some essential ingredient; at least half of your counterexamples must come from the literature studied in class
▷ For each example and counterexample, a *warrant* that clearly explains why the rule is or is not being met
▷ For your whole argument, a *counterargument* expressing the viewpoint of someone who might disagree with you
▷ For the counterargument, a *rebuttal* in which you defend your position
▷ Conventional grammar, spelling, punctuation, and usage throughout your essay
▷ Evidence of having written at least one rough draft that has been submitted for peer evaluation

responsibilities for you as a teacher. If you are going to grade something, then you need to teach students how to do it.

You might narrow this topic so that instead of defining discrimination broadly, they define it under more particular circumstances. If the texts focus on issues of race, gender, bodily status, physical appearance, social class, neurological makeup, or some other more specific topic, you could provide the opportunity for students to define discrimination in these arenas alone. Given that many adults have difficulty making such distinctions, it seems reasonable to help young people narrow the topic to a single area that they find accessible and can get a handle on.

Literary Analysis

Literary analysis is often the focus of writing instruction. In most cases, however, students are evaluated on their ability to write an analysis of a literary work already studied in class, inevitably relying on the teacher's interpretation for their own analysis, and are evaluated on their skill at low-level mimicry. This approach implies that the teacher's role is to provide a good interpretation for students to replicate on the assessment. Consider, however, what would happen if students were evaluated on their ability to analyze a work of literature that they have never seen before. This approach would evaluate their independent analytic abilities, suggesting that the purpose of instruction is to *teach analytic skills* rather than to provide a preferred interpretation, shifting the focus of instructional attention from declarative knowledge to procedural knowledge.

Let's say, then, that in the sophomore unit on coming-of-age literature, the teacher helps students see a common pattern in such stories. Coming-of-age stories typically provide some illustration of a protagonist's immature behavior at the outset, move to a critical experience that results in a major realization, and conclude with a transformation to more mature behavior by the end. Class activities could focus on seeing how protagonists negotiate the threshold of this critical experience and thinking about what kinds of transformations they undergo. As part of this literary analysis, students could engage in reflection on personal transformations they have made following from critical experiences, thus recognizing this pattern in their own lives.

The teacher could then evaluate students' ability to recognize and interpret this pattern with an essay based on a choice of literary works, none of which has been covered in class. Their task is then to identify and analyze the transformation that they see in the independently read story, possibly through a culminating text produced in response to the following prompt:

From the literary choices provided, read one work of literature, and write an essay in which you analyze the protagonist's coming-of-age experience. In your essay, make sure that you

> ▷ Provide a general thesis for the paper, explaining the protagonist's primary transformation during the course of the story
> ▷ Describe the protagonist's immature behavior at the beginning of the story, including specific examples from the text

▷ Describe clearly the key event that causes the character to change; in doing so, explain why this event, rather than others in the story, causes the protagonist to come of age

▷ Describe the significant changes taking place in the protagonist following the coming-of-age experience, including specific examples from the text

▷ Draw a conclusion about how people change as a result of significant events and how these changes can be considered as a coming-of-age

▷ Follow rules of conventional grammar, spelling, punctuation, and usage throughout your essay

▷ Give evidence of having written at least one rough draft that has been submitted for peer evaluation

Argumentation

Argumentation is another staple of school writing, a common form of writing in many professions, and the way in which most conflicting points of view come into contact. In order to prove your point, you need to argue it; that is, you need to:

✦ Have a thesis (e.g., a belief that conflict between peer groups in school must be resolved).

✦ Support it with a set of claims (e.g., that antagonism has increased, tension is greater in hallways, there is less unity at school functions, administrators have taken steps to provide greater security, etc.).

✦ Back each claim with evidence (e.g., that fights have grown more frequent, students self-segregate in the cafeteria, some students have posted hateful comments on websites, administrators have hired additional security guards, etc.).

✦ Anticipate a counterargument (e.g., that the problem is not so great because for the most part, students in the school are safe; that the school cannot afford the cost of yet more security guards; that increased security guards make the school a hostile environment for learning and socialization).

✦ Rebut the counterargument (e.g., that the problem must be addressed before a crisis takes place, rather than after it happens).

Even if you never become a lawyer or serve on a political talk show panel, knowing careful argumentation can help you see clearly on issues you care about yet over which people disagree. At the same time, it helps to recognize that argumentation is not purely logical, but has a strong emotional dimension. I have argued, drawing on Haidt's (2014) work in moral reasoning, that most arguments begin with gut feelings that are then rationalized (Smagorinsky 2018c). This phenomenon explains why arguments conducted on the US Supreme Court, presumably populated by the nation's most judicious thinkers, are often decided according to the justices' entering ideologies rather than the power of their argumentative clarity.

Much of the English curriculum can provide opportunities for instruction in argumentation. Students can argue for interpretations of literature or for ways to view literary movements. For the sophomore curriculum, the unit on conflict with authority is a good occasion for students to argue for a particular interpretation of a character's actions. The students could write their arguments in response to the following prompt:

From the literary choices provided, read one work of literature, and write an argument in which you analyze the protagonist's conflict with an authority figure. In your argument, evaluate the protagonist's approach to resolving the conflict. In producing your argument, make sure that you do the following:

▷ Provide a governing *thesis* in which you explain the conflict and provide a general evaluation of the protagonist's actions.
▷ Support this thesis with a set of *claims*—that is, the reasons that support your interpretation.
▷ Back up each claim with *evidence* from the story and a *warrant* that explains why it supports the claim.
▷ Anticipate and explain a *counterargument*, which is a disagreement with your interpretation.
▷ Rebut the *counterargument* with additional reasons in support of your argument.
▷ Follow rules of conventional grammar, spelling, punctuation, and usage throughout your essay.
▷ Give evidence of having written at least one rough draft that has been submitted for peer evaluation.

Research Report

Another conventional kind of assessment found in school is the research report. Such reports are produced in many disciplines and professions, and they often are required in school curricula. A good report on a significant topic can make an important contribution to people's knowledge about issues that matter to them.

In English classes, students could write research reports on issues related to the unit concept they are studying. The Shakespeare unit from the sophomore curriculum, for instance, could involve students in doing library research on the historical context of *Julius Caesar*. This research could serve a variety of purposes: evaluating the historical accuracy of the play, learning more about particular characters of interest, informing an understanding of the play's plot, and so on.

For the discrimination unit, students could conduct research on the Black Lives Matter movement, the women's Me Too movement, various "religious liberty" cases, or any variety of discrimination battles waged in local, US, or world history. By sharing these reports with their classmates, students could provide a good context for discussing questions of discrimination that arise in the literature.

Research reports tend to follow a particular written formula in schools. This traditional means of presentation was established before other media became available to students. I think that, in circumstances where resources allow, teachers ought to take advantage of opportunities that students have to use computers, videos, and related technologies to produce their research reports. The form of the report, then, might vary if students have the capability to produce a documentary film instead of a written report.

A research report might be produced in response to the following prompt:

We have been studying questions of discrimination in the literature we have read and in your personal knowledge of the world. For your culminating project, produce a research report on some historical instance of discrimination. The topic may be of international significance (e.g., apartheid in South Africa), important in American history (e.g., the denial of women's right to vote), or of local or community interest (e.g., a skateboarding restriction on community sidewalks). Your report should meet the following requirements:

▷ You may produce it in any form of your choice: writing, film, interview recordings, computer graphics, and so on, or any combination of these forms.

> ▷ The report should be guided by some perspective you take on the issue.
> ▷ If written, your report should include a minimum of one thousand words (roughly four typed pages).
> ▷ If produced in some other medium or combination of media, your report should require at least a ten-minute presentation.
> ▷ Your presentation should exhibit some clear organizational pattern that follows from your report's thesis.
> ▷ The information you provide must come from a minimum of five sources and may include secondary sources (i.e., sources such as books or encyclopedias that someone else has written and that you take information from) and/or primary sources (i.e., sources that you personally investigate, such as interviews you conduct, observations you make, or documents you study).

Summary

Conventional assessments of the sort usually outlined in state and district curriculum guides do not need to be reductive and needn't make school learning an exercise in memorization, testing, and forgetting. By working paradigmatically in conventional genres, students have rich opportunities to learn about themselves, social history, literary themes, and other illuminating topics. The key is to focus on content over form initially and to teach procedures that students may use to guide their own inquiries.

Performance Assessment Prep

This chapter will matter in your performance assessment dossier, given that assessment is one of the three major categories in most such evaluations. In your dossier, your account of your assessment procedures will be presented after you have taught kids, so you'll be demonstrating your assessment plan in action. At this point, you aren't prepared, I assume, to have examples of how you've responded to student writing, how you've revised your teaching after reflection, and so on. Rather, you are thinking about assessment prior to having classes of your own to teach.

Nonetheless, this chapter provides you with an understanding of the sorts of assessments often conducted in schools, and how they emerge from pedagogical traditions. You could use the information in this chapter to justify your assessment choices in your commentaries, and then use your experiences to verify or disconfirm the assumptions you made in your planning.

5

Goals for Unconventional Assessments

Now we'll take a look at some alternative kinds of culminating texts that can form the basis of assessment. Although less frequently assessed in schools, they are every bit as legitimate in terms of how people think, act, communicate, and represent meaning throughout society.

Exploratory Thinking and Writing

Previously I reviewed Barnes' (1992) views of exploratory and final-draft uses of speech. Much of what you evaluate in school will be final drafts. One problem with schooling in general is that it focuses on these products without providing opportunities for students to engage in—and be rewarded for—the informal, tentative, experimental processes that lead to them. Following are four kinds of exploratory work you can evaluate: portfolios, journals, rough drafts, and student-generated questions about literature.

Portfolio

The process *portfolio* is a tool through which you can evaluate students on what they have learned about their learning during your course, often through reflection on exploratory texts they have produced on their way to more formal products. You could also use portfolios in individual units.

Course-Long Portfolio Preparation

Process portfolios call for preparation during each unit of study. For each unit, students should identify exploratory work that has generated significant new learning and include it in the portfolio they are preparing for the course as a whole. You could periodically devote class time to having students discuss which of their exploratory efforts have been significant learning experiences and work with them on the process for preparing a reflective statement for an individual exhibit.

Portfolios for Individual Units

You could have students keep shorter portfolios for individual units of study, or perhaps for each marking period, requiring exhibits gathered from a more limited pool of possible items.

Journal

Students can also keep journals in which they think through their engagement with the unit topics, allowing writing to serve as a tool for discovering new ideas. Journals come in a variety of forms, such as personal journals, reading logs, and dialogue journals.

Personal Journal

A personal journal is an open-ended opportunity for students to write whatever they think or feel in response to the unit's content and processes. Ideally, the journal will involve a strong component of reflection, of thinking through ideas and emotions, of developing a personal response to the unit. It should not simply summarize readings or discussions. You can make reflection part of the requirements of the assignment and include attention to reflection in your assessment.

Some people find such reflection to be invasive. Some parents, for instance, protest strongly when teachers require introspective writing because they feel that a student's personal life is of no importance in learning an academic discipline and is none of a teacher's business. Some students are very private and don't wish to produce writing on personal topics that others will read about. One solution is to make them optional, so that students who benefit from them will have the opportunity, whereas students who are discreet or whose families discourage introspection in school will not be caught in a conflict. You could present the journal as follows:

Keep a journal in which you think through thoughts and feelings that you have in response to the material we study, the class discussions and activities that we engage in, and any other experience you have with the unit topic. The following issues will be factors in the way I grade your journal:

▷ Your journal does not need to follow the conventions of textbook English. Rather, the purpose is to think about the class without worrying about the form your thoughts take.

▷ Do not simply summarize literature we read in the class. Though you need to refer to these texts, the primary purpose of your journal is to think about your response to them, rather than to provide summaries of what they say. In other words, your journal should focus on how you have engaged with the literature.

▷ You are welcome, though not required, to reflect on personal issues that occur to you in relation to your consideration of the literature.

▷ Your journal should include a minimum of five hundred words of writing (roughly two typed pages) per week. For each entry, put the date of the writing at the beginning.

▷ Keep in mind that *I am required to share any thoughts or suggestions of violence, suicide, substance abuse, family abuse, or other harmful behavior with the school counselors.*

▷ If there are any pages in your journal that you do not want me to read, please mark them with an *X* at the top.

These last two items raise one of the trickiest questions about journals: how to treat issues of confidentiality. You want students to write honestly in their journals, yet they know you will read them. You are also obligated to report destructive or dangerous behavior, and the thoughts associated with it, to parents and/or school authorities. At my own university, teacher candidates working in schools are considered "mandatory reporters" under state law, which requires them to report suspected child abuse or risk liability themselves. Students need to know how you are going to read their journals and what you will do with certain kinds of information. Often, students use assignments like this as a way of asking for help when they don't know of any other way.

Reading Log

A more structured kind of journal, with a more specific purpose, is the reading log. The purpose of such journals is to encourage students to attend carefully to the language of the texts and to read reflectively, pausing to think about particular passages before moving along, or perhaps reading longer sections and writing about the text in retrospect. A reading log could follow from a prompt like this:

> Keep a reading log in response to the literature we are studying during this unit. To keep your log:
>
> ▷ Write informally in response to the literature read for class. Your writing may come in response to anything you find interesting, puzzling, compelling, challenging, or otherwise worthy of your consideration. Feel free to pose questions without answers; explore your ideas through the process of writing; rant, rave, or respond in whatever way best helps you to think about what matters to you in the literature.
>
> ▷ Write a minimum of three entries for each work of literature studied.
>
> ▷ Remember that your journal does not need to follow the conventions of textbook English. Rather, the purpose is to think about the literature without worrying about the form your thoughts take.
>
> ▷ Keep in mind that *I am required to share any thoughts or suggestions of violence, suicide, substance abuse, family abuse, or other harmful behavior with the school counselors.*

Dialogue Journal

A dialogue journal is a journal shared by two or more people, where they carry on a discussion about a shared topic. Students might share a dialogue journal through electronic mail or online shared document, and could include any number of participants, providing a forum for discussion beyond what the classroom offers.

A dialogue journal might be prompted as follows:

With at least one other person, maintain a dialogue journal in which you discuss the issues raised in class. In keeping your dialogue journal, remember the following:

▷ Your journal does not need to follow the conventions of textbook English. Rather, the purpose is to think about the class without worrying about the form your thoughts take.

▷ Do not simply summarize literature or other texts that we read in the class. Your discussion should include questions, analysis, reflection, and evaluation. It should be evident that you are learning something new through your dialogue.

▷ Make sure that you include attention to each text studied in the unit.

▷ You are welcome, though not required, to reflect on personal issues that occur to you in relation to your consideration of the literature.

▷ All participants in your dialogue journal should make roughly equal contributions.

▷ *I am required to share any thoughts or suggestions of violence, suicide, substance abuse, family abuse, or other harmful behavior with the school counselors.*

Rough Drafts

Another way to evaluate exploratory thinking is to have students turn in rough drafts of their work. You can provide feedback in several ways.

For each piece of extended writing they do, students could be required to produce one or two rough drafts. For each of these drafts, they could get in small groups to evaluate one another's work and provide recommendations for improvement.

They could also turn in these drafts to you for feedback or seek a reader from outside class, including their parents or other significant adults or knowledgeable readers. Keep in mind that in school, teachers are almost exclusively the evaluators of students' work. Having students write for others can help them learn about the notion of audience, which many rhetoricians stress is essential to effective writing and communication.

Asking Questions

Students rarely pose questions in school. Observers of classrooms have found some rather astonishing things about how frequently students initiate inquiries of their own. In one study, for instance, students asked, on the average, one question each month. Most questions students ask are procedural, such as how long a paper should be or if they may go to the bathroom. It's hard to imagine establishing a school culture based on principles of inquiry and constructivism when students so rarely pose the questions that guide their learning.

Simply telling students to ask questions is often frustrating because they have been conditioned to view school as a place where every question has a correct answer. In school, then, when you ask students to ask questions, they often come up with questions that sound a lot like the ones you'll find at the end of their textbook chapters: Which character did what? What was the name of the character who did such and such? The mirror they provide for schooling is not one I find attractive to look into.

One way you can evaluate students is to teach them to ask questions, requiring exploratory talk because they will need to talk about the texts in order to generate their questions, and the questions they pose ought to inquire into the open-ended territory that exploratory talk helps them investigate.

I created this assignment for the study of *The Outsiders* in a unit on gangs, cliques, and peer-group pressure, but it can easily be adapted to any unit. The assignment places the job of literary discussion entirely in students' hands. After many years of leading class discussions myself—relying on my own clever questions to guide our analysis—I shifted this responsibility to students with the following assignment:

To discuss S. E. Hinton's *The Outsiders*, the class will organize into six small groups, with each group being responsible for leading a discussion of two chapters of the novel. Each group will conduct a class discussion on its two chapters for one full period. To lead your class, you may adopt any format you wish: regular English class, reasonably civilized talk show, town hall meeting, courtroom, or other mode of your choice. Your discussion should involve all of the following:

> ▷ Each group member should take a roughly equal part in leading the discussion.
> ▷ You should make an effort to include each other class member in your discussion.

> ▷ The questions you pose should not ask for factual information from the story, unless those facts serve to help explore open-ended questions (i.e., those without a single correct answer).
> ▷ The questions you pose should include at least one of each of the following categories:
> > ▷ *Inferences* about characters or events within the text (e.g., which character do you believe that the author has the greatest sympathy for? Why?)
> > ▷ *Generalizations* from the text to society at large (e.g., where in our school do we see characters like those in the novel?)
> > ▷ The *effects of literary form or technique* (e.g., why is the novel called *The Outsiders*?)
> > ▷ The *purpose of a particular event* in terms of the text's meaning (e.g., what do you think is the most significant point in the novel? Why?)
> > ▷ *Evaluations* of the literature (e.g., what parts of the story do you like best and least? Why?)
> > ▷ *Emotions* that students have in response to the story (e.g., did anything in the novel make you angry? Please explain.)
> > ▷ *Personal connections* to the story (e.g., which characters from the novel do you most identify with? Why?)
> ▷ During the discussion, you should also work at getting students to elaborate on their initial comments.

Narrative Knowing

Recall Bruner's (1986) contention that narrative knowing has just as crucial a role in human history as paradigmatic knowing. Much literature is presented around some kind of story, one that portrays something about the human condition. Often readers relate to literature by recounting a personal story that parallels the issues depicted in the literature. One thing that students can do, then, as a way of engaging with the unit themes is to write, act, or otherwise produce a personal narrative in which they relate a significant event from their own lives. For the hypothetical sophomore curriculum I have developed, these events would involve the negotiation of a threshold, with particular attention to one of the unit concepts.

Let's say, for instance, that the students are studying the unit on conflict with authority. Their task might be the following:

> Write about a personal experience in which you had a conflict with someone in authority. The authority figure might have been an adult (a parent, teacher, coach, etc.) or a peer in an authority position (a team captain, student government leader, etc.). Through your narrative, you should convey the following:
>
> ▷ Your relationship with the person with whom you came in conflict
> ▷ The nature of your conflict
> ▷ How both you and the other person viewed the conflict
> ▷ If you resolved it, how; if you didn't, what happened
> ▷ What you learned through the experience
>
> You do not need to explain these things in this order and don't need to announce or label any of them (that is, you don't need to have a paragraph beginning, "My relationship with so-and-so was . . ."). Rather, you should, at some point in your narrative, relate these things in some way.

Connected Knowing

Previously I reviewed ways in which schools do not provide many opportunities for relational or connected learning. Here I suggest a few ways in which you can plan assessments that take connected knowing into account.

Collaborative Learning

One way you can be responsive to connected knowers is to provide opportunities for collaboration on graded work. For instance, you can allow students to conduct their research reports or creative and multimedia projects in teams or plan to include collaborative learning in the activities that lead to the production of culminating texts.

Affective Response

Through the use of journals, student-generated discussions, narratives, and other kinds of assessment, you can increase the opportunities for students' affective responses to texts to be included in your evaluations of their schoolwork.

Exploratory Learning Opportunities

Connected knowing is often associated with tentative, exploratory learning. I have reviewed a number of possible ways to allow for exploratory expression in assessed schoolwork: journals, student-generated discussions, process-oriented writing instruction, and so on.

Multimedia or Multigenre Productions

Some of the most remarkable work I have seen from high school students has come through multimedia productions, including art, music, dance, live or video recorded performance, and various combinations of these modes and others. Some rather intriguing multimedia productions do not necessarily reveal deep engagement with the literature. In one class I observed, for instance, a student baked a cake and decorated it in the fashion of a story's setting, and the class then ate it. It was never clear what the student had learned from this process, although the cake was mighty tasty. You might want to ask students to either write or verbally present an explanation of their project's significance to help you evaluate it. Multimedia composing can provide a powerful medium for high-level engagement with literature and serve a very important function in students' interpretive process, helping them generate images of literature that can then form the basis for a response or interpretation.

Here is one very open-ended assignment that you can adapt to a variety of units:

You have read a complex work of literature in Shakespeare's *Julius Caesar*. To show what you have learned through your engagement with this play, create an interpretive text in any form of your choice: collage, painting, poetry, music, drama, sculpture, performance art, or other textual form. You are also welcome to combine forms to produce your text. Furthermore, you may use different forms within a form—that is, you can include a gravestone with epitaph, a haiku, a song, an encyclopedia entry, a movie review, and so on, all within a single interpretive text. Keep the following in mind when producing your text:

▷ It should in some way depict your understanding of the play. This understanding might be about any of the following:
  ▷ The play's characters and their actions and relationships
  ▷ How the play has helped you learn something about yourself and your world
  ▷ Roman history
  ▷ Shakespeare as a playwright
  ▷ Other topic of your choice

> ▷ It should make some kind of reference to the play, even if it focuses on you and your current world.
> ▷ You may produce your text individually or in a group of any size up to five.
> ▷ You will have two class periods in which to work on your text and must do all additional work outside class.
> ▷ You must prepare a three- to five-minute presentation of your text to the class in which you explain its significance and what it says about your understanding of the play.

Unconventional Genres

Another type of assessment is to have students write (perhaps in combination with other media) in genres that are not ordinarily produced by students for school. The following list is hardly exhaustive and is intended primarily to prime the pump of your imagination. When making assignments, you need to identify the traits that should be involved in such texts, specify what they are, and make yourself responsible for teaching students how to produce them.

Book or Film Review

Book and movie reviews are available through a variety of media, with newspapers, television, and the Internet providing countless examples of the genre. Students could study the genre and its elements and produce reviews of texts they read in class. This kind of assessment might be particularly useful if you choose a book club arrangement for a unit or if you have opportunities to publish the reviews for other students to read.

Guide Book

Students could also produce a guide book. In a unit on peer groups, for instance, students could write a guide book for incoming students. The book would review the different social groups among the student body. The book could include pictures, descriptions, interviews, and other ways to characterize the different groups inhabiting the school. Students should try to present each group in a fair and respectful manner and not portray groups they don't belong to in unflattering ways.

Letter to the Editor

Students could write letters to the editor of a publication in which they express their opinions on some topic of importance to them. This task might follow from instruction in expository or persuasive writing, but students could see that letters to the editor often lack the formality of the kinds of analytic writing they learn to do in school.

Children's Book

Students could produce a children's book related to the unit's theme. For the unit on *Julius Caesar*, for instance, students could retell a scene from the play, presenting it in the style of a set of children's books that they study. The assignment could conceivably bridge two different units, with students producing their book in the form of a parody.

Creative Writing

Students can also generate creative work of their own, produced in a variety of forms. By creative writing, I mean works of poetry, fiction, drama, and other fictive modes. Following are two examples.

Writing Related to the Unit Concept

Students can produce a poem, play, story, and so on that concerns the unit concept. They might, for instance, produce some kind of literary work that includes a conflict with authority. You could either have students produce a particular form (poem, story, etc.) or leave the assignment open-ended, allowing them to choose their own medium or combination of genres.

Evaluating creative writing has proven to be difficult for many teachers who find it too subjective to assess. As a result, they don't assign it. Eliminating creative work from the curriculum because it's hard to grade, however, can limit the ways in which students learn through their engagement with literature and other texts. Instead of disallowing open-ended thinking and writing, you should think of open-minded ways to assess it. The following assignment is one way to specify assessment criteria without compromising the open-ended manner in which students may proceed:

During the unit we have read a variety of literary works concerned with the theme of conflict with authority. Now it is your turn to write one. Using a medium of your choice, or a combination of media, produce a literary work that includes a conflict with an authority figure. In producing your literature, keep in mind the following:

▷ You may use any literary form or combination of literary forms.
▷ You may supplement your writing with other media: graphics, sound, movement, and so on.
▷ Your text should in some way involve a conflict with an authority figure.
▷ Although you needn't resolve the conflict (many conflicts go unresolved), you do need to show in some way the aftermath of the conflict and its consequences.

Genres

Students can also produce literature in a particular genre. In the sophomore unit on parody, for instance, they can both study parodies and create them. An assignment that George Hillocks thought up long ago still works quite well. The idea is for students to study a writer with a distinctive style, such as Edgar Allan Poe or J. D. Salinger. After characterizing that style, the students parody it with a kind of text that provides a humorous contrast, such as a children's story or nursery rhyme. Following a careful reading of Poe's style and characterization of his tendencies—dark images, macabre themes, recurring terms—students could retell Humpty Dumpty, Jack and Jill, or another children's story using his style. The prompt for students might appear as follows:

Take a Mother Goose rhyme or other children's story, and retell it in the style of Edgar Allan Poe. In your parody:

▷ Remain faithful to the main elements of the children's rhyme or story.
▷ Tell the story in a voice that uses elements of Edgar Allan Poe's narrative style, including:
  ▷ Common themes
  ▷ Typical sentence structures
  ▷ Recurring words

▷ Method of narration (e.g., first person)
▷ Narrative perspective

▷ Exaggerate these elements so that they are clearly recognizable and humorous.

Summary

My focus on detailing assignments is only part of the story. Each pearled item in each assignment is also an assignment to myself: I have a responsibility to teach the students how to produce the elements I'm calling for.

Performance Assessment Prep

This chapter is similar to the previous one in helping you prepare your commentary. You should also consider the possibility that your safest choice in this assessment is to go with what is expected and not what is unconventional. As I say in this book's final chapter: Preparing for performance assessment should matter only in performance assessment. How you teach when not getting assessed is far more liberating and should not be confused with passing this test.

6

Responding to Student Compositions

You have identified the texts that students will produce in your class. Now you'll need to evaluate them. Several considerations figure into the ways in which you read and respond to the work that students do, both during their composing processes and when they submit papers for a grade.

In-Process Response

Most responses to student writing tend to come solely from the teacher, and only at the end of the final draft that students would submit for evaluation. However, students benefit from feedback as they work, rather than just at the end. This shift is not simply organizational but implies a change in philosophy about learners. By providing in-process feedback, teachers become more oriented to the growth of the learners than to the perceived quality of their final products. This shift is consistent with a constructivist approach, helping learners understand how to produce satisfying and communicative texts and, in the process, develop in terms of both their literacy skills and sense of self.

For school purposes, "prewriting" often has an official beginning and end, circumscribed by the teacher's allocation of time to this "stage" of the writing process. I use quotations around these terms because in practice, they are not so discrete. Attention to learning processes makes for very untidy conceptions of teaching. If we think of meaningful compositions as provisional texts in a long-term project of making sense of the world, then what students write for school may or may not contribute to that effort. If students' lives outside school are considered irrelevant to textual interpretation, then I imagine that school writing is mostly irrelevant and disruptive to that quest for meaning.

Response at Conception

One way to enable students to get feedback and to explore ideas collaboratively is to have them work initially in small groups on a problem similar to the one that they will later approach in greater complexity, perhaps independently. Let's say, for instance, that you have designed a thematic unit on loss of innocence, with J. D. Salinger's *Catcher in the Rye* serving as the unit's major work. Among your unit goals is the composition of a parody of Holden Caulfield's narration. Most students are familiar with parody through their experiences with the media.

Using their prior knowledge as a basis, and providing some information about the features of parody—emphasis on typical traits, exaggeration—you can have students work together to generate a topic for a parody and plan how to carry it out. At this stage, students might focus on something brief and distinctive, such as TV commercials for trucks to learn procedures for parody before writing one on Holden Caufield.

By working collaboratively on an open-ended problem of this sort, the students get immediate feedback on their ideas. The point is that at this early stage in students' efforts to try something new, they work in a setting in which they may engage in exploratory, experimental, playful discussion through which they mutually arrive at ideas that they put into practice. Further, they receive immediate feedback on everything they say from the other members of their group. By including such opportunities throughout the composing process, teachers build response to composing into students' efforts during their work.

Response to Drafts

Peer Feedback

Another in-process opportunity for response to student compositions is to provide peer feedback following the completion of a draft. Many people advocate using a small-group response session so that students may critique one another's work. There are two advantages to this approach. First, students get feedback on their compositions that helps them in the next draft. Second, students get experience as critical readers that may help them in reading and revising their own work.

Response groups may be conducted in a number of ways. One way is simply to have pairs of students exchange their work and provide each other holistic evaluations, either through marginal commentary or writing conferences. The same approach can work with larger groups, with students reading and evaluating more than one composition. Be aware, however, that many teachers believe that, without guidance in how to respond constructively, peer response opportunities may provide little value and might result in students following questionable suggestions.

You might also assign particular reading roles. Let's say that you've taught a unit on the British Lake poets, and among the students' tasks is to write an argumentative essay interpreting a poem such as Keats' "Ode on a Grecian Urn." After supporting their understanding of both how to interpret such a poem and how to write a critical argument, you could have students produce a draft of their interpretive essay. You could then organize the students into groups of roughly four and have them evaluate in turn four qualities on which the paper will be assessed. They can go through the following procedures:

1. The students pass their papers to the person on the left. After receiving a classmate's paper, each person reads for a specific quality such as general argumentative structure, including the presence of an overall thesis, a related set of claims, and examples from the poem and/or other British romantic poetry supporting each claim. Each critical reader makes marginal comments to help the writer sharpen the argument according to this criterion.

2. Students rotate their papers again to the left so that each is reading a new classmate's paper. Again, the students have a specific responsibility, this time critiquing the paper for the degree to which the claims are orchestrated to support the general thesis and to which the evidence convincingly supports the claims. Again, each reader makes marginal comments.

3. Students rotate their papers to the left a final time. For this reading, they evaluate for coherence, including the writer's attention to form and mechanics, transitions between paragraphs, and other qualities that contribute to a fluent presentation.

4. Students then receive their papers back and have an opportunity to discuss their papers with one another before beginning their next set of revisions.

This approach might require some training and practice, particularly if students are unfamiliar with responding to one another's compositions. You should caution the students to evaluate the feedback and incorporate only that which they judge to be valuable.

Writing Conferences

Writing conferences are simply meetings between a teacher and a student to discuss either a piece of writing or a collection of papers. The main advantage is the personal attention that the students receive in terms of their writing growth. The main problems concern the amount of class time (or out-of-school time) that writing conferences require and the managerial issues that follow from a teacher's dedication of undivided attention to a single student. If a class includes twenty-five students, and if a single writing conference occupies about ten minutes, that's roughly four hours of conferences that a teacher must conduct to reach everyone, and four hours in which the rest of the class gets little attention or supervision. Writing conferences, then, occupy about a week's worth of instruction and possible free-range opportunities for the rest of the class, requiring the teacher to provide some sort of worthwhile activity that the remainder of the class can pursue without being supervised closely, an assumption reliant on students' maturity and dedication to academic work.

Writing conferences tend to be conducted in one of two ways. One is a nondirectional approach in which the student does most of the talking and the teacher primarily poses questions. The idea here is for the student to develop agency and ownership with respect to writing and for the teacher to provide a supportive role in the conferences. The other approach is more directive, with the teacher providing an evaluation and recommendations for how the student might improve.

Response to "Final" Products

I put the word *final* in quotation marks because I don't think that a text is ever finished, any more than a person ever is. Rather, a composition is tied to a person's growing sense of self. It serves as a temporary, provisional statement of where the person is at the point of composition. It further contributes to the growth process that leads to that sense of self by providing an opportunity to explore and represent ideas and beliefs. A final draft, then, is final only for purposes of assessment; if it has any meaning, it then serves as a point of reflection and further revision of the ideas.

Correctness

Let me start by relating an experience I often had as a younger, more single heterosexual person attending parties. I'd strike up a conversation with a woman who came within range. Inevitably, we'd exchange the "So, what do you?" question. Here's when I always knew that the party was over for me. "I'm a high school English teacher," I'd say.

She'd get a nervous look on her face. "Oh, English was always my worst subject," she'd reply. And then the inevitable: "I'd better not make any mistakes in my grammar," offered with a ruffled chuckle. And within a few minutes, or seconds, she'd spot someone far, far across the room and excuse herself to escape my corrective presence. That's the image that English teachers have developed over time. And I think that's unfortunate for the domain.

English teachers are often focused on correcting errors in both speech and writing. Shaughnessy (1977) has provided a different conception of errors that I think is more complex and provocative and more sensitive to the growth trajectories of writers. She found that errors were often encouraging signs of growth, rather than discouraging signs of ignorance. This perspective on errors is consistent with a constructivist teaching approach in which learners are viewed developmentally, as works in progress, as is their writing. As such, violations of conventions needn't be flooded with red ink but should be viewed as efforts by the writer to try something new, a venture that inevitably produces errors somewhere along the line.

The dreaded red pen is problematic in other ways as well. Hillocks (1986) found that teachers who mark each and every infelicity on a student's paper end up intimidating and terrifying all of the confidence out of young writers. He suggests instead that response to student writers be focused on a few features, preferably those that have been emphasized during instruction. If a conceptual unit features writing narration and the student incorporates dialogue, sequences events appropriately, explores a feeling, and otherwise attempts to tell a story in accordance with the instruction, feedback should focus largely on those qualities. Teachers should offer encouragement, include commentary that is conversational and not just corrective, and not mark each and every error in spelling and mechanics that occurs while the student's focus is elsewhere.

Hillocks further found that when interviewed, teachers *say* that they value a student's ideas over all other considerations, that mechanics are a distant second to content in their treatment of student writing. Yet studies of the feedback provided by these same teachers to their students found that they responded almost exclusively to grammar and usage.

On language, then, I suggest taking a sympathetic, developmental approach to the whole of what students are trying to accomplish through their writing. Responses to student writing should be positive and encouraging so as to help build confidence in what is for many people an onerous task. I'm not saying that you should never draw a student's attention to an inappropriate use of language or punctuation; if writing can't communicate, then it's got problems. Rather, I'm suggesting you consider the overall qualities of writing, especially in relation to your teaching, and respond to student writers accordingly. Think of something that you're awful at and are intimidated by—learning to prepare a complicated meal, growing roses, repairing a plumbing problem—and think about how you'd benefit from being supported as you learned to do it. I doubt if you'd ever want to do it again if all you got was negativity and correction in response.

Rubrics

Grading student work can be a perplexing task. How do you know that all work that receives a B has similar qualities that can be distinguished from all work that receives an A or a C? Making this distinction is especially important when a student or parent questions your grading decisions. How can you answer their challenge in ways that are defensible?

One way is to develop a *rubric* to guide your decisions. A rubric is a scale that specifies how to differentiate between one level of performance and another. In its simplest form, a rubric for a one-hundred-question multiple-choice test might simply say:

90–100 items correct: A

80–89 items correct: B

70–79 items correct: C

60–69 items correct: D

59 or fewer items correct: F

Yet life in a constructivist classroom is not so clear-cut. When grading essays, portfolios, narratives, multimedia projects, drama, and so on, you need to specify how you will distinguish between an A and a B, a B and a C, and so on. We'll use the portfolio as an example of how to develop a scoring rubric for an open-ended assignment.

The following is a series of questions you might ask in thinking about assessment:

✦ What might students learn from doing this task and producing this text, and how do I know that they've learned it?

✦ What conventions do students need to follow to produce an acceptable form of this genre? These could include issues ranging from the need for a particular form of English (e.g., textbook English) to the need for criteria in an extended definition.

+ What level of detail is required to treat the topic sufficiently?

+ What degree of cohesion should a student achieve?

+ To what degree has the student met each point in the assignment?

The portfolio assignment includes some very clear, unambiguous requirements, and some requirements that are more open to interpretation. Assume that your school follows the traditional A–F grading system. The following is one possible rubric for assessing the portfolio project described in Chapter 4. Note that the assessment points map well onto the assignment's criteria. In turn, you'll need to take responsibility for teaching students how to do the things you'll be grading them on.

A grade of A will be awarded to portfolios that

+ Are turned in on time;

+ Include the minimum components;

+ Meet minimum expectations for each component (e.g., word minimum);

+ Clearly explain how each exhibit served as the source of significant learning about oneself, the materials, and/or the student's learning process; and

+ Clearly explain in the synthesis paper how the individual exhibits contribute to an overall set of related learning experiences explained in terms of a related set of points.

A grade of B will be awarded to portfolios that

+ Are turned in on time;

+ Include the minimum components;

+ Meet minimum expectations for each component (e.g., word minimum);

+ Clearly explain how each exhibit served as the source of significant learning about oneself, the materials, and/or the student's learning process; and

+ Do not clearly explain in the synthesis paper how the individual exhibits contribute to an overall set of related learning experiences explained in terms of a related set of points.

A grade of C will be awarded to portfolios that

+ Are turned in on time;

+ Include the minimum components;

+ Meet minimum expectations for each component (e.g., word minimum);

+ Do not clearly explain how each exhibit served as the source of significant learning about oneself, the materials, and/or the student's learning process; and

+ Do not clearly explain in the synthesis paper how the individual exhibits contribute to an overall set of related learning experiences explained in terms of a related set of points.

A grade of D will be awarded to portfolios that

+ Are turned in on time;

+ Include the minimum components;

+ Do not meet minimum expectations for the components (e.g., the synthesis paper does not provide a synthesis, the commentaries are less than a page long or do not indicate reflection on learning);

+ Do not clearly explain how each exhibit served as the source of significant learning about oneself, the materials, and/or the student's learning process; and

+ Do not clearly explain in the synthesis paper how the individual exhibits contribute to an overall set of related learning experiences explained in terms of a related set of points.

A grade of F will be awarded to portfolios that

+ Are turned in after the specified due date; or are turned in on time but do not include the minimum components (cover page, eight exhibits, eight commentaries, synthesis paper);

+ Do not meet minimum expectations for the components (e.g., the synthesis paper does not provide a synthesis, the commentaries are less than a page long or do not indicate reflection on learning);

+ Do not clearly explain how each exhibit served as the source of significant learning about oneself, the materials, and/or the student's learning process; and

+ Do not clearly explain in the synthesis paper how the individual exhibits contribute to an overall set of related learning experiences explained in terms of a related set of points.

While not solving all problems, a rubric of this sort will help you evaluate the portfolios in a fairly consistent manner. You will find rubrics especially useful as you experience fatigue from grading: when you've been grading for a while and your attention begins to slip, and you need a reference point for making distinctions among performances. If your rubric makes clear distinctions and you can demonstrate how your grading is informed by these distinctions, you will have fewer headaches to contend with.

Not everyone believes in rubrics. Kohn (2006), for instance, says that "rubrics are, above all, a tool to promote standardization, to turn teachers into grading machines or at least allow them to pretend that what they are doing is exact and objective" (12). I believe, however, that a carefully designed rubric can lead to richer reading. I also think that if rubrics become "'arbiters of quality and agents of control' over what is taught and valued," to quote Kohn, the problem is that the rubric is out of synch with the teaching and the values the rubrics are meant to embody, not that rubrics themselves are inherently off target. A well-crafted rubric that is in tune with the instruction helps a teacher not only read the students' writing sympathetically but also provides a systematic method for reflecting on how well the students have been taught how to produce the assessed qualities.

Yet a rubric can result in fairly rigid approaches to assessment. It's important to think of the effects of using any particular evaluative tool on student work. At the risk of belaboring the metaphor, a code designed for one kind of building in one part of the country might not work well for buildings designed elsewhere for other purposes. Similarly, a grading rubric provides both constraints and affordances for how students will construct their texts in school.

Is there only one code available for evaluating the soundness of a student text? No, there are many available, each encouraging the production of a different kind of text. The question then becomes this: What kind of text are you encouraging students to produce? Does the rubric limit students more than it enables them? Does the rubric take into account the possibility that a student's idea for a functional text might be judged as insufficient by the teacher's rubric? Does the rubric deny students the opportunity to construct an innovative text by specifying the terms of production?

The question of which standards to use when evaluating writing raises an important issue about the nature of writing. Is a piece of writing good or bad, without respect to who's reading it? Think about the idea proposed by Nystrand (1986) that the quality of writing is a function of the relationship between writers and readers. In this view, good writing is writing that is *in tune* with its readers. A highly technical research report might be a splendid piece of work to other researchers, yet might be obscure gobbledygook to the person on the street. The text itself is not good or bad; rather, different readers are more or less in tune with the writing conventions used by the writer, the topics it covers, and other textual matters.

Evaluation is one of the inevitabilities of life in school. You can't teach without giving a grade in most schools. And you need to grade in ways that students (and often their parents) find consistent, equitable, and defensible. A rubric is a way to specify the code you're using to evaluate student work.

If you're uncomfortable writing the code by which you assign students their grades, you could look for alternatives, such as dedicating class time to having students produce the rubrics. While helping with the question of who's building whose building, it would raise a different set of questions, such as: Do students' expectations for a soundly constructed text meet expectations by which these texts will be judged elsewhere? Is the process of arriving at these judgments an experience so worthwhile that it outweighs the importance of meeting adult standards for text production? I recommend http://rubistar.4teachers.org/index.php, which provides information and models for designing rubrics and is used by many teachers.

Summary

The issue of response to students' compositions is broad and complex. In spite of my dependence on things like rubrics, I have often labored over whether a student's work should get a B– or C+; even with criteria in mind, these decisions can be very vexing. And they make a big difference to students, whose futures often depend on the ways in which teachers tip the scales in high-stakes grading decisions. I've taken classes where my grade average for a marking period was a 79.4, and the teacher gave me the C+. Those sorts of decisions always really honked me off because they seemed so arbitrary and punitive, and if anything, it made me dislike and distrust the business of schooling even more than ever. I encourage you to give a lot of thought to how you evaluate students, what you evaluate them on, and what the consequences of your evaluations will be for them.

Performance Assessment Prep

Documenting your teaching effectiveness may require you to include samples of student writing to which you have written a response. Although you may not have graded student papers yet, it's time to think about how you would go about it and how you would explain your process to an assessor.

This chapter should help you align your dossier with key values of the assessments, in particular the alignment of goals/assignments/outcomes, instruction, and assessment. The better you can learn to explain the relation across the three, the more likely you will achieve a passing score; and I also think that the more effective a teacher you will be in terms of setting clear expectations and teaching so that students may achieve them.

Finally, this chapter has laid out some pros and cons of using rubrics to standardize grading and make expectations clear. Rubrics have their critics, but you won't find them among your assessors. I suggest at least learning how to develop them, demonstrating this ability for this assessment, and then determining later on whether and how to use them in your own teaching.

PART THREE

Planning for
Planning Instruction

7

Why Conceptual Units?

A conceptual unit of instruction dedicates a period of time—roughly four to six weeks of fifty-minute classes or two to three weeks of ninety-minute classes—to *sustained attention to a related set of ideas*. These ideas are pursued through a variety of texts, both those read (often literary) and those produced (usually written). This sustained attention allows students—and, given a provocative topic, the teacher—to consider a related set of issues from a variety of perspectives with increasing understanding.

This consideration ultimately provides opportunities for each student to construct a personal interpretation or perspective, ideally one that takes into account and synthesizes the various ideas explored through the unit texts and discussions. By considering the same topic, the class can work toward a sense of community, where it is expected that students will appreciate and critique the ideas their classmates produce in response to the unit texts. By considering other student texts in conjunction with commercially published ones, the class can work toward a contemporary vision of how a particular topic might be imagined in their own society.

The Parts That Make Up the Whole

A conceptual unit is designed to organize students' learning around a particular emphasis. Literature, nonfiction texts, and related artistic texts provide the stimulus for student inquiry into the unit topic. The texts include those produced outside the class (typically in published form) and those produced by students. Students do not simply react to texts and consume previously produced knowledge. Rather, they have an active role in constructing new knowledge through their engagement with the unit concepts. They produce texts of their own that contribute to the class's exploration of the key unit questions and raise new questions.

A conceptual unit involves students in a conversation that deepens as they progress through the texts, activities, and discussions. To be considered conceptual, the unit must focus on a set of key concepts that students engage with over time. This extended consideration is designed to help students pursue a set of ideas that will help them

+ Come to better personal understanding of the topic and their related experiences;

+ Gain fluency with tools that will enable them to read and produce new texts in the future; and

+ Work within a social context in which they can develop this new knowledge to the best of their potential.

A conceptual unit typically includes all or most of the following: a rationale, an inventory, goals, assessment, lessons, activities, discussion, texts, tools, and composing.

Rationale

A rationale is the argument that you make to justify your selection of a unit topic and its contents: its materials, activities, assessments, and so on. I believe that writing out this rationale is the most effective way of articulating reasons for teaching decisions. At the same time, I recognize that doing so takes precious time that busy teachers might decide to invest instead in the lesson plans themselves, in doing bureaucratic paperwork, in reading and thinking about the texts included in the unit, or in taking a break from all this work. Yet the better prepared you are to explain your decisions, the less stressful these occasions will be. Having a persuasive rationale is especially important if you teach in a school in which a constructivist approach is not widely employed and you need to justify why you are teaching against the grain.

Inventory

An inventory is a vehicle that helps you learn about your students. Most school textbooks are written for a generic student. However, you will have all kinds of students. If you view your role as teaching students as well as teaching the subject, then it's a good idea to know who they are, including:

+ What they're interested in;

+ What their goals are for being in your class;

+ What they know about particular topics;

+ What they've already read;

+ How they use language and how they write; and

+ What other skills they have that you can build on in the classroom.

Knowing this information can help you design appropriate instruction. You won't make the mistake of teaching them things they already do well, or pitching instruction too far beyond what they know, or teaching in ways that have nothing to do with their own purposes. It's possible that you teach in a district that restricts your decision-making in these areas. Even so, teachers often develop ways to meet their own goals and their students' goals while also satisfying other people's requirements.

Inventories can be taken in a variety of ways. You can learn a lot about students, for instance, by having them write an introductory letter about themselves. You will not only learn about their interests but also get a sense of their writing fluency. You can develop some kind of questionnaire that asks about their background in education, their interests in school, their interests outside school, their reading experiences and preferences, their attitudes toward writing, and other information you would find useful in planning your teaching. Chapter 14 includes examples of such inventories. You could provide them with literature of different degrees of difficulty and ask them to respond to it, which would help you to identify appropriate reading material for the class. All of these possibilities help you understand whom you are teaching and how you can build on their knowledge and interests.

Goals

Instructional goals refer to the unit's destination. This destination is the ultimate learning that you anticipate for students as a result of their experiences during the unit. Their learning comes about through their production of a *culminating text*— that is, something that they create that synthesizes their learning. Note that I refer to this final assessment as a learning opportunity, rather than simply as a test of content mastery. I strongly believe that assessment and learning ought to go together hand in hand; each assessment ought to provide an occasion for new learning as students extend their thinking through producing the unit's culminating texts. Most commonly these texts are some kind of extended writing. Students, however, should have opportunities to learn through the production of other kinds of texts as well, including those grounded in the arts and those available through digital devices. The goals you set imply a path for the instruction to follow. Identifying worthwhile goals, then, is a key facet of planning worthwhile instruction.

Assessment

Goals are tied to the inevitable question of *assessment*. Whether or not you like it, or whether or not you have philosophical objections to grading, you will almost certainly have to issue a grade for each student. In fact, you will assign many grades that ultimately produce a "final" grade for each marking period, and eventually a semester or year. The unit goals you set should provide students the opportunity to create culminating texts that you can assess in ways that you and your students believe reflect their learning during the unit.

Lessons

A lesson is a shorter unit of instruction within the larger conceptual unit. If, for instance, you are teaching a unit on animals as symbols and have a goal of enabling students to see how symbolic animals can represent human characteristics, you might include a lesson in which students are introduced to the idea that literary animals can symbolize people and their (often negative) tendencies. This lesson might include different parts of the unit that I describe here: *discussion* of *texts* such as a set of fables, an activity in which they *compose* a fable of their own using the tool of writing, and an *assessment* of their fable.

It's important to remember that, although lessons are identifiable as pieces of the larger unit, they should be integrated and sequenced rather than discrete. You are, after all, designing a *unit*, which means that the lessons need to be related to one another and to the overall conceptual knowledge that students construct.

Activities

An activity is a hands-on experience, often taking place within a lesson. It is related to the unit concepts and helps to prepare students for reaching the unit goals. It typically involves:

+ Interaction with other people;
+ The manipulation of ideas and/or objects;
+ The production of an idea and/or text;
+ The inductive development of strategies for learning; and
+ An open-ended task.

Let's say that you would like to teach students how to make inferences in their reading. One accessible way to introduce this idea is through an activity such as a spy game (see Hillocks 1972). First you tell small groups of students that a spy has been captured. Then you present them with the contents of the spy's pockets, which you assemble before class and might include coins from foreign countries, a scrap of paper with code on it, a set of paper clips strung together, a ticket to an event, and/ or any other clues you want to provide. I've even assembled these randomly, using effluvium from students' pockets and purses, without compromising the activity. Each group then makes inferences about the spy's personality, qualities, characteristics, and mission. Because there is no real spy, each group may legitimately arrive at different inferences, as long as it can explain them. The groups then discuss their inferences with the class, comparing and critiquing one another's ideas.

Following this activity, the class may move to examining characters from literature to make inferences that will help them construct a response. These activities could lead to individual efforts to analyze literature in terms of the inferences they can make about narrators or other characters.

Discussion

By *discussion* I mean talk in which multiple participants exchange ideas. I distinguish this variety of talk from a *lecture* in which one person provides information or opinions for others to record. To count as a discussion, an exchange needs to be

+ *Open-ended* (i.e., not having a specific or correct answer or destination);
+ *Authentic* (i.e., concerned with the purposes and interests of all or at least many participants, not just a few); and
+ *Democratic* (i.e., equally open to all and involving the greatest possible number of willing participants).

In my experience, discussions include people with roughly two different dispositions. One disposition is that of *arguing to win*. Lawyers do this: Right or wrong, their goal is to win the argument. Participants who take this stance typically do not view themselves as learners in the discussion; rather, they see themselves as contestants. The other disposition is that of *arguing to learn*. Participants who take this stance typically view discussions as opportunities to think through ideas and learn from the others involved. For them there are not winners and losers. They cannot help but benefit from the discussion, even if they ultimately change their minds about the ideas they express.

Alternatives to Teacher-Led Discussions

Teachers tend to talk a lot in class. When teachers create openings for students to speak, it's typically a small space within which they can slot information that fits with the teacher's broader interpretation. A common pattern has been identified to characterize typical classroom talk: IRE. A teacher *initiates* a topic or question, students *respond* briefly, and the teacher *elaborates* or *explains* the students' responses in a monologue, often adjusting students' contributions so that they fit better with the preferred interpretation.

To help shift the balance so that students have more and longer speaking turns and greater validation for their own ideas, educators have come up with a rich variety of ways of structuring discussion so that students are entrusted with larger, more important roles. I've collected them at http://www.petersmagorinsky .net/TEBD/UnitLibrary/Activities_that_Promote_Discussion.htm and encourage you to see the possibilities that await.

Texts

A text is any meaning-laden product that students read or produce, including literature, art, dance, film, and other artifacts of human expression.

Tools

Tools are important to all builders, including teachers and students. For a carpenter, the hammer, saw, and other accoutrements are the tools of the trade. Students who construct knowledge also use tools. Through the tool of speech, they can communicate, explore ideas, and impose order on their worlds. Students can use speech to argue, to tell stories, to classify, to amuse, and to deceive. Students can also use nonverbal artistic devices to construct meaning-laden texts. The key to all of these actions is that they must be used in service of the construction of meaning.

Teachers, too, use *pedagogical tools*. These include *conceptual tools*, such as an educational theory like constructivism that can be applied broadly to guide thinking about teaching. Teachers also use *practical tools*. These include any methods that you use to enact your teaching: lesson plans, small-group activities, handouts, and so on.

Composing

Composing describes the act by which people produce *texts* that have meaning and/ or use for them. These acts of composition involve

✦ The use of an appropriate tool or set of tools;

✦ An understanding of the conventions and genres within which one is working and an understanding of the effects of breaking these conventions;

✦ An extended process that usually includes planning, drafting, feedback, reflection, and revising;

✦ Building on prior knowledge and understanding as a basis for the construction of new ideas and a new text;

✦ New learning that takes place through the process of composing; and

✦ Regarding both the process of composing and the ultimate text as sources of meaning.

Writing is typically considered synonymous with composing. Much school writing would not meet the criteria for my definition of a composition (e.g., writing factual short answers on an exam). Other kinds of production (writing a musical score, choreographing an interpretation of a story) do meet these criteria and thus are compositions.

Eight Types of Unit

I next review eight kinds of organization for conceptual units. Any unit design ought to lead class members into new understandings. As such, it needs to be complex enough to generate thoughtful consideration about whatever thread ties the unit texts and lessons together. Units need to help students develop frameworks for thinking about issues so that they can think about new situations through that perspective.

Therefore, a unit on friendship ought to do more than have students read stories about friends. It should approach these texts so that students develop frameworks for thinking about new situations that develop in their experiences with friends, observations of friendships, or textual experiences with friendship. One of a teacher's responsibilities in designing a unit, then, is to think about how different sequences of activities and readings will contribute to students' ability to develop these generative frameworks for thinking about the unit concept. The conceptual growth of students during a unit was aptly described by Hillocks, McCabe, and McCampbell (1971): "One of the most important things that any literature unit can do is to provide a conceptual matrix against which the student can examine each new work he reads. Insights into any given work are partly the result of experience in reading others because concepts grow by comparison and contrast" (254).

The kinds of units that I outline are described in terms of the kinds of texts that students read and produce. In some ways student compositions are the unit's most important texts, because they distill what students have learned through their engagement with the unit. These texts are important not only for assessment purposes but for all students in the class to learn from, and so a conceptual unit should provide opportunities for students to read and think about what their classmates have produced in relation to the unit concepts.

Theme

A *theme* provides an idea or motif that ties together the texts, activities, and discussions of a unit. A theme often refers to a set of experiences, ideas, concepts, or emotions shared by people within and often across cultures. Themes include common experiences such as rites of passage, dealing with peer groups, coping with loss, social responsibility, and other topics.

Themes provide a compelling way to organize an English curriculum, one that is responsive both to recurring patterns in art forms and to students' authentic interests in learning. Students are engaged in integrated inquiry into topics that parallel their social development or that help to lead their development. Texts and readers should be mutually informative; that is, texts should bring new understandings to their readers, and readers should bring their own histories of experiences to project meanings into the texts. The themes that students study can

+ Help them consider pivotal experiences in their lives, such as their relationships with their friends or families; and

+ Introduce them to issues that they may not yet have considered, such as what it means to be a responsible citizen.

By studying thematic units, then, students can potentially see literature and related texts as useful tools and touchstones in their own development toward adulthood.

Archetype

An *archetype* refers to a recurring symbol or motif in literature, art, or mythology such as a type of character or event type, often one that appears in a variety of cultural narratives. There are a variety of lists of common archetypes, often centering on roles such as the hero, the caregiver, the trickster, the magician, and others. An archetypal event might be the journey, a sort of quest that often includes archetypes such as the mentor, the helper, and other types. Organizing a curriculum by archetype can enable both the exploration of typical cultural actions in art and literature, and these same issues in the lives of students.

Genre

A *genre* refers to works that share codes: westerns, heroic journeys, detective stories, comedies of manners, and so on. These genres are often produced through a variety of media: short story, drama, novel, film, graphic novel, and so on, which themselves are referred to as genres. I use *genre* to refer to the first of these two meanings rather than to the one that describes textual forms. Authors of satire, for instance, typically use a set of devices such as exaggeration, voicing opinions different from their own, creating foolish characters, and so on, that are designed to invite particular responses. A genre includes a variety of textual forms that rely on common interpretive, genre-based codes.

Period

A *period* can also provide the basis for a conceptual unit, particularly when authors from that period write from a cultural perspective that provides them with a common set of themes. The era known as the Victorian period, for instance, encompassed the sixty-three-year reign of Queen Victoria of England. Its literature reveals the sentiments, beliefs, tastes, and accomplishments of the English people of that time. Victorian literature was often staged around the class struggle that followed the Industrial Revolution in Great Britain, creating tensions among the working class, the new industrial middle class, and the old aristocracy. The literature of Dickens typifies the Victorian period, with sympathy extended to the poor, the working class, and their children, thus giving it a thematic character.

Movement

A *movement* is a belief system that is expressed through a variety of media and is part of a broad philosophical perspective. Romanticism, for instance, had a coherent set of principles, even when it took specific directions in different social or national circles. It emphasized the imagination and emotions over intellect and reason, believed in the innate goodness of people in their natural state, had a reverence for nature, held a philosophical idealism, believed in individualism, rejected political authority and social convention, celebrated the human passions, and embraced religious mysticism. Movements thus tend to be thematic at heart. Designing a unit around a movement enables the inclusion of historical and philosophical writing as well as art, architecture, and other artifacts that embody the beliefs of the people who subscribe to the movement.

Region

Often, a geographic region can serve as the means for organizing a conceptual unit. Authors and artists from a particular region often share common outlooks, themes, and styles. You may have studied, for instance, Southern fiction, Great Lakes authors, the British Lake poets, or the Harlem Renaissance. You might consider having students design units around their own local sense of place as a way to link their studies to their own regional grounding and heritage.

Works by a Single Author

If an author has produced a body of work that is highly compelling or holds a significant place in literary history, then that author's work could provide the basis for a unit of instruction. The work of a single author is amenable to a unit approach because the works tend to rely on a set of themes and techniques that students can follow across texts. Studying a single author, as I've detailed previously, can lead to such possibilities as writing parodies based on that person's style.

Learning a Key Strategy

Literature is a very particular kind of text. You don't read it the same way you read a science report. A unit can be organized around strategies for recognizing and interpreting literary codes (not memorizing lists of literary terms). A unit built around this approach would take a technique and have students analyze it in a series of increasingly sophisticated texts. Michael W. Smith (1991), for instance, has written an extended unit on understanding unreliable narrators in which students begin by reading Calvin and Hobbes comics and move from there through more sophisticated literature. Having formal strategies for recognizing and interpreting literary codes can be very useful for students in their subsequent reading.

Benefits of the Unit Approach

Learning design principles based on unit organization were very beneficial to my high school teaching career. Although I obsessively thought about my teaching and was constantly tinkering with my plans, I was not plagued by daily uncertainty because I had learned to plan ahead and design conceptual units. I therefore found teaching to be less stressful than did many of my colleagues, because I was not always struggling to figure out what to do next. I was also happier with my teaching because my students saw continuity in what we did from day to day and week to week and saw it within the context of questions that mattered to them. In various units, we considered questions such as:

+ What does it mean to be a success?

+ What does one do in the face of peer pressure?

+ How does discrimination affect society and its individuals?

+ What is a social conscience, and at what point and in what form does one register a protest against a social wrong?

+ How does it feel to be an outcast?

This approach made my classes far more interesting to me, because the answers were different for each class. Instead of explaining the same interpretation to students class after class, year after year, and having them repeat it to me on tests, I had the opportunity to be involved in discussions that were as infinitely varied as the students themselves. My classes were places where I did a lot of learning as I listened to my students construct for themselves an awareness of how they understood and acted within their worlds.

A Rationale for Teaching with Conceptual Units

The study of literature by means of conceptual units may be justified in a number of ways. If you can't defend something, then you shouldn't teach it.

The Need for Integrated Knowledge

Many curriculum theorists argue that effective instruction seeks to help students make connections that cohere around principles. Applebee (1993), for instance, conceives of curriculum "as a domain for culturally significant conversations" that take place across a course of study (200), suggesting the need to explore a set of questions across a series of related texts. Conceptual units are well suited for integrated learning, enabling students to explore a topic over time through the lenses offered by a variety of texts. Such an approach will avoid the problem of fragmentation that Applebee (1996) sees as characterizing much of the English curriculum. This fragmentation in turn works against students' ability to integrate knowledge and experience the domain coherently.

A well-designed conceptual unit can promote integration and continuity in which students actively participate and help to construct with their own contributions and compositions. Furthermore, Applebee argues that learning for the whole year should contribute to the development of an *overarching concept* that helps to connect class discussions and student productions from unit to unit. This conception of curriculum focuses on ideas, particularly as students enter and transform the subject of English and grow through the process of their inquiry.

A literature curriculum that students experience and contribute to, that provides them with a domain for developing themes to guide their life's actions and decisions, can make two key, related contributions to their education. First of all, through transactions with provocative texts, it can provide them with a strong literary education and thus enable them to participate in and contribute to a major tradition in arts and letters. Second, it can enable them to experience this tradition in a way that allows them to understand the social conditions, life experiences, and literary conventions that guide the production of literature and other texts—including those that they produce—and help texts serve as vehicles for their growth into happy, productive citizens.

Schemata and Scripts

Another rationale for conceptual units comes from cognitive psychologists' *schema theory*. A schema is a network of knowledge that includes both elements and processes. Most if not all schemata are *cultural* in that they embody an ideology and set of values. Having schematic knowledge enables a person to understand situations that are new yet related to ones already known. An effectively designed conceptual unit will help students understand new material that is related to familiar material. This approach to schooling is quite different from the approach in which assessment tests students' recall of what they have already covered.

Organizing instruction by conceptual units fits well with schema theory. If prior knowledge helps people anticipate new situations, then studying texts that are conceptually unified makes sense. Often students already have prior knowledge that can help them engage with the unit concepts. Coming-of-age experiences, for instance, are common among young people. Anyone who has had a coming-of-age experience has a script for such events. The prior knowledge from personal experience (and textual engagement) can form the basis for understanding how the theme works in newly encountered literature, film, and art. In a reciprocal process, these newly encountered texts can provide the basis for reflection on the prior experiences.

Furthermore, each text can serve to develop a schema that in turn helps a reader to understand both the experiences that are at the heart of the theme and the textual conventions that authors use to help convey a theme. For instance, a coming-of-age story typically involves a character who exhibits immature behavior at the outset, has a transforming experience, and gains greater wisdom or maturity at the end. This script parallels the kinds of experiences that young readers have as they negotiate adolescence. By organizing literature according to literary themes or genres, teachers can thus help students refine their schemata for both their own unfolding experiences and their knowledge of narrative conventions.

Transactional Learning

Additional support for using conceptual units within an integrated curriculum comes from Rosenblatt's (1938, 1978) transactional theory of response to literature, derived from Dewey (1934). Rosenblatt argued for a democratic view of reading that gives the ordinary reader as much authority in determining a literary work's meaning as that accorded to a professional literary critic. Rosenblatt asserts that readers need to attend carefully to the words a writer uses to craft a work of literature. What those words might mean, however, is a matter of personal construction. This construction is based on

+ A reader's personal experiences;
+ The cultural factors that shape both readers and texts;
+ The social environment of a classroom and its effects on a reader's response; and
+ The psychological makeup of individual readers that provides a particular frame of mind for interpreting events in particular ways.

The same text might be read quite differently by two readers in the same class who bring different cultural expectations to the experience, or who have different personal experiences, or whose psychological makeups provide different frameworks for interpreting events.

Transactional theory's emphasis on what readers bring to texts and, in turn, construct from them contributes to a rationale for organizing literature according to concepts. If, for instance, themes represent universal experiences, then they can serve students well in two ways. First of all, students will bring critical prior knowledge to their reading, giving them authority as savvy readers of literature. If students have had experience with justice, or Puritan values, or satire, or whatever topic is covered, then those experiences provide them with knowledge about the topic that deserves acknowledgment and respect in the classroom.

Second, their consideration of the concept through textual engagement ought to provide them with opportunities to reflect on their experience and construct new knowledge. They can thus develop a relationship with literature and classmates that potentially enriches their understanding of themselves, the ideas, and one another. This approach does not promote an anything-goes classroom where any interpretation by a student is acceptable. It does, however, honor the ways in which students can find meaning that has a basis in the actual language of the text, whether or not that meaning matches the teacher's or professional literary critics' readings.

Summary

I've created the Virtual Library of Conceptual Units, available at http://www.petersmagorinsky.net/Units/index.html, and a set of unit outlines at http://www.petersmagorinsky.net/Units/Unit_Outlines.htm to provide you with mentor texts and general ideas for your unit design. Planning a yearlong curriculum around an overarching concept, and providing attention to that concept through units of study, enables coherence and continuity for both teachers and students, helping students revisit critical issues in their worlds or important learning strategies as they continue to delve into new texts and ideas. Teaching thus avoids the sort of fragmentation that can discourage students' synthesis of ideas and promotes integration of learning across texts and experiences that are both diverse and related. Beginning with the next chapter, we'll turn our attention to the nuts and bolts of planning units of this sort.

Performance Assessment Prep

If you are able to provide a persuasive rationale for your teaching, you should have plenty of useful material for satisfying a performance assessment. Throughout the dossier, you will be asked to explain your decisions and ground them in prior research and theory. I've provided ways of justifying instruction that could easily be adapted to any demands to explain the contexts for learning in your dossier. For instance, you might be asked to identify the focus of instruction (the theme, archetype, strategy, and so on that you build instruction around) and how your knowledge of your students informs that teaching (e.g., how a unit concept helps to build on what your students know and might need to know). You could justify your teaching according to any of the means I've reviewed in this chapter, or others, and select from that rationale in order to meet specific demands of the assessment prompt.

8

The Basics of Unit Design

Although this chapter suggests a particular order for the process of beginning your planning of a conceptual unit, it's entirely possible that you will not strictly follow these steps in designing your own unit. In fact, it's likely that you will not plan a unit strictly in stages but instead will jump around: You will consider good books to teach, think of how they'd fit together into a unit of instruction, think of good reasons to teach them, think of additional texts to include, refine the topic of the unit, and so on. However, it would be confusing if I were to write this book so that it made spontaneous leaps the way your mind will while planning a unit. My intention, then, is to treat each area separately with the understanding that you will employ each in conjunction with others, in whatever sequence works for you.

Identifying Unit Topics

Identifying a unit topic is a complex process that involves the consideration of a variety of factors. In the best of all possible worlds, you—perhaps in conjunction with your students—would pick topics and teach them. However, every decision you make comes within the context of a range of factors that constrain your choices. A number of influences may enter into your deliberation of what topics will work well for you and your students. I present them in no particular order; the relative importance of each will vary from setting to setting.

The Curriculum

The curriculum may have been set in place before you were hired, or perhaps before you were born. Perhaps before I was born. Here's how it might both constrain and afford your thinking about what and how to teach.

Curricular Restrictions

One constraint that most teachers deal with is the confines of the curriculum for the course they are teaching. To give an obvious example: Most US high schools dedicate the senior year to British literature. It would be hard to justify teaching a unit on the Harlem Renaissance in a British literature class, although teaching Shakespeare in American literature is often required. Understanding the confines of a curriculum, then, is an important step in determining what is and is not available to teach to particular groups of students.

If you teach out of an anthology, you are likely in safe territory with regard to the topics and texts you and your students read because the anthology has been approved at so many levels. If you teach beyond the anthology, things can get more interesting, because individual works of literature can include themes or actions that may be controversial in some communities.

Curricular Overarching Concept

Another concern in planning units is the overarching concept that unifies the curriculum over the whole course. You should ask, to paraphrase Applebee (1996): What larger conversation should students be engaged in that in turn suggests good topics around which to build units? I'll suggest a few possibilities. An American literature curriculum might ask, for instance, *What does it mean to be an American?* The question assumes that America refers to the United States and not any of the nations to its north or south. Students might explore this question through a variety of units, possibly including the following:

+ *Protest literature*, beginning with the colonial rhetoric that helped launch the American Revolution and inscribe American values in the Constitution and/or key protest literature from other eras, such as the various women's and civil rights movements

+ *The Puritan ethic*, which would seek to understand what this ethic is and how it has endured throughout American history and helped to shape the American character

- *Success*, in which students would consider what a successful person is in the United States and whether one person's notion of success works for others or whether the same actions would be considered successful in different situations

- *Frontier literature*, including literature that gives the pioneers' perspective on western expansion and literature that provides the native people's view

- *The works of Maya Angelou*, who approaches the American Dream from an African American perspective

- *Cultural conflict*, which would help illuminate the issues involved when (1) a country is inhabited by natives whose society is affected by the arrival of people from radically different cultures, or (2) a nation designed to embrace immigrants engages new arrivals whose ways conflict with established customs, and so on

- *Gender roles*, which might look at how those roles have changed over time and examine how a conception of gender plays a role in fulfilling the American Dream

- *The authors and artists of [your state]*, which would help students see how their own state fits in with broader themes and perspectives of US society and help acquaint them with significant authors and artists from their own part of the country

Students

When asked, "What do you teach?" some teachers answer, "Students." Rather than viewing themselves as subject-area specialists, they see themselves first as teachers of the people who are in their care. Taking this approach will make you different from some people in the teaching profession, who feel that they teach a subject rather than students. When you believe that you are teaching the subject, you release yourself from much responsibility to make sure that your students are learning. You also can ignore the particular characteristics and needs of your students, since it's their job to learn the subject. What matters is that you know your subject well and present it effectively.

Where you fall on the continuum of teaching students or the subject is a personal matter. If you find this book useful, you probably think that it's important to teach both. In thinking about which units to teach, reflecting on who your students are can help you make good choices. Following are some considerations that ought to enter into your thinking.

Culture and Community

As a teacher you are caught amid many tensions. One that you no doubt feel every day is the tension between viewing everyone as being equal or the same and viewing everyone as unique and different. Teaching students of different races is a good example. On the one hand, you will be encouraged to be *color blind*, to try to view your students as being the same, regardless of race. On the other hand, you will be encouraged to understand cultural differences that require you to acknowledge and respect the perspectives and behaviors of students whose cultural upbringing has been different from yours. Understanding culture, while important, can also be dangerous if the understanding results in limiting stereotypes. And, of course, race is only one aspect of culture. Ethnicity, region, religion, gender, neurological makeup, socioeconomic class, and countless others are all factors. Knowing each can help you understand your students but may also cause you to operate according to limiting stereotypes.

Developmental Level

Although your students' age or grade level is not an absolute indicator of what they should study, it does provide some broad guidelines for what is appropriate to teach. In a class at one grade level you will have students of differing ages, levels of maturity, levels of knowledge, and so on. This variation makes it hard to say that something is an especially ripe topic for students at a particular grade. On the other hand, some things are more appropriate to teach particular groups than others.

Developmental psychologists have described some tendencies that could help us make decisions about what is developmentally appropriate. Over the course of adolescence, most children in Western societies move in thought, feeling, and action from

- Simple to complex;
- Concrete to abstract;
- Personal orientation to impersonal or multipersonal orientation;
- Spontaneous activity to thought with less activity;
- Conception of objects themselves to conception of their properties;
- Literal to symbolic; and
- Absolute to relative.

In general, then, they develop an ability to step back and see the big picture. As they grow older, students are able to grapple with problems of greater abstraction and are increasingly able to stand back and view themselves as participants in a larger society. Thus, topics for young adolescents might be centered on the immediate social worlds of young protagonists, often in young adult literature: peer pressure, friendship, new kid on the block, and so on. Toward the end of high school, they might consider topics that place the individual in relation to broader society, with the topics requiring the contemplation of more abstract terms: success, justice, progress, changing times, and the like.

Interests

Another factor in deciding on unit topics is students' interests. In suggesting this emphasis, I am not saying that you ought to pander to students' more trivial pursuits. Instead, I'm saying that if one of our goals is to make school learning something that students view with anticipation, then we should consider what they find interesting when evaluating possible topics of inquiry.

Knowing students' interests can be useful when these interests coincide with topics related to unit concepts. In addition to careful observation, you can invite formal accounts of their interests, such as by having students write you an introduction to themselves, or having them write a user's manual for themselves, or having their parents, guardians, or other significant adults write you a letter about them.

Needs

I see needs as being different from interests. Interests refer to those things that, when all is relatively well, students want to learn about. Needs refer to deeper psychological issues. Some of these are developmental and shared by just about everyone passing through a certain point in life, while others are created by particular circumstances.

Common needs result from certain kinds of predictable experiences. I've already referred to the coming-of-age experience as an archetypal passage that can provide the basis for a good, developmentally appropriate unit of instruction. Others might include units on conflict with authority, the trickster, peer pressure, the outcast, rites of passage, and any other social rite or character type that most students are likely to be dealing with in their lives.

Needs that are created by particular circumstances might be tied to archetypal experiences, but they have a more local impact because of events affecting the community. Let's say that a community is experiencing a rise in gang involvement among its youth. It might be appropriate to teach a unit that deals with gangs, cliques, and peer pressure. Or perhaps there are increasing instances of bullying and violence in school. Studying a topic such as discrimination or alienation and discussing the material in terms of events in school might help students think through the causes and effects of such behavior.

Unless you are trained as a psychologist or counselor, you should be very careful about how you deal with students' needs and equally careful about how you solicit and respond to their thoughts and feelings on sensitive topics. You also need to be prepared to allow students to resist efforts to have them reveal their feelings. Literature and writing can serve as vehicles for people to reflect on and understand better the experiences of their lives. Yet teachers have no right to require personal revelations from students who don't want to share them. Keeping to oneself is a right that all students have, and that should be respected, no matter how much a teacher believes in the power of spoken and written reflection.

At the same time, you have an obligation to ensure a healthy environment for your students. If you think that your students' withdrawal has its roots in depression, drug use, suicidal thoughts, abuse, or other threat to their well-being, then you should share your concern with a counselor or school psychologist who can intervene in knowledgeable and appropriate ways. As I've reviewed, in Georgia teachers are viewed as "mandatory reporters" under state law and are liable if they do not share sensitive information about students' well-being. Knowing local laws, then, may help guide your actions in these cases.

Teacher

Teachers ought to consider their own interests and needs when deciding what topics to teach. They should reflect on the value of their judgment in knowing what students might benefit from studying, even if the students haven't identified it as an interest. To meet your own needs, think about your interests and your knowledge.

Interests

Just as classes should be of interest to students, they should also be intriguing to their teachers. Students know when teachers are going through the motions. Many student evaluations of teachers that I've read over the years have stressed the importance of teachers being enthusiastic and passionate about their work, usually extended to being caring about students. Nothing kills enthusiasm like teaching topics and books that you don't like.

The corollary of this axiom is that you should not teach something just *because* you find it interesting. Millions of students have been punished because teachers persistently teach their favorite books, year after year, no matter what students think. Consider your interests, yes, but consider them in the context of other factors.

Knowledge

A second factor for teachers to think about is their own knowledge. What do you know about? Teaching within your area of expertise can make you an excellent resource for students in their learning. On the other hand, some teachers decide to teach a topic or work *as a way to learn about it*. Some have even suggested that it's a good idea to teach a book every so often that you haven't read before, so as to share the students' experience of reading without knowing the outcome. This approach is quite different from the standard image of the English teacher, who knows in advance where all of the foreshadowing and rising action and alliteration are and is primed to point it out and require students to identify it on a quiz.

Reading a book for the first time with students, however, is a good way to stay in tune with their experiences with literature and to model a different conception of what it means to know something. It shows the teacher in the role of reading tentatively and provisionally, as readers do the first time around, instead of in the role of knowing the book as a concrete, well-dissected whole, as most teachers are accustomed to doing.

Selecting Materials

If you view teaching as primarily concerned with the content of your discipline, then the traditions of your discipline will provide you with a canon of literary works that students should read. Although the traditional canon can provide excellent reading for secondary school students, it should be one of several factors in settling on the materials for your unit. The issue of broadening the canon raises an old conundrum for teachers of literature. The problem concerns the long-standing tension between the idea that certain works are required reading of all educated people and the idea that the canon meets the needs of professional literary critics more than it does the needs of the general reading public, adolescents in particular.

Teachers are caught in this tension. For the most part they have earned degrees in English and so have taken part in traditional literary study as a kind of formal scholarship. Most of their students, however, will not view literature as a field of scholarship and will instead read for pleasure, escape, fulfillment, knowledge, personal connection, or other personal reasons. How teachers manage the tension between their own love of classic literature and their students' preference for other kinds of reading will influence the choices they make about the content of the literature curriculum. In particular, Young Adult Literature has begun to challenge classic works for a role in the curriculum because it speaks so well to youth concerns, often in ways that alarm adults and require strong rationales to include in your teaching.

In selecting materials, you should take into account the following concerns.

Tracking

Many schools group students according to their perceived ability or level of performance. A typical school will have two or three tracks; I know of schools with five, plus various boutique programs, especially for the high achievers. The presence or absence of tracking should influence your decisions about teaching. If your school is untracked, you need to be prepared to meet the needs of the whole range of students in your school, all in a single group, suggesting the need for differentiated materials within single classes. If your school uses tracking, then your decisions about materials should be responsive to the reading abilities and interests of your students, and you should be alert to the ways in which race- and class-based discrimination can account for the different populations you find in different tracks.

Tracking is controversial among university academics, less so for teachers. Searching around can help you understand why it is viewed as problematic, and also why it is persistent. My goal here is less to persuade you that it's good or bad and more to alert you to this typical curricular means of separation.

Literary Value

Educators have often disagreed about the extent to which certain types of texts are sufficiently scholarly to serve as educational materials. The very existence of a literary canon and of a Great Books program suggests that at least some people would differentiate between literature of high quality and literature of lesser value. The question of what makes something literary is one that all teachers should consider. Furthermore, it is one that students should contemplate. Having students establish criteria for identifying works of literary merit can be a central aim of a literature curriculum.

This book is not designed to answer the question of what distinguishes literature that is great from literature that is not. Rather, it is designed to get you to think about how and why you make decisions. In considering literary value, then, you might ask

+ To what extent should I rely on the wisdom of literary critics in identifying works of literary merit? That is, is relying on the traditional canon sufficient?

+ Are the criteria for excellence the same for adolescents and for adults? For mainstream adolescents and college English majors? For students in high and low tracks? For members of one cultural group and members of another? If they are different, whose criteria should prevail in decisions about what to read for school?

+ When choosing a text for a particular thematic unit, will any text that fits the theme do, or are some better selections than others? If some are better selections, are they universally better or better relative to different groups of readers?

+ What is important in having a satisfying experience with reading? How can one distinguish the traits that result in such satisfying experiences? Are these traits the same for all people? If they are different, how do teachers and students make decisions about which texts are appropriate for reading in school?

Variety of Textual Forms

Another consideration should be the range of textual forms available to illuminate the themes of the literature. Unless your unit topic is restricted to an author who specializes in a particular medium, or that focuses on reading particular types of literature, you should look at what is available in short story, novel, poetry, drama, film, music, fable, sacred story, myth, essay, art, architecture, dance, and any other artistic form.

Appropriateness

By appropriateness, I refer to the extent to which texts meet the rules of propriety that govern life in your school and community. You need to differentiate between what you think is a good text and what people in your community will find objectionable. The texts you personally find riveting may include sex, violence, profanity, and ideologies that may create problems between you and your students' parents. You don't have free rein with text selection, so be careful out there and make wise choices.

Variety of Authorship

Studies of high school literature curricula (see Applebee 1993) have shown that most books taught in American public high schools have been written by what are known as either DWMs (dead white males) or PSMs (pale stale males). There's a good economic reason that literature anthologies feature works by the deceased: Dead men collect no royalties. The preponderance of white males troubles many, however. Look for variety in authorship, particularly when that variety provides for different points of view and matches your classroom demographics. When selecting materials, make an effort to include both canonical works and works from underrepresented traditions and cultures. You may find that items from your broadened list will not always be available, but if you teach so that students have options for their reading, you may find that students who want different kinds of experiences will find the books or other texts on their own.

Summary

Developing unit topics and choosing materials are the beginning stages of designing a unit. It's unlikely that I've eliminated all surprises; schools, while designed to be repetitive and predictable, always defy the odds and provide their inhabitants with new situations all the time. Undoubtedly, something will come up that I haven't anticipated. Yet this review should help acquaint you with much of what you need to know to get your unit design off the ground.

Performance Assessment Prep

Your selection of materials will always come in relation to a variety of factors. You may have little discretion at all in what your students read, depending on how "tightly held" or heavily scripted your curriculum is. This chapter may help justify the types of materials and specific texts you use in your evidence of effective teaching.

9

Your Unit Rationale

A rationale is a persuasive essay in which you explain why, of all the things on earth you could possibly teach, you've decided to teach this unit. In selecting your unit topic, you've already gone through an informal process of providing a rationale for your unit. You've thought about the community you teach in and how its characteristics might suggest topics. You've thought about the students' developmental needs and the topics that might help meet them. You've given a lot of thought to the concepts that the unit texts will involve. You've also considered the merits of possible texts to include and what students might learn from them. However, there are other reasons that might help you justify your unit topic.

Think of your rationale as serving rhetorical needs. One useful way to think of the rationale is this: If someone were to challenge your teaching, how would you defend it? Teachers are under attack from various quarters. The media are always criticizing schools for one reason or another. Irate parents frequently come to school to voice their displeasure with this or that. Taxpayers often claim that schools are overfunded. Students frequently complain about instruction being irrelevant or tedious. Teachers are known to snipe at one another's methods and decisions for various reasons. If any combination of these people asked you to defend your teaching, what would you say? Your rationale is your ticket to teaching in ways that you believe in. It's important, then, to write a good one.

Your rationale may focus on one of the following justifications or include attention to several. For each type of justification, I have listed units from the Virtual Library of Conceptual Units that employ it.

Psychology or Human Development

Many units can be justified because they respond to the psychological needs of students. Literature often deals with common human experiences about the pressures, changes, dilemmas, aspirations, conflicts, and so on that make growing up such a challenge. Adolescent literature in particular often features youthful protagonists dealing with the kinds of problems that students are likely experiencing, both those that have endured across the ages and those that are more current. The field of developmental psychology has provided abundant descriptions of the stages that most people in Western cultures go through during their maturation and can help provide a rationale for a number of units that deal with youth culture and the challenges of growing through it.

In the Virtual Library of Conceptual Units, see examples of this type of rationale in the following:

Adu, Glenn, Johnson, and Moore: "R-E-S-P-E-C-T: Finding Out What It Means to Me"

Aveni, Barbakow, Ingram, and Stewart: "Testing the Boundaries: A Unit on Censorship in America"

Brown, Hummel, Mann, Taylor, and Wright: "Freedom and Identity"

Davis: "Family"

Evans: "The Dynamics of Family"

Feldman, Lynn, and Winter: "A Sense of Self"

Ficco: "Negotiating Boundaries: Making It Through Adolescence Alive"

Headrick: "Life Paths and Destinations: Toward Meaningful Textual Transactions for a 12th-Grade British Literature Class"

McDaniel: "Individual Liberty"

Cultural Significance

Some units are worth teaching because they are culturally significant. In other words, the material within them is worth engaging with because their themes are central to an understanding of a particular culture, whether national, local, or distant. Here are a few examples of culturally significant topics from each of these three categories.

National

Some topics are related to themes that are central to national concerns. Learning strategies for distinguishing "real" from "fake" news, for instance, has emerged as a critical literacy skill in the current world and could be considered a national imperative.

Local

Learning about a local culture can help establish a sense of pride and identity between students and their communities. A unit on a sense of place or local authors (e.g., the writers of Ohio; prairie literature) can allow a teacher to feature local writers and help students engage with themes that have historically been central to their region and culture.

Distant

School should do more than help students know their own cultures; it should also help acquaint them with others. These cultures needn't be situated across the globe; they can be "distant" even while in close proximity. It might be useful, for instance, to have students read a body of literature by members of a race other than their own to learn about how life is viewed and experienced differently, even within the same general setting.

In the Virtual Library of Conceptual Units, see

Bogdanich and Butler: "Passing to the American Dream"

Wright, Rosenberg, Hellman, and Furney: "Beyond Tacos and Piñatas: A Unit on Hispanic Literature"

Literary Significance

Another way to justify a unit topic is to argue that its literary significance makes it essential to any kind of cultural literacy. The works of Shakespeare, for instance, have been performed for nearly four centuries across the world's stages. Therefore, you might mount a convincing argument that studying Shakespeare is central to understanding the themes of Western culture and the metaphors that are invoked to explain it.

You could also argue that particular periods or regions have produced literature that has historical and cultural significance. The Harlem Renaissance, for instance, served to establish African American writers as a significant group in American letters, the first non-white group to achieve this stature in the United States. Constructing these arguments would require some research into the genre and likely the reading of some cultural or literary criticism that establishes its significance.

In the Virtual Library of Conceptual Units, see

Berry, Donovan, and Hummel: "Romeo and Juliet"

Ehret: "Teaching Cultural and Historical Literacy Through Satire"

Ficco: "Negotiating Boundaries: Making It Through Adolescence Alive"

Headrick: "Life Paths and Destinations: Toward Meaningful Textual Transactions for a 12th-Grade British Literature Class"

Mann: "Mary Shelley's *Frankenstein* and the Responsibility of the Creator to His Creation"

Civic Awareness

Some units of study help students to understand their roles as citizens in their communities, states, and nation. In units on topics such as justice, social responsibility, self-reliance, and protest literature, students consider the role of the individual in society. In justifying such units, you might consider the importance of developing a citizenry that knows its history, laws, customs, rights, and responsibilities and uses that knowledge to act responsibly for a more equitable, democratic, and dynamic society. In preparing a rationale for such units, you might argue that throughout American history, citizens have taken action to achieve what they feel is just and that these actions have been driven by different social goals, different types of conscience, and different understandings of law. A unit oriented to civic awareness can find its justification in the historical background that students can learn through the unit texts and in the code of civic ethics they will develop through their engagement with the problems they read about.

In the Virtual Library of Conceptual Units, see

Aveni, Barbakow, Ingram, and Stewart: "Testing the Boundaries: A Unit on Censorship in America"

Buxton and Kramer: "Educational Issues as a Medium Through Which We Educate"

Davis: "Family"

Dyer: "Science Fiction: Critiquing the Present, Exploring the Future"

Ehret: "Teaching Cultural and Historical Literacy Through Satire"

McDaniel: "Individual Liberty"

Focus on a Current Social Problem

Some units of study find justification in their effort to help adolescents understand and make choices about problems they face in their lives. A unit on peer pressure, for instance, would be justified in a community where teen smoking, drinking, drugs, bullying, and other behaviors are a threat to the security and health of teens. In a community that has experienced a devastating loss, a unit on coping with loss might help students find the tools they need to work toward an understanding of their tragedy.

In the Virtual Library of Conceptual Units, see

Dyer: "Science Fiction: Critiquing the Present, Exploring the Future"

Estey: "I Will Speak Up! For Myself, for My Friends, and for What I Believe In!"

Evans: "The Dynamics of Family"

Ficco: "Negotiating Boundaries: Making It Through Adolescence Alive"

Frilot and Tubiak: "The Exploration of Self Within Society"

Headrick: "Life Paths and Destinations: Toward Meaningful Textual Transactions for a 12th-Grade British Literature Class"

Lancaster and Warren: "Mental Illness"

Preparation for Future Needs

Teaching is a future-oriented career. Most of what teachers do in the classroom is in preparation for what they think students need next. Teaching students what they will likely need later on is therefore a good justification for a unit, although teachers' projections about students' needs for the future are often better suited for students like themselves than those different from themselves.

College

One reason that teachers often give for teaching something is that it will help students succeed in college. I never found this reason to be terribly compelling. Among other things, it doesn't help those who don't go to college. It's also based on the idea that if you know something before you go to college and are required to learn it there, then you're ahead of the game because you've already learned it. This assumption defines knowledge a little too narrowly for my taste.

Nonetheless, it's conceivable that you could justify teaching some things on the basis that students will need them later in college, particularly if what students get are tools rather than simply facts.

Social Needs

Teachers might also teach a topic because they feel that they will be preparing students to help construct a better society in the future. Teachers might note, for instance, that people in general do not act with care and inclusion for those who are different from the way they are. Anticipating the need for a more compassionate society, you might decide to teach a unit on the outcast or the effects of discrimination.

In the Virtual Library of Conceptual Units, see

Cooney: "Technology and Progress"

Dodd, Garrard, and Welshhans: "Humanity and Voice in Literature: Building Bridges Among the Past, Present, and Future"

Relevance

Many teachers justify their instruction by arguing that it is relevant to students' interests and personal situations. This relevance often comes in terms of a correspondence between students' current life situations and the actions of characters in the texts they experience. Many readers find that they empathize with, learn from, see hope through, or otherwise relate to characters' dilemmas and predicaments. The quality of relevance often justifies the use of young adult literature in school classrooms.

In the Virtual Library of Conceptual Units, see

Berry, Donovan, and Hummel: "Romeo and Juliet"

Brown, Hummel, Mann, Taylor, and Wright: "Freedom and Identity"

Dyer: "Science Fiction: Critiquing the Present, Exploring the Future"

Kee: "Researching the World"

Robinson: "Greed"

Alignment with Standards

Aligning instruction with various standards documents may serve as a sound justification for teaching decisions. Many states and districts provide core curricula that outline in considerable detail the particular skills and knowledge that students should develop in school. A rationale based on the instruction's alignment with standards may persuade colleagues and administrators that instruction is appropriate and in accordance with such centralized expectations for teaching and learning.

In the Virtual Library of Conceptual Units, see

Culjan: "A Different Dimension: Fantasy, Folktales, Myths, and Legends"

Estey: "I Will Speak Up! For Myself, for My Friends, and for What I Believe In!"

Writing a Rationale

A rationale is a type of argument, a genre that typically includes a number of key elements. Your rationale should be based on a consideration of a related set of questions.

+ What *concepts* are central to the topic of this unit?

+ *Why* am I teaching this unit and its concepts?

+ What *type(s) of justification* am I primarily relying on to support my rationale (e.g., psychology or human development, cultural significance, etc.)?

+ Within each justification, what are the main *claims* I can make about its relevance to the unit I'm proposing (e.g., studying protest literature is important because it helps students understand the role of conscience in social action)?

+ For each claim, what kinds of *evidence* can I provide that would be persuasive to others, and how can I include a *warrant* that explains the ways in which the evidence I present supports my claim?

+ What *counterarguments* against my rationale can I anticipate, and how can I provide a rebuttal for them?

+ How can I provide a rationale for each of the texts that my students will read in conjunction with the unit focus?

With these criteria in mind, you have the framework to construct a rationale for your own proposed unit. Although there is no single procedure for writing a rationale, there are some kinds of planning you might want to try. Ultimately you will be producing a persuasive piece of writing, so however you proceed, you should think in terms of coordinating a set of related claims that support a general thesis, each supported by some kind of evidence. You should also keep a potential audience in mind for this argument. If you decide to teach a controversial book, whom must you convince that it's acceptable? The answer to this question might depend on where you teach. If you teach in a mixed-race community and wish to assign *Huckleberry Finn*, which includes language offensive to many African Americans yet which is often admired by middle-class white teachers (Smagorinsky 2016b), how will you pitch your rationale? Considering your audience, and the sorts of claims and points needed in order to persuade these readers or listeners, will work to your advantage in providing a sound, convincing justification for your curricular choices.

Summary

You must be ready to justify your teaching decisions, especially when they fall outside the range typical in your school. Inevitably, you will have your teaching contested. The better prepared you are to defend your instruction, the more likely it will be that you can teach in ways that you find important and satisfying. Because the teaching profession can often be frustrating, it's important to have as much control and authority over your teaching practices as possible in order to feel that you are having the effect on students' lives that you hope for. Providing a convincing rationale for your choices is one way to become both a contented teacher and perhaps ultimately a curriculum leader in your school and district.

Performance Assessment Prep

If you are able to provide a persuasive rationale for your teaching, you should have plenty of useful material for satisfying a performance assessment. Throughout the dossier, you will be asked to explain your decisions and ground them in prior research and theory. I've provided ways of justifying instruction that could easily be adapted to any demands to explain the contexts for learning in your dossier. For instance, you might be asked to identify the focus of instruction (the theme, archetype, strategy, and so on around which you build instruction), and how your knowledge of your students informs that teaching (e.g., how a unit concept helps to build on what your students know and might need to know). You could justify your teaching according to any of the means I've reviewed in this chapter, or others, and select from that rationale to meet specific demands of the assessment prompt.

10

Outlining a Unit

In this chapter I take one unit of instruction from the sophomore curriculum and identify a set of goals that students could work toward; the unit itself is detailed in Chapter 13. I've designed the third unit of the year, on discrimination, to illustrate how I might think as I plan a conceptual unit. My teaching of the unit should keep whole-course goals in mind. For the whole semester, for instance, students will be keeping a portfolio. I need to include regular attention to what might go into the portfolio: what the purpose is, what might make a good exhibit, how to reflect on an exhibit's contribution to the student's learning. Because many students will never have kept a portfolio before, I need to devote some explicit instructional time to how to select and reflect on an exhibit.

I can also assume some learning responsibilities of my own. I could produce some portion of these texts along with my students. I might keep my own portfolio about what I learn about teaching from my experiences during the year. In doing so, I would be *teaching reflectively*. Through my evaluation of students, I should always be evaluating my teaching. If students are not learning, how can I change the environment or the structure or content of the lessons? Do some groups of students perform better in my class than others, and if so, why? Do I find myself less patient with some students than others, and if so, can I identify a reason and consequences for my response to them? How do students treat one another in my class, and are there changes I can make to promote better relationships?

In turn, the students have the responsibility to take advantage of the opportunity I will provide. If my instruction is designed in thoughtful ways, they ought to use these tools and activities to grow to the greatest extent possible in their quest toward the unit goals. Through our production of these texts, the class can become

129

a construction zone where there is an ethic of productivity within a respectful environment. Though I'll rarely have 100 percent success in achieving such a classroom, I can set up my class to encourage most students toward that end.

Whole-Course Considerations

I began by identifying a small set of overarching concepts for the sophomore curriculum as a whole, providing a brief rationale for each.

+ *Negotiating Thresholds* (theme): Sophomores tend to adopt a group orientation and can benefit from considering ways of negotiating the contact they have with other groups. These groups include social groups within their peer culture, the groupings provided by different age and grade levels within their school, and the general distinction between the adolescent and adult worlds that they are in transit between.

+ *Self-Determination* (stance): I want my students to develop the stance that they are capable of learning on their own. My role, then, is to help them *learn how to learn*.

+ *Dramatic Images* (strategy): Students should know how to generate images that help them visualize literature. Students can render their understanding of literature through art, drama, dance, digital texts, and other artistic and theatrical forms.

Earlier I identified a series of culminating texts that students could produce for final exams in relation to these overarching concepts. Now I will narrow my scope to a single unit within this whole course and identify goals for that unit.

Conceptual Unit on Discrimination

The year begins with a unit on coming of age, which provides an opportunity to explore the kinds of transitions that students make in moving from ninth grade to tenth. Often the summer has placed them in situations that have enabled significant transformations of the sort explored in coming-of-age literature. By beginning with the coming-of-age unit, I have an opportunity to include attention to the writing of narratives, through which the students may recount, reconstruct, and reflect on critical personal experiences in relation to the unit theme. From there, we move to an open-ended writing workshop in which students work for several weeks to develop writing of their choice.

Given that students often choose personal narratives for their workshop writing, the unit on discrimination provides a good opportunity to move to analytic writing. The primary writing that they do in this unit is an *extended definition of discrimination*. Because discrimination is subject to so many permutations, I provide an element of choice by allowing each student to pick a particular kind of discrimination to define: racial discrimination, religious discrimination, discrimination based on age, gender discrimination, discrimination based on physical or mental conditions, or whatever other topic interests him.

I also include a multimedia production in this unit. In the coming-of-age unit, I start by having students write narratives and then get into small groups to dramatize a narrative based on their writing. In this way, prior to reading, the students have exposure to a series of stories that are concerned with coming-of-age experiences. The opening unit thus includes a formal kind of writing of the sort often found on high-stakes writing assessments as well as a more kinesthetic means of relating a story that contributes to students' ability to generate images for their reading. The discrimination unit also has a balance between formal writing and multimedia composing.

In the coming-of-age unit I teach students to maintain double-column reading logs (see Chapter 2). We return to these logs as well in the discrimination unit. This time, however, I don't need to teach them how to produce the logs; I can simply assign them. We thus have both formal and informal writing in this unit.

Finally, in this unit I teach students how to generate questions in relation to a text and to lead their own discussions. The main feature that all four of the culminating texts share is that they are open-ended and require students to construct knowledge for themselves through the available tools.

Materials

For the unit's major work, I've selected a canonical text, Richard Wright's autobiography, *Black Boy*, a staple of many sophomore curricula. I also want other types of texts represented. For this unit, because discrimination has historically been the subject of many kinds of expression, I include songs, poetry, and short stories. I might also use an image search engine to find statues, paintings, political cartoons, and other works of art featuring discrimination.

The materials I've selected follow. In making these selections I've tried to seek a balance of authors according to gender, race, geography, and other demographic categories. I've made other efforts to include multiple perspectives on this complex topic. I recognize that any given school might have limitations in terms of what's available to teach, so these choices may need revision in particular settings. Also note that my own taste in music is undoubtedly dated to the adolescent mind and that you might search for more contemporary selections than my ancient affections can provide.

SONGS

The Weavers: "Sixteen Tons"

Vanessa Williams: "Colors of the Wind"

Dave Matthews Band: "Cry Freedom"

Bob Marley and the Wailers: "War"

Johnny Clegg and Savuka: "Inevitable Consequence of Progress"

Randy Newman: "Short People"

The Crüxshadows: "Leave Me Alone"

Neil Young: "Southern Man"

Creedence Clearwater Revival: "Fortunate Son"

POEMS

Maya Angelou: "On the Pulse of Morning"

Peter Blue Cloud: "The Old Man's Lazy"

Elizabeth Brewster: "Jamie"

SHORT STORIES

Maria Campbell: "Play with Me"

Leslie Marmon Silko: "Tony's Story"

Kurt Vonnegut: "Harrison Bergeron"

Shirley Jackson: "After You, My Dear Alphonse"

José Antonio Burciaga: "Romantic Nightmare"

Ray Bradbury: "All Summer in a Day"

AUTOBIOGRAPHY

Richard Wright: *Black Boy*

Note that this text narrates life in a legally segregated society from nearly a century ago. As you'll see, it would be possible to exchange it for a more contemporary work that exposes discrimination in today's world.

Unit Goals

For the major unit goals, I selected assessments that evaluate a range of ways of knowing. I also included assessments of two types.

1. *In-process texts and activities*—that is, those that students do as part of their learning during the unit. These texts and activities are designed to be exploratory and formative, with attention primarily to what students learn. The final look of their product is of less concern.

2. *Culminating texts and activities*—that is, those that students do toward the end of the unit. These texts and activities should be more concerned with expectations for form while also serving as opportunities for new learning.

The *in-process* texts and activities ought to contribute to students' ability to produce satisfying *culminating* texts and activities. There are dozens of worthwhile goals you could set for any unit of instruction. To help focus the students' attention on culminating texts they can produce in rich and productive ways, I suggest identifying a small set of goals to serve as the major assessments for the unit. These goals should be consistent with the overarching concepts of the course as a whole. When you plan other units within the curriculum, you should vary the goals and assessments to account for students' multiple ways of knowing. Let's take a look at one possible set of goals for this unit.

In-Process Texts and Activities

Self-determination is among the year's overarching concepts. I hope that during the course of the year, students will develop the stance that they are in control of their learning. I want them to believe that they know what they want to learn and know how to learn it.

But hoping isn't enough. I need to make sure that I teach them ways of learning that contribute to that kind of confidence and authority. Teaching for self-determination, therefore, requires that I help students learn procedures for setting goals and posing questions that they would like to answer. If they have had a typical education, they are probably inexperienced at posing their own questions about their schoolwork; they have spent most of their school life answering questions asked by teachers.

Because of their inexperience at asking questions and undertaking inquiries in school, I want to give them opportunities that have the following two features:

1. The students may take risks and make mistakes without being punished by a bad grade.

2. They have the opportunity to work collaboratively and receive feedback while learning as part of an instructional scaffold.

Two goals that could potentially provide these opportunities are keeping a *response log* and leading *student-generated discussions*.

DOUBLE-COLUMN READING LOGS

Keep a reading log in response to the literature we are studying during this unit. To keep your log, do the following:

▷ Divide each page with a vertical line down the center.
▷ On the left side of each page, record significant passages from the literature you read.
▷ On the right side, across from each passage, include at least one question of each type for each work of literature studied.
  ▷ Ask *open-ended questions* that would help you understand the passage better.
  ▷ Give your personal response to the passage (i.e., any thoughts you have in connection with it).
  ▷ Give your personal evaluation of the passage.
  ▷ Think through a possible interpretation of the passage.

Three Rules

1. Remember that your journal does not need to follow the conventions of textbook English. Rather, the purpose is to think about the literature without worrying about the form your thoughts take.

2. Turn in your response log every two weeks. I will read your log and respond to your comments. *If you make an entry that you do not want me to read, place an X at the top of the page, and I'll skip it.* Really.

3. Keep in mind that *I am required to share any thoughts or suggestions of violence, suicide, substance abuse, family abuse, or other harmful behavior with the school counselors.*

STUDENT-LED DISCUSSIONS

To discuss Richard Wright's *Black Boy*, the class will organize into five small groups, with each group being responsible for leading a discussion of four chapters of the novel. Each group will be responsible for conducting a class discussion on its chapters for one full class period. You may adopt any format you wish: regular English class, talk show format, town hall meeting, courtroom, or other mode of your choice. Your discussion should meet all of the following requirements:

▷ Each group member should take a roughly equal part in leading the discussion.

▷ You should make an effort to include each class member in your discussion.

▷ The questions you pose should not ask for factual information from the story, unless those facts serve to help explore open-ended questions.

▷ The questions you pose should include at least one of each of the following categories:

  ▷ *Inferences* about characters or events within the text (e.g., how does joining a gang affect Richard's life?)

  ▷ *Generalizations* from the text to society at large (e.g., in what ways is Richard's story from the first half of the twentieth century relevant to today's society?)

  ▷ The *effects of literary form or technique* (e.g., do you think that Richard's presentation of his experiences is realistic?)

  ▷ The *purpose of a particular event* in terms of the text's meaning (e.g., how does Richard's life in the orphanage shape his perspective on life in the United States?)

  ▷ *Evaluations* of the literature (e.g., what parts of the story do you like best and least? Why?)

  ▷ *Emotions* that students have in response to the story (e.g., how did you feel when Richard burned down his grandparents' house?)

  ▷ *Personal connections* to the story (e.g., what connections do you feel with Richard during his employment at the optical company?)

▷ During the discussion, you should also work at getting students to elaborate on their initial comments.

Because I turn the discussion-leading over to students and focus largely on teaching them how to run a class, I could easily substitute a more contemporary work for this classic memoir of the segregated South.

Culminating Texts and Activities

The in-process assessments are designed to teach students strategies for learning both stance and procedures for personal inquiry. They focus on the process of inquiry more than on the precision of the final product. For culminating texts and activities, your focus includes attention to the final form of the effort and how it meets particular conventions. A reading log does not call for correct answers or conventional English because the emphasis is on using writing as a tool for thinking, rather than on producing an impeccable product. A reader who expects standard conventions might consider students to be bad writers when they are in fact using the logs as intended. It behooves a writer to know which conventions to call on in producing particular kinds of writing. Culminating texts should be responsive to the need for appropriate conventional form.

Following is a set of assignments for culminating texts that meet all of these goals for the unit.

EXTENDED DEFINITION OF A PARTICULAR KIND OF DISCRIMINATION

Throughout the unit we have considered the effects of discrimination, on both the person who discriminates and the person who is being discriminated against. We have looked at questions of discrimination in a variety of situations, using examples from current events, from your personal experiences and observations, and from literature. In some cases, there has been disagreement on what counts as discrimination.

Your task is to write an essay in which you provide an extended definition of discrimination of a particular kind, such as gender discrimination in the workplace, racial discrimination in housing, religious discrimination in school, age discrimination in hiring, or any other sort that interests you.

To do so, provide the following:

▷ A general introduction in which you provide an overview for your definition

▷ A set of criteria or rules that state clearly what discrimination is and is not

▷ For each criterion, an example from literature or other texts, current events, or your personal experiences that illustrates the rule at work; at least half of your examples must come from the texts studied in class

▷ For each criterion, a counterexample from literature or other texts, current events, or your personal experiences that appears to meet the conditions of the rule yet that lacks some essential ingredient; at least half of your counterexamples must come from the literature or other texts studied in class

▷ For each example and counterexample, a warrant that clearly explains why the rule is or is not being met

▷ For your whole argument, a *counterargument* expressing the viewpoint of someone who might disagree with you

▷ For the counterargument, a *rebuttal* in which you defend your position

▷ Conventional grammar, spelling, punctuation, and usage throughout your essay

▷ Evidence of having written at least one rough draft that has been submitted for peer evaluation

MULTIMEDIA PROJECT

You have read a number of literary works that concern the theme of discrimination. To show what you have learned through your engagement with this literature, create an interpretive text in any form of your choice: collage, painting, poetry, music, drama, sculpture, performance art, digital text, or other textual form. You are also welcome to combine forms to produce your text. When designing your text, keep the following in mind:

▷ The project should in some way depict your understanding of experiences with discrimination.

▷ It should make some kind of reference to at least one work of literature or other text studied during the unit.

▷ You may produce your text individually or in a group of any size up to three.

▷ You will have one class period in which to work on your text and must do all additional work outside class.

▷ You must prepare a three- to five-minute presentation of your text to the class in which you explain its significance and what it illustrates about your understanding of discriminatory experiences and/or literature or other texts.

Summary

We now have a simple outline of the unit goals. I'll flesh out each as I put them into practice during the unit design. A few reminders: For each of these assignments you'll need a rubric for assessment; for each responsibility you assign to students, you must simultaneously assign yourself the task of teaching them how to meet the responsibility; and the whole range of assignments should allow diverse students access to success in learning about the topic and performing well on the assessments.

Performance Assessment Prep

Unit goals correspond to the assessment segment of your dossier, so this chapter should inform how you conceive of worthwhile culminating assignments, phrase them for utmost clarity, align them with rubrics, and teach your class so that students are likely to perform well on them.

Setting Up the Construction Zone

11

The next step is to plan classes so that students can work productively toward the unit goals. I continue using the construction metaphor I have used throughout the book, characterizing the classroom as a *construction zone* where teachers help students build and reflect on texts that they find useful and important.

If the unit goals are thoughtfully set so that they help students engage with the unit concepts, they should enable students to work toward the production of texts that are meaningful in the following two ways:

1. The *process* of planning and constructing texts will enable students to synthesize prior knowledge and build new knowledge. Both the teacher and other students are available to co-construct or provide help during this process. This process of composition is usually *exploratory*, with new ideas discovered as the work of construction unfolds.

2. The *product* will be a text that the student can reflect on for continued learning. The text also serves to communicate students' understandings to others and enable them to reflect on the unit problems in new ways. *Product* does not describe only the finished text. It also refers to the text at any point during the composing process, when its builder(s) can step back, consider its form, and either revise or build on it. If the text matters to the student, then it will undergo continual revision, if not tangibly then psychologically, as the student continues to think through the ideas that generated the text.

You will help students learn how to use tools effectively, draw on necessary resources, act as productive crew members, and understand the nature and purpose of the texts they are constructing. At times you might be a facilitator. Other times you might provide clear and explicit information. At yet other times you might turn over leadership responsibilities to students. You might work along with students, constructing texts according to the same guidelines they are following. You might also produce texts from research that you are conducting on the relation between your teaching and their learning, on the kinds of human relationships that follow from your teaching in your classroom, or on students' lives outside the classroom so that you better understand how to build on their knowledge and strengths.

You will use your good judgment about which role is most appropriate for which circumstances and needs. You will make all of these judgments with an awareness of the overall context in which you are teaching, including your department, your school, your community, and your state. You should be a good citizen of all of these social groups, keeping in mind that one responsibility of citizenship is to work for change when systems don't serve their constituents well.

Teaching Language

Speech is a tool through which students may express themselves, construct meaning, communicate, and accomplish other ends. To the grammarian, this tool has great limitations when used in the classroom, with speech produced according to a single set of conventions. I see language as much more malleable and flexible and do not believe that rigid rules do much except discourage people from wanting to write in school. You should familiarize yourself with some important debates surrounding the teaching of grammar so that when setting up your classroom as a construction zone, you will be prepared for students to use language in many and varied ways to build meaningful texts in relation to your curriculum.

Textbook English and Problems with Teaching It

The teaching of grammar separately from speaking and writing is among the most widely employed, yet least effective, practices in the English teacher's repertoire. Educational researchers have reached an astounding consensus for more than 100 years: Isolated grammar instruction does not move students' speech or writing toward the norm established in textbooks (Hillocks 1986; Weaver 1996). Hillocks found that isolated grammar instruction actually has a *negative* effect on the quality of student writing, probably because it takes time away from teaching writing. There is remarkable agreement that isolated grammar instruction is at best futile and at worst harmful, yet it remains a ubiquitous classroom practice. Teaching grammar can be more difficult than it seems, for several reasons. I would not mention this finding at job interviews, however, where a traditional grammarian might be preferred over someone with a flexible understanding of language usage.

There Are Many Sets of Rules

One assumption behind grammar instruction is that people agree on what correct grammar is and so can distinguish right from wrong in students' usage. Yet in spite of claims that there is a well-defined standard for the English language, what is right according to one set of rules is wrong according to another. Let's take one recurring within-sentence structure, the list consisting of three or more items. According to the Harvard comma rule, a writer inserts a comma following the penultimate item (e.g., the good, the bad, and the ugly). The *Publication Manual of the American Psychological Association* (American Psychological Association 2001) prescribes the use of the Harvard comma rule. Yet the Modern Language Association does not; writers using MLA eschew the comma that precedes the final item in the set. Not only are rules meant to be broken, some sets of rules break each other.

Students Rarely Hear Textbook English Actually Spoken

Students are surrounded by people who speak English. Few people, however, actually speak the textbook version stressed in English classes. Young people hear ungrammatical structures daily from musicians, athletes, movie stars, DJs, newscasters, and others whom they admire and emulate, including teachers, administrators, and university professors. Even high-level politicians—including those who demand elaborate accountability systems to make sure that children are being taught their grammar—are known to butcher a phrase now and then. Students end up conforming to the everyday speech of their surroundings rather than the quaint and curious rules that their textbooks and teachers say are correct, raising concerns about which grammar to teach, if any.

"Errors" Can Be Signs of Growth

Shaughnessy (1977) was among the first to take a developmental approach to her students' use of language. Instead of punishing her students for making errors, she viewed errors in a more hopeful light. People make errors, she reasoned, when trying something new, and they will rarely try something new if they will be penalized for their errors. She hoped to accomplish two goals simultaneously: to encourage her students to experiment with new sentence structures and syntaxes and to educate them about textbook English *over time*. She saw errors, then, as potentially positive indications of students' willingness to grow as writers and did not mark down papers initially for deviations from the norm that ultimately would be expected of them.

What's Important Is Knowing How to Speak for Different Listeners

Many people question the idea that a standard version of English even exists, arguing instead that there are many dialects of English, of which textbook English is but one. What counts as proper is a function of who is speaking and who is listening, and what matters most is knowing the codes that provide the basis for what others find appropriate. Delpit (1995) relies on this premise to argue that speakers of varieties such as African American English benefit from expanding their repertoires to include the syntax, vocabulary, and other aspects of diction that are current in the work environments in which they seek employment. Others have argued that African American English has its own logic and legitimacy and should be honored (Smitherman 2006). I suggest flexibility and the understanding that correcting spoken speech may be more debilitating to a student's sense of self than correcting written speech produced for readers who expect fidelity to textbook rules (at least, those they know).

All Errors Are Not Created Equal

Each of the following sentences contains at least one error:

> Your continuous complaining is getting on my nerves.

> The warts on my nose is getting bigger.

Let's assume that you are the rare person who can distinguish between *continuous* and *continual* and knows that for people to complain continuously, they would complain without pause, including while asleep. Then let's assume that you can identify a plural subject and single object of the adjectival prepositional phrase and know that the verb should agree with the subject of the clause and not the nearest noun.

Which of these two errors bothers you more? If you're like most people who can identify the errors, the subject-verb disagreement is more bothersome to you. Errors that really get people's dander up are known as "status" errors (Connors and Lunsford 1988; Hairston 1981). Subject-verb agreement errors offend language purists much more than do dangling prepositions and thus should get greater instructional attention. Teachers, rather than viewing grammar instruction as a field that must be covered in its entirety, should concentrate on educating students about a relatively small number of usage rules, the mastery of which will give them greater status when communicating with those to whom the English language has a pure form.

Methods of Teaching Grammar

Thus far I have outlined why the teaching of grammar is such a controversial topic and bewildering school subject for many students and teachers. Critiquing the state of affairs is not sufficient. Within these limitations and competing interests, I need to find ways to teach students about language usage that they will find relevant to their communication needs.

There are several reasons language study is justified. First, as readers of student writing, teachers want to be able to understand what students are trying to say. Papers written with rambling syntax do not communicate ideas effectively, and in other, more high-stakes settings in which writing is expected, writing produced with deviations from the textbook norm will reduce students' prospects for advancement, and often suggest that the teacher is not getting the job done. Second, in spite of the problems I have outlined, test designers continue to include large sections on language use that have great consequences for students, teachers, and schools. And so attention to language usage has an important, if problematic, place in the English curriculum.

Principles Guiding Grammar Instruction

Based on my understanding of the issues I have outlined and my experience as a teacher, I endorse the following general guidelines for teaching students about language in the English curriculum:

✦ Don't teach grammar in isolation. Grammar instruction is most relevant when related clearly to students' writing and reading. Although there may be occasions when you correct students' spoken grammar, reserve most of your corrective work for students' writing.

✦ Treat grammar as an enabling *tool* rather than as a subject to be learned or a way to measure students' deficits relative to textbook English. Long ago, Pooley (1954) identified the following four points as germane to the tool approach:

1. Postpone grammar instruction to the point where it can really become useful to the student. Too much grammar is commonly taught too early.

2. Teach a few concepts at a time, slowly and thoroughly.

3. Emphasize the elements of grammar which lead to improved sentence structure.

4. Teach correctness in specific situations, and use grammar as the explanation of, rather than the means toward, greater correctness (143; quoted in Reid 2006, 13).

[Fun grammar game: In writing about grammar usage, which error did Pooley make?

If you answered that in Item #3 he used "which" when he should have used "that," then you are right . . . . if you're in the United States. In England, "which" is typically used in this structure.]

+ Teach language lessons in limited doses. Perhaps these lessons might be daily oral language segments that are clearly tied to students' experiences with their reading or writing.

+ Grammar instruction should be selective and targeted to language issues that may (1) raise questions with some about the speaker's or writer's status, such as subject-verb agreement, unintentional sentence fragments, and comma splices, or (2) result in confusion, such as dangling modifiers and pronoun-antecedent ambiguity. I also see a role for correcting pet-peeve errors in usage, such as using nominative forms in objective structures (e.g., "My teacher taught the preposition lesson to she and I.").

+ Although some grammar instruction is inevitably corrective, it should also be generative. Knowledge of how to generate various syntactic structures (e.g., through sentence combining or generative imitation) helps students produce more varied and sophisticated writing.

+ Focusing on labels of grammatical components is useful largely for testing students on such knowledge, and even then not so effective. I recommend focusing on attending to linguistic structures without getting carried away by the terminology, while also being aware that this terminology might matter when outside assessors lurk.

+ When responding to student writing, focus on a few recurring problems rather than flooding papers with red ink, which can overwhelm writers because there is too much diffuse information for them to process effectively. Your best bet is to help students understand a few things at a time, rather than to try to effect wholesale change all at once.

+ Speaking of red pens, think about marking papers with some other color. That color has a lot of bad associations for many students.

Contexts of Teaching

You do not teach in a vacuum. Rather, you teach within a set of confines or constraints. These parameters can be useful in that they provide a set of guidelines for appropriate decision-making. They can also, of course, restrict your choices. Whether or not you like them, however, they exist and provide the context for your teaching. It's important, then, to understand where you teach, whom you teach, and those with whom you teach. In this book I'll offer two unit designs. The first is for a rather suburban, reasonably affluent context; the second is for a school in a financially stressed community.

Setting Up Shop: Getting Started with Students

Teachers and students often view the return to school in the same bittersweet way: sad to see summer and its pace come to an end but glad to be back in school with their friends. Mostly, the first day of school is a time of getting reacquainted, of getting back into the routine of school.

One way to get started is to take an *inventory* of students' interests and performance levels. Throughout the first few weeks of school, you should look for opportunities for students to tell you about themselves. You could do this in a number of ways.

Personal Experience Writing

You might ask students to provide you with a piece of writing in which they tell of some significant event from their recent past that will help you get to know them and their interests better. It's possible to build this writing into the first conceptual unit of the year by including narrative writing as a way to explore the unit theme.

Owner's Manual

You could learn about your students by having them provide you with an owner's manual for themselves. You might need to review what this should include.

- ✦ A description of the product and its intended use
- ✦ Instructions on how to assemble it (optional)
- ✦ A diagram of what it looks like in action
- ✦ Instructions on how to operate and maintain it
- ✦ How to know when it's not working properly
- ✦ What steps to take to fix it

Students usually have fun writing about themselves in this way, and you can learn about their personalities, interests, and writing.

Parent/Guardian Introduction

You could ask a parent, guardian, or other significant adult provide a letter of introduction. You might contrive a situation: The student is new to a setting, and this person is writing the letter that will provide entrée. You should always be careful about requiring parental involvement, given that some students come from troubled homes or no homes at all.

Survey

You could also prepare a survey in which you ask students to tell you things about themselves. For example, you could create a survey like this:

> Please answer each question as honestly as possible. Your answers will help me to get to know you as a person and also help me to know how to teach this class well. If you do not enjoy doing the things I'm asking about and haven't done any over the summer, just say so. There's no penalty for being honest.
>
> 1. What kind of reading did you do over the summer? Please tell the following:
>   - ◆ The *type* of reading (news sources, magazines, novels, Internet pages, social media, text messages, etc.)
>   - ◆ The *amount* you read (one hour a day, two pages a week, none, etc.)
>   - ◆ The *names* of things you read (specific websites, names of books, people followed online, etc.)

2. Who is your favorite author? What have you read by this author? Why do you consider this author to be your favorite?

3. What kinds of things do you particularly dislike to read? Why do you find them so awful?

4. What's your favorite thing about school?

5. What's your least favorite thing about school?

6. What kind of writing did you do over the summer? Please tell:

   ♦ Tthe *type* of writing (messaging, email, social media, a novel, none, etc.)

   ♦ The *amount* you wrote (100 words a day, thirty tweets a week, none, etc.)

7. What purposes do you use writing for outside school?

8. If you could change one thing about the writing you do in school, what would it be?

9. If you could change one thing about the reading you do in school, what would it be?

10. What would you like to learn about the most in this class?

11. If you could give me one piece of advice about how to teach this class, what would it be?

12. If you could change the way school is run, what changes would you make?

13. What are your favorite things to do outside school?

14. Do you think that your favorite things from outside school should be part of what you do for grades in school? Please explain.

15. Do your grades in school accurately reflect how smart you are? Please explain.

Response to Literature

Finally, you could do a kind of diagnostic inventory to see how students make sense of their reading. You could have them read a short work of literature and have them write a response in which they explain how they make sense of it. Their responses could come in the form of either a short essay, an imaginative piece they produce, or short answers to a series of questions you ask about the reading.

From whatever combination of inventories you use, you should get a sense of where the students stand academically and where their interests lie. This knowledge can help you choose appropriate texts to read and develop a suitable set of expectations.

Summary

The construction zone metaphor characterizes how you might set up your classroom and anticipate your teaching needs. Doing so involves knowing not only your students but the community in which you teach so as to anticipate the various situations in which you might find yourself as the year unfolds. You can never anticipate everything that will happen. Good preparation, however, can ward off too many unexpected surprises of the sort that can complicate your teaching in ways that you'd rather avoid.

Performance Assessment Prep

From this point on, I detail what specific instructional plans might look like, with the understanding that my approach may not correspond to what your school will require. At the same time, the basic elements should be in place for you to adapt your planning skills to local bureaucratic needs. The remaining chapters on unit planning should provide models for instructional scaffolding, the alignment of goals/assessment with instruction, the means of adapting instruction to particular communities and learners, and many of the other expectations on beginning teacher performance assessments.

12

Introductory Activities

You and your students now know what you are building toward. It's possible that things will happen along the way to cause these plans to change somewhat, but for the most part you have a set of goals to guide your planning of the unit.

How, then, to begin? I suggest providing a particular kind of instructional scaffold, called an *introductory* or *gateway* activity. An introductory activity is designed to help students develop the kind of schematic knowledge they need to understand the unit's key concepts and problems. It thus provides them with a blueprint for the knowledge they will construct during the unit.

In designing your unit, you should ask, What knowledge will students need to work successfully toward the unit goals? I will review some possible ways through which you can introduce students to concepts that will likely be central to the literature they study. As you will see, all provide some opportunity for reconstruction by students. All of the types of introductory activities I describe are designed to have students wrestle with problems similar to those faced by characters in literature.

The activities either directly or indirectly ask students to draw on their own experiences in similar kinds of situations to think about either the structure of experience (e.g., the script for a coming-of-age experience) or the substance (e.g., evaluating characters' decisions in problematic situations). By thinking through these questions prior to reading, students will be able to use the blueprint for experience, and the script for action based on this blueprint, to help them understand the characters' actions in the texts they read (see Smagorinsky, McCann, and Kern 1987).

The assumption behind this approach is that students typically have some kind of experience or knowledge that they can draw on to assist them with new learning. Unfortunately, students often view their personal knowledge as irrelevant to understanding schoolwork and flounder in areas where they could flourish. The introductory activities I describe in this chapter are designed to help students recognize and use their knowledge to make connections with the literature they read and to help provide them with material for the texts they produce.

The activities in this chapter fall under four categories: personal experience writing, opinionnaire or survey, scenario or case study, and writing about related problems. Each of the four types of activity is linked to one of the units in the sophomore curriculum. It is beneficial to vary the kinds of introductory activities that you use so that your teaching doesn't become too predictable. I offer these four types of introductions as possibilities, rather than as the only ways in which you could introduce a unit. I hope that you think about the metaphor of the cognitive map and generate your own approaches to designing introductory activities. The Virtual Library of Conceptual Units is filled with scores of examples for you to consult.

These introductory activities are designed to help students draw on their prior personal knowledge to help them understand issues that come up in literature and other texts. In turn, the students' engagement with the unit's material should help them come to a better understanding of their personal knowledge and experiences. You can help students make these connections in your instructional design by having them return to the introductory activity after their engagement with the texts. For instance, I suggest that when students write about relevant personal experiences prior to reading, they return to these narratives later in the unit and develop them into more formal pieces of writing. Doing so has the added benefit of providing the class with a range of student-generated texts to help illuminate the central concepts of the theme.

Writing About Personal Experiences

Students can write informally—perhaps in journals or reading logs—about experiences that are similar to those of the characters they will study. The act of writing can promote reflection about important experiences that will help students relate to the problems confronted by the characters in the literature or other texts with which they engage. In having students produce appropriate personal experience writing, you need to think about the key concepts and problems in the texts and design a writing prompt to help students think about experiences they've had that would help them understand these concepts and problems.

For my hypothetical sophomore curriculum, half of the units are thematic. The key theme should provide you with the topic for your prompt. Other kinds of units can also allow for personal experience writing as an introduction, particularly if they involve a theme. The unit on *Julius Caesar*, for instance, includes a set of related themes with which students are likely to have had experience: loyalty, betrayal, ambition, and so on.

For the sophomore curriculum I've designed, students could write about a personal experience they've had in which they came of age. Doing so would meet a number of curricular ends.

+ It would make their first writing of the year in the narrative genre, which many argue is more familiar and accessible, and more developmentally appropriate, for sophomore students than writing in the paradigmatic mode. Students' initial writing, then, would be something they have an opportunity to feel successful about.

+ It would introduce students to the key problems and concepts of the unit.

+ It would give them explicit knowledge of the script of coming-of-age literature.

+ It could serve as the basis of a classroom drama.

+ It could provide the first draft for the unit goal of writing a personal narrative.

+ It could provide the class with a host of texts that illuminate the unit theme.

One option with personal experience writing is to have students interview a significant person in their lives, perhaps a parent or guardian, and then prepare a narrative of that other person's experience. You do need to be careful about requirements to involve parents, however. You can't always assume that students come from stable, happy, and emotionally safe homes. It's a good idea, then, to build in options rather than to require parental input, perhaps allowing students to substitute a significant adult for a parent if they wish.

The prompt for the students' personal experience writing should ask them to describe the situation in ways that will prepare them for their subsequent reading and writing. The prompt should be specific enough to get students to think about the full range of problems involved, yet not so detailed as to override the spontaneity of their writing. One possible prompt would cue the students as follows:

Write about a personal experience you've had in which you had a coming-of-age experience—that is, one that caused you to grow up in some way. Make sure to explain

▷ The immature behavior that you exhibited prior to the experience;
▷ A transforming experience through which you gained significant new knowledge and maturity; and
▷ The mature behavior that you exhibited following the experience.

You are not required to explain these events in this particular order, although you may if you wish. Keep in mind that other students will read about the experience you write about.

The last statement is necessary any time you ask students to share their writing. You shouldn't require students to share what they've written if you haven't advised them of this step ahead of time. Students should always have the option of not sharing if they feel uncomfortable reporting their experiences to others. Also be aware that in some communities, parents will not allow teachers to ask students to engage in any form of introspection or experiential reflection, which they will view as a violation of their privacy and often of their religious convictions. Always know where you are teaching and how that shapes your choices.

This prompt is less detailed than the prompt for the culminating text that they produce for their unit goal. The idea is to get them writing freely about the experience, to use writing as a tool for helping them to think about how experiences can contribute to maturity. The prompt includes a brief, accessible definition of *coming-of-age experience* to help set the stage for the rest of the unit.

Have some kind of follow-up to an introductory activity of this type so that students compare their responses with those of other students, and so that the whole class has an opportunity to benefit from one another's reflections. Here are some possible ways to follow up personal writing:

✦ Have students get in small groups, read one another's narratives, and characterize the kinds of experiences that result in significant change. Then, have each group report to the whole class, with the teacher orchestrating the contributions into a discussion on significant experiences and the kinds of changes they can promote.

✦ Have students get in small groups, read one another's narratives, and choose one or several to use as the basis for short plays to be performed before the class. Following these plays, have the class discuss the kinds of scripts developed by each group for coming-of-age stories. These scripts could serve as the basis for the analyses of stories during discussions and ultimately for an analytic essay students write on an unfamiliar story based on the coming-of-age theme.

✦ Have students get in small groups and describe the characteristics of a good coming-of-age narrative. Have each group report to the whole class, with the teacher orchestrating a discussion on the traits of good narratives of this type. Have students revise their narratives based on the qualities identified during this discussion as a second draft of the narrative they will produce as a culminating text.

Opinionnaire or Survey

An opinionnaire, or survey, is a set of controversial statements designed to get students thinking about issues they will later encounter in the literature. At times the statements might come directly from the texts to be read by the class. For instance, I once developed an opinionnaire for an American literature unit on protest literature, and one statement on the list was paraphrased from one of the texts we would read, Thoreau's "Civil Disobedience": "The best government is the one that governs the least." If the texts provide no such provocative statements, then you will need to develop them yourself based on the issues that students will eventually think through while reading.

For the sophomore unit on discrimination, you could use an opinionnaire as a way to get students to think about issues prior to reading. One possible set of statements follows:

Each of the following statements expresses an opinion. Rate each statement from 1 (strongly disagree) to 5 (strongly agree).

▷ Any set of beliefs is OK, as long as you believe in them sincerely.
▷ I tend to go along with whatever my friends are for, even if I disagree with them.
▷ People should always try to understand and include other people, no matter how different they are.
▷ If you move to a new country, you should adapt to its culture as quickly as possible so that you fit in.
▷ I try not to notice people's physical characteristics. That way, I treat everyone the same.

> ▷ A person's religion is never a factor in the kind of relationship I develop with him or her.
> ▷ I never judge people on the basis of their appearance.
> ▷ If you know where people live, you can tell a lot about them.
> ▷ It's harmless to tell jokes about people in which they appear stupid because of their race, hair color, nationality, and so on; people who take offense should be able to recognize that it's all for the sake of fun and humor, and just lighten up.
> ▷ Laws are designed to make society fair for all of its citizens.

The key to writing an effective opinionnaire is to write statements that will invite disagreement among students. This disagreement should lead to discussions of issues central to the problems that will arise in the unit. All of these statements are designed to help students think through what they already know about discrimination and to refine their ideas in light of contrasting opinions expressed by classmates.

You can use opinionnaires in a variety of ways.

+ Pass them out and go over the items in order, having a discussion of each.

+ Have students complete the opinionnaire individually, have them discuss their responses in small groups, then follow this with a whole-class discussion.

+ Have students answer the opinionnaire questions in small groups, then follow up with a whole-class discussion.

The advantage of the second and third approaches is that they enable all students to participate in the discussion. In a whole-class discussion on a topic that invites strong opinions, less assertive students have few opportunities to speak. By adding the small-group stage, you will allow for greater participation, particularly among students who feel inhibited by the whole-class setting or who benefit from engaging in exploratory talk.

Scenario or Case Study

Scenarios and case studies describe problematic examples of people who find themselves in thorny situations that parallel the circumstances of the literary characters. Scenarios tend to be brief and intended for small-group discussion followed by a whole-class comparison of the small-group decisions. Case studies tend to be more detailed and complex and used for more extensive study, such as when small groups lead the whole class in an analysis of a single case.

The basic structure and design process of the two are similar, however. Once again, you should write the scenarios or case studies at the intersection of what the literature and other texts provide and what the students have experienced. In the sophomore-year unit on conflict with authority, you could design an introductory activity based on a set of scenarios requiring students to evaluate how such problems are negotiated. The following activity could serve this purpose:

Each of the following scenarios involves an individual coming in conflict with an authority figure. In a small group of four students, read each one carefully. Then, as a group, rank the characters according to how much you admire them, putting 1 by the scenario in which you admire the character's behavior the most, 2 by the scenario in which you admire the character the second most, and so on. You must rank all five of the scenarios. No ties.

1. Justin Time was on his high school football team. He didn't start but was a reserve linebacker who often played when the team went into special defenses. After a tough loss, the coach mistakenly thought he heard Justin laugh at something as the team was walking back to the locker room. Enraged that a player was not taking defeat seriously enough, the coach ordered Justin to crawl across the parking lot on his elbows in front of the whole team and a few hundred spectators, while the coach yelled at him at the top of his lungs the entire time. Justin thought that a good team player always does what the coach says, so although he initially denied that he had been the one who'd laughed, he ended up following his coach's orders without arguing.

2. Sybil Rights was a bright young woman, although her grades didn't always reflect it because she didn't always do what her teachers wanted her to do. One time her history teacher gave the class an assignment in which they were to outline the entire chapter from the textbook that dealt with the American government's decision to drop the atomic bomb on Japan. Although every other student in the class did the assignment, Sybil refused, saying that it was just busywork and that she would not do assignments that she thought were a waste of her time. She decided that she could spend her time better by actually learning something about this incident, so she wrote an essay on the morality of the bombing that she intended to enter in the school's annual essay competition. She ended up getting a zero on the assignment, which lowered her grade for the marking period from a B to a C.

3. Ryan Caraway was a young American soldier stationed in Europe in World War II. His troop was one of many battling the enemy in a hilly region of the war theater. They had the enemy outnumbered, but the enemy was well positioned at the top of a hill, and his unit couldn't seem to gain any ground in spite of their superior numbers. Finally, an order came down from the commanding officer that Ryan's troop should charge the hill. It occurred to him that his troop was being sacrificed to create a diversion so that other troops could rush up and make a sneak attack from the flanks while the enemy was fighting off his troop. Ryan thought that this was a risky plan that was doomed to failure and that his life was going to be sacrificed needlessly. Yet, he followed his orders, charged the hill, and, like everyone else in his troop, was killed. Sure enough, the master plan failed. After Ryan's troop was wiped out, the flank attack was foiled and the enemy still held the hill.

4. Frieda Hostages had a job working at the local hardware store after school. Usually, she did whatever was necessary, such as unpack boxes, work the cash register, or put price tags on merchandise. She almost always had something to keep her busy. One day, however, a heavy rainfall kept business down. At one point there were no customers in the store and she had taken care of all the little jobs, so she was standing around doing nothing. Her boss hated to pay her for nothing and so told her to scrub the linoleum floor of the store with an abrasive cleaner, a job that Frieda reckoned hadn't been done in years. She thought that this task was utterly ridiculous and a waste of her time, but she didn't want to risk losing her job, so she got a bucket, a brush, and some cleanser and went to work.

5. Frazier Nerves stayed out too late with his girlfriend one night, and his parents reacted by grounding him, confining him to his room every night for a month. He thought that this was excessively harsh but knew that arguing would only make matters worse. Still, he had a great desire to see his girlfriend; not only was he madly in love with her but he also knew of other boys who found her attractive, and he thought that if they were not to date for a month he might lose her to someone else. Desperate to maintain his relationship with her but fearful of parental repercussions, he started sneaking out through his window every night after his parents had gone to bed for a late-evening rendezvous with his girlfriend. He made it through the month without getting caught and with his relationship still intact.

An alternative to writing the scenarios yourself is to take a set of stories from the news. A typical year provides an abundance of current events related to many thematic units. For conflict with authority, you might use stories about athletes coming in conflict with their coaches, workers challenging their bosses, citizens demonstrating against political leaders, students in adversarial relationships with teachers and administrators, and so on. The main thing to keep in mind is that the stories should illustrate a variety of kinds of conflicts and resolutions (or nonresolutions) so that students think about the problem in complex ways.

Another labor-saving device is to create activities using "found" materials: those already at hand so that you can reduce preparation time. For instance, Berchini and Smagorinsky (2018) describe an activity in which students discuss their cell phones, an exploration that could lead to comparison and contrast writing, narratives about experiences with phones, arguments about which phone is best, extended definitions of a quality cell phone, research papers on aspects of cell phone development and usage, interview reports on other people's cell phone beliefs, and perhaps other types of writing.

Writing About Related Problems

My friend and collaborator Tom McCann has spent a great deal of time thinking of ways to teach students how to write arguments. One of his ideas works well as an introductory activity. The format for the activity is based on advice columns such as Dear Abby. The idea is to think of situations that come up in literature and then present students with a letter to an advice columnist that describes a similar kind of situation. Their job is then to write to the person, offering a solution to the problem.

In the sophomore curriculum, the unit on gangs, cliques, and peer pressure would be well suited for an introductory activity of this type. Let's say that the class will read S. E. Hinton's *The Outsiders* as the unit's major work of literature. You could prepare a letter to the Answerline columnist that anticipates the dilemmas raised in the novel and have students write a letter back arguing in favor of a particular solution. The prompt for their writing could look like the example shown on the next page.

The students' job is to write to Fearful, offering a solution to the problem. After all students are done, you could follow the same sequence that I outlined in the other introductory activities: Have students compare their answers in small groups, then have a whole-class discussion in search of a solution.

This introduction, like the personal experience narrative introducing the coming-of-age unit, could additionally serve to prepare students for more formal writing

Pretend that you are a famous newspaper columnist who gives advice to people who write letters to you. Often their problems concern crucial moments in their lives that they need advice about. What kind of guidance would you give to the following person? Make sure that when you write your response you are supportive of the person's problems and give a thoughtful answer. Make sure too that whatever your advice is, you give several reasons that the person should follow it. Also make sure that you explain why your recommended course of action is better than others that the person might follow.

Dear Answerline,

I have a problem that I need your advice about. I have to go to you because I can't tell my parents. They'd just yell at me and ground me if they thought I was in any kind of trouble. Please help me figure out what to do.

The problem actually starts with my best friend. We're both part of a group that always hangs around together. We always stick together, right or wrong. If one of us gets in a fight, the rest are there to help out. If one of us is in trouble, the others are always there. Every time I've ever had a problem, my friends were there to make things right. I could never let any of them down, especially my best friend, Chris, who's always been there for me.

But now I'm worried that things have gone too far. There's another group in our school that we've always had trouble with. They think they're better than we are and always put us down. Usually we just yell things back at them, or sometimes get in a fight, and it's over till the next time. But last week they slashed Chris's tires. Now everybody wants revenge. And Chris has got a gun and wants to use it.

I don't know what to do. If I say I think it has gone too far, they'll call me chicken. If I say I don't want to go along with them, they'll think I'm disloyal. If I call the police, my best friends might get arrested. If I warn the other group, my friends may get hurt. If I lose my friends, I won't have anybody left.

What should I do?

Sincerely,
Fearful in Fredericksburg

later in the unit. In a unit using this kind of introduction, you could have a goal of producing an argument about problem resolution related to an independently read work of literature. The Answerline letter, then, could introduce students both to the literature and to argumentative writing. Subsequent instruction could focus on making, supporting, and warranting claims and rebutting alternative solutions.

Summary

Introductory activities should prepare students for issues that come up during the unit. They often draw on prior knowledge that students can connect with new knowledge. The questions you should ask are these: What does one need to know to read this text with the appropriate expectations? How can I help students access the knowledge that will prepare them for this reading? You should also be aware that many people in the field would prefer that readers go ahead with their readings without such preparation. They argue that students' initial constructions are part of their process of meaning making and should not be tainted by the teacher's sense of what's important to know.

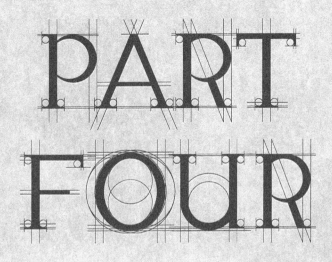

Designing the
Conceptual Unit

13

Down and Dirty 1

Planning Instruction for a Suburban School and Community Setting

This chapter is written as though I am thinking aloud while planning a unit. I plan each class very specifically, right down to an anticipated amount of time I will spend on each activity. Some might find such microlevel planning to be a bit too heavily scripted. The purpose, however, is not to write a script but to try to anticipate how classes will go from day to day, with the understanding that I might seize the moment, or many of them, and shift during the course of action.

For the sake of convenience, I start teaching the unit on a Monday, although life does not always allow for such neat scheduling. I want to move straight into the introductory activity right after the initial class routines of attendance, announcements, and other duties. I could introduce the unit on discrimination in a variety of ways. I could do an Internet search, for instance, and locate a number of short newspaper articles on controversial incidents of discrimination. I could then create a scenario activity out of them, perhaps simply asking students to rate each incident as involving discrimination or not. By doing so, they would begin the process of working on criteria for their extended definitions of a particular kind of discrimination.

I think, however, I'll try something new and different. Let's say that our school has a set of computer labs and that my state core curriculum emphasizes technology. I can dovetail several possibilities into a single activity by beginning the unit with collaborative webquests that investigate discrimination. I might even take this activity one step further and combine the introductory activity and webquest with a jigsaw activity. This activity could also serve as a vehicle through which students will identify the specific topics on which they'll write their extended definitions of discrimination.

The School and Community Contexts

Your teaching should be responsive to your students and their needs. I don't claim that you can simply take the unit I outline in this book or the units in the Virtual Library of Conceptual Units and teach them anywhere without modification. I will therefore provide a context for the unit, based on schools where I've taught as well as schools I've observed. The school's profile is typical of many schools across the country. The unit is very similar to units I've taught in schools like these.

Our hypothetical school is a comprehensive public senior high school of two thousand students. It lies in the metropolitan area of an urban center and includes students from across the economic spectrum. It has a three-track system, with the tracks labeled honors, regular, and basic; for upper grades there are more specialized tracks such as Advanced Placement and vocational. The sophomore curriculum I've designed will be for students in the regular track.

Racially, students are 50 percent European American, 20 percent African American, 10 percent Asian American, 10 percent Latin American, 5 percent Native American, and 5 percent mixed race. Slightly under half of the students come from homes that include both biological parents. Eighty percent of the senior class will have a part-time job at some point during their senior year. Sixty percent of each freshman class will graduate within four years. Of the remaining 40 percent, 15 percent will move to another district, 10 percent will drop out, 1 percent will be expelled for disciplinary reasons, and 14 percent will graduate following additional coursework. In a typical graduating class, 40 percent of seniors go to a four-year college, with half of them eventually receiving degrees. Of the remaining 60 percent, 20 percent go to a two-year college, 20 percent go to a trade school, and 20 percent enter the workforce, including the military.

The school is the crucible for many of society's broader concerns. It is the one arena that the community's parents all have in common, making it the primary theater in which broader conflicts about values and social posturing are played out. It would be difficult to find consensus on the faculty over what the mission of the school is, much less to develop agreement among the citizenry about the best way to conduct school.

Time Considerations

My school has fifty-minute class periods, a common amount of time for school organization. The school year as a whole is divided into two semesters, each of which is partitioned into nine-week quarters. Grades are due at the end of each quarter, with final grades due at the end of semesters. At the halfway point of each quarter, the euphemistically named progress reports must be sent home for any student who is struggling.

These grading periods and the time length of individual classes help define the limits of your units. If you decide to teach eight units for the year, you should plan on roughly four to five weeks per unit. You will need to provide closure to your unit as the grading period comes to an end so that the students' report card grades will reflect their performance on the unit's culminating texts. The main consequence of this deadline is that your instructional planning is never ideal but designed and modified to function within the parameters of your school's schedule.

WEEK 1

Day 1 (Monday)

3 minutes: Attendance, housekeeping.

5 minutes: Walk to the computer lab and get seated and settled (I've reserved the lab ahead of time).

10 minutes: Provide hard copy of the following prompt, and review the assignment with the students:

> For the next month or so, we are going to be reading and thinking about what it means for one person to discriminate against another, or for one group of people to discriminate against another. To begin our consideration of discrimination, we will go to the computer lab and do collaborative webquests. The procedures are as follows:
>
> - Each of you will get in a group of no more than five students and pick a particular kind of discrimination: against old people, against young people, against foreigners, against people of a particular race, against women, against men, against LGBTQ+ people, against people of particular religions, against left-handed people, against conscientious objectors to war, against war veterans, against short people, against tall people, against people with mental health issues, or whatever other kind of discrimination that your group agrees to investigate on the Internet. The only limitation is that no two groups may research the same topic.
>
> - To create your webquest, several good instruments are available on the Internet. One way to locate them is simply to type "webquest" into a search engine, and you will find links to sites such as http://webquest.org. These sites will guide you through the process of conducting your webquest and provide you with all of the tools you'll need to produce it, including examples of webquests. Ultimately, you may submit your webquest to be displayed at http://webquest.org.
>
> - Your task is to search the Web for information about your topic and use the links you find to construct your collaborative webquest.

32 minutes: Students work on their webquests until the bell. Teacher circulates to make sure that students are on task and working according to the webquest requirements.

Day 2 (Tuesday)

The class meets in the computer lab.

3 minutes: Attendance.

47 minutes: Students complete their webquests and, if they wish, post them to a website.

Through these first two days, each student should have become knowledgeable about a particular kind of discrimination. The webquest activity thus serves as the first stage of the jigsaw activity in which students participate in small-group discussions on one aspect of a text or problem. On Day 3 the class will move to the second stage of the jigsaw, in which each group member will go to a separate group—each consisting of one member from each webquest group—and report on and discuss the five different forms of discrimination investigated thus far.

Day 3 (Wednesday)

3 minutes: Attendance, housekeeping.

5 minutes: Explain the jigsaw procedures as follows:

Each webquest group will now disperse into new groups according to the following procedures:

1. In each group of five, assign each student a number from 1 to 5.

2. Those assigned 1, assemble in one corner; those assigned 2, assemble in the next corner going clockwise; those assigned 3, assemble in the next corner going clockwise; those assigned 4, assemble in |the next corner going clockwise; those assigned 5, assemble in the center.

3. Each group now includes one person from each webquest group. Your task is for each student to lead a discussion of roughly seven minutes on what you learned from your webquest.

40 minutes: The groups discuss the webquests according to these instructions, with the teacher circulating to help students stay on task.

2 minutes: Return the desks to their original positions; exeunt.

So far the teacher has done little talking aside from setting up activities and monitoring them. The students, meanwhile, have been involved in the open-ended task of investigating some sort of discrimination and working through possible criteria for their extended definition of discrimination. Further, each class member has now been designated as an expert in an area of specialization, and every student has been exposed to the findings from all five groups. Now, some sort of whole-class follow-up is appropriate, in which the teacher orchestrates the ideas and contributions of the students based on both stages of the jigsaw activity.

Day 4 (Thursday)

3 minutes: Attendance, housekeeping.

47 minutes: The teacher orchestrates a discussion based on the two phases of the jigsaw activity, querying each group on the following questions:

- What is, and what is not, discrimination of the type you investigated during your webquest?

- On what basis did you decide that a particular action is an act of discrimination?

- How can you formulate a rule (aka criterion) that helps you distinguish discrimination from nondiscrimination?

- Provide an example of something that is discrimination according to your criterion and something that almost meets the criterion but is not discriminatory.

- Explain why the example meets the criterion and why the contrasting example does not meet the criterion.

This discussion maintains the open-ended approach established through the webquest and jigsaw activities and provides an opportunity for the whole class to follow the reasoning of each group. It begins the process of writing extended definitions by having the students develop criteria, examples that illustrate the criteria, contrasting examples that do not meet the criteria, and warrants that explain the examples and contrasting examples in terms of the criteria. By going through this process, students should be reasonably well prepared to begin their reading of texts that focus on discrimination.

Day 5 (Friday)

3 minutes: Attendance, housekeeping.

It's possible that this Friday will extend the previous day's discussion. If we've wrapped up the discussion, I think I'll give everyone a break and play a vocabulary game. When I taught high school English, I tried many approaches to teaching vocabulary, few of them resulting in students learning new words. I finally settled on a set of games modeled after TV game shows: *Jeopardy*, *$25,000 Pyramid*, *Password*, *Family Feud*, and *Balderdash*. The games were all based on some sort of strategy for understanding the meaning of unfamiliar words, in particular using context clues and using knowledge of roots and affixes. Today we'll play a vocabulary game from the ones described at http://www.petersmagorinsky.net/TEBD/Books /Vocabulary_Games/ExpansionsIndex.htm.

WEEK 2

In Week 2 I'll continue to scaffold the students' understanding of the concept with something both familiar and enjoyable: music. A lot of popular music across the decades has dealt with issues of discrimination, so I'll work with a selection of tunes that I'm familiar with that will help the students explore the topic. I'll also encourage them to bring in their own music on the off chance that they find mine a bit musty.

Day 6 (Monday)

3 minutes: Attendance, housekeeping.

45 minutes: Provide copies of song lyrics and recordings of the songs listed below or other songs that feature various types of discrimination (with school-appropriate lyrics, of course). Have each group select one song either from the list or from their own collections, with each group picking a different song. Their task is to create a storyboard for a music video for the song. Doing so will require them to pay careful attention to the lyrics, particularly the images concerned with discrimination. Their task is as follows:

> In small groups of three to five students, select one song from the following menu or a song of your choice (with school-appropriate lyrics) that deals with discrimination, and create a storyboard for a music video about the song.

> The Weavers: "Sixteen Tons"

> Vanessa Williams: "Colors of the Wind"

> Dave Matthews Band: "Cry Freedom"

> Bob Marley and the Wailers: "War"

> Johnny Clegg and Savuka: "Inevitable Consequence of Progress"

> Randy Newman: "Short People"

> The Crüxshadows: "Leave Me Alone"

> Neil Young: "Southern Man"

> Creedence Clearwater Revival: "Fortunate Son"

A storyboard is a set of drawings that outlines the major events in a sequence of action, such as the major scenes in a music video. As of this writing, you can find an example of a storyboard at www.danhausertrek .com/AnimatedSeries/Storyboard.gif.

To prepare your storyboard, you should consider the following questions about the song:

- What or who is being discriminated against by whom?

- How is the discrimination carried out?

- What images might tell the song's story?

- What is the role of color, lighting, and other effects in telling the story?

- What images best portray the song's story of discrimination?

Your storyboard should consist of five to ten panels that you will first draft on paper, then revise into presentable form to show the class as you play the song. Distribute the song's lyrics to accompany your presentation.

2 minutes: Return the desks to their original positions; exeunt.

Day 7 (Tuesday)

Day 7 will either continue with the storyboarding or begin with the presentations. I'll plan to complete the storyboards, and if the students finish, we can always start the presentations ahead of schedule. The plan, then, might look like this.

3 minutes: Attendance, housekeeping.

45 minutes: Complete the storyboard activity.

2 minutes: Return the desks to their original positions; exeunt.

Day 8 (Wednesday)

3 minutes: Attendance, housekeeping.

47 minutes: Students play their songs and present their storyboards. Each of the groups in the audience should prepare at least one question for each of the presenting groups. We might not get to all of the questions, but groups should be prepared to ask them.

Day 9 (Thursday)

We move at this point from songs to poems. For the purposes of this unit, I've located a set of poems that fit well with the unit on discrimination. My selection of this set of poems is illustrative rather than prescriptive.

Maya Angelou: "On the Pulse of Morning"

Peter Blue Cloud: "The Old Man's Lazy"

Elizabeth Brewster: "Jamie"

Because the students are keeping reading logs, we'll dovetail the poetry reading with the reading log assignment to generate an analysis of the poems. The day's activities, then, might look as follows.

3 minutes: Attendance, housekeeping.

20 minutes: Pass out a copy of the first poem, Peter Blue Cloud's "The Old Man's Lazy."

Provide the following prompt for students:

Use your double-column reading log to generate a set of responses and questions to the poem. We will use your responses and questions as the basis for a discussion about the poem.

This task helps to establish a routine for the class: using the reading logs as the source of discussion questions and response, trusting students' ability to take control of their own learning by putting the onus and direction for response to literature in their hands.

25 minutes: Small-group follow-up: Students work in small groups of their choice to use their reading log responses as the basis for an exploration of what the poem reveals about discrimination.

2 minutes: Return the desks to their original positions; exeunt.

Day 10 (Friday)

Here I want to help establish the routine sequence of thinking individually, sharing ideas in small groups, and then moving to a whole-class discussion that builds on and synthesizes the various small-group ideas.

3 minutes: Attendance, housekeeping.

47 minutes: Whole-class discussion based on the previous day's individual and small-group work. There are many different ways in which to conduct this discussion. One is simply to ask for students to come forward with their ideas and hope that a free-flowing jam session follows. If students are more reticent, a methodical approach might be necessary, such as calling on each group individually to report on its discussion and have the remainder of the class pose questions to the group afterward. Each of my five small groups would then have about nine minutes to report on its response log and small-group ideas.

WEEK 3

The beginning of the third week might call for some evaluation of how well the unit has gone. If students have been slow to grasp the issues, I might want to backtrack a little and include some more work with accessible materials. Let's assume, though, that the kids are moving along well in terms of their consideration of issues of discrimination. In this week, we'll read some short stories that explore questions of discrimination. I want to continue with the activity-based approach to provide varied structures for thinking about the unit concepts.

One reason I want to vary the classroom organization is to escape the rut that students often find themselves in when teachers do more or less the same thing every day. Varied structures keep students on their toes and add a sense of intrigue to the class in terms of how they'll approach the topic each day they enter the class. Another reason to vary the ways in which students approach the texts is to provide the broadest possible access to success for the widest range of students imaginable. By making activity and collaboration central to most classes, you will allow for more students to find ways to connect to the unit concepts. And so we'll continue to approach each text in a different way, while maintaining our focus on the same unit theme.

Day 11 (Monday)

Today we'll move to a short story from the list of materials. Because the students will be largely in charge of their own discussions, I can be flexible in terms of which story I select; I could even provide a menu of choices from which students may pick, although the ensuing whole-class discussion might lack the coherence that would follow from having all students read a common text. Students benefit from reading texts that approach discrimination from different angles and discussing them in different ways. From the menu I've prepared, let's go with Leslie Marmon Silko's "Tony's Story" and José Antonio Burciaga's "Romantic Nightmare." Two discussion techniques that might work well are the *found poem* and the *body biography* (see http://www.petersmagorinsky.net/TEBD/UnitLibrary/Activities_that _Promote_Discussion.htm).

Here's how the beginning of Week 3, then, might work with these texts and formats in mind:

3 minutes: Attendance, housekeeping,

47 minutes: Teacher begins by making three reading assignments, with students having Monday's class to work on as many as they can complete:

> Leslie Marmon Silko: "Tony's Story"
>
> José Antonio Burciaga: "Romantic Nightmare"
>
> Richard Wright: *Black Boy*

Students then have the remainder of the class to read, with the understanding that they will discuss the two short stories on Tuesday and Wednesday of this week. They will have several weeks to complete their reading of *Black Boy*, which will constitute their homework for the bulk of the unit.

Day 12 (Tuesday)

3 minutes: Attendance, housekeeping.

25 minutes: Working in small groups, students produce a found poem based on "Tony's Story," in response to the following prompt:

> In small groups of three to five students, produce a found poem based on "Tony's Story," by Leslie Marmon Silko. A found poem is a "poem" that consists of significant words and phrases found in a source text such as Silko's short story. Your task is to discuss the story in your group with the goal of identifying the story's most important words and phrases, which you then put into the form of a poem. All words in your found poem should come directly from the Silko story. You will write your found poem and share it with the other groups in the class using whatever means of presentation or projection is available (whiteboard, projector, etc.). Your presentation of the found poem may suggest additional meanings by the colors you choose and the ways in which you position the text. In other words, your poem needn't look like a regular poem consisting of a series of black-print words on a white background; it may also include shapes, images, and other ways through which you convey the meaning of the text.

22 minutes: The students present their found poems to the group, with the opportunity to field questions following their readings.

Day 13 (Wednesday)

3 minutes: Attendance, housekeeping.

45 minutes: Students construct body biographies in response to José Antonio Burciaga's "Romantic Nightmare," using the following prompt: (There are body biography models on the Internet that are available through search engines, which you might download and provide to students. They are described by O'Donnell-Allen 2006.)

> In small groups of three to five students, select one character to represent and interpret through a body biography. A body biography is a visual and written portrait illustrating several aspects of the character's life within the story.
>
> You have many possibilities for filling up your text. The choices you make should be based on the text, for you will be verbally explaining (and thus, in a sense, defending) them at a showing of your work. Above all, your choices should be creative, analytical, and based on the story.
>
> After completing this portrait, you will participate in a showing in which you will present your masterpiece to the class. This showing should accomplish these goals. It should
>
> - Review significant events, choices, and changes involving your character;
>
> - Communicate to us the full essence of your character by emphasizing the traits that make him who he is; and
>
> - Promote discussion of your character.

Body Biography Requirements

Although I expect your biography to contain additional dimensions, your portrait *must* contain the following:

- A review of significant happenings in the story

- Visual symbols

- An original text

- The three most important lines from the story

Body Biography Suggestions

- *Placement*: Carefully choose the placement of your text and artwork. For example, the area where your character's heart would be might be appropriate for illustrating the important relationships in the character's life.

- *Spine*: Actors often discuss a character's spine, representing a major task within the storyline. What is the most important goal and motivation for your character, and how can you represent it in the body biography depiction's spine?

- *Virtues and Vices*: What are your character's most admirable and worst qualities? How can you help viewers of your body biography visualize them?

- *Color*: Colors are often symbolic. What color(s) do you most associate with your character? Why? How can you effectively work these colors into your presentation?

- *Symbols*: What objects can you associate with your character that illustrate the character's essence? Are there objects mentioned within the story itself that you could use? If not, choose objects that especially seem to correspond with the character.

- *Formula Poems*: These are fast, but effective, recipes for producing a text because they are designed to reveal a lot about a character.

- *Mirror, Mirror . . .* : Consider both how your character appears to others on the surface and what you know about the character's inner self. Do these images clash or correspond? What does this mirroring tell you about the character?

- *Changes*: How has your character changed within the story? Trace these changes within your text and/or artwork.

2 minutes: Return the desks to their original positions; exeunt.

Day 14 (Thursday)

3 minutes: Attendance, housekeeping.

25 minutes: Students present their body biographies to the class, with time following each presentation to field questions and comments from the teacher and other students.

22 minutes: If there is no further discussion of the short story or the issue of discrimination, students may read ahead in *Black Boy*.

Day 15 (Friday)

My next task is to teach the students how to write an extended-definition essay. I'll start this instruction on a Monday rather than a Friday, because the weekend's hiatus is likely to erode whatever understanding of the activity students gain today. So Friday may be devoted to one of two things: in-class reading of Black Boy or a vocabulary game from the activities listed at http://www.petersmagorinsky.net/TEBD/Books/Vocabulary_Games /ExpansionsIndex.htm. This decision will be a judgment call, depending on how I see the unit going thus far. My plan for Friday, then, might be as described next.

3 minutes: Attendance, housekeeping.

47 minutes: Either in-class reading of *Black Boy* or vocabulary game based on *Family Feud*.

The unit is now about half over. The approach I'm taking requires more work outside class in terms of planning; and less work in class because the students are engaged in activity. To me, however, the planning is challenging and enjoyable, so it's not such work after all, because I love my job.

And the infinite variety of work that students produce when they're given open-ended opportunities makes my classroom life more interesting and educative for me. I see things in literature that I might not have noticed because my students are enabled to bring their myriad resources and experiences into their interpretive process. To me, that's far more challenging and interesting for both them and me than my repeating the same official interpretation over and over, class after class, year after year, even though it might not be the best interpretation for young readers and requires so little of them cognitively, not to mention that it asks so little of me as a professional.

WEEK 4

In the fourth week I'll begin scaffolding students' writing of extended-definition essays. This effort will require systematic scaffolding for analytic thinking, which will work in conjunction with the narrative and alternative ways of responding to literature to help give students a well-rounded understanding of the unit concept.

We won't jump right into defining discrimination. Rather, we'll produce two essays. The first will be on a topic of great familiarity to the students so that they can learn the procedures without the additional burden of learning new content. After this initial experience, the students will define a kind of discrimination of their choice, perhaps the type on which they did their webquest. Although everyone will write extended-definition essays, both the specific topics and the definitions produced will be open to seemingly infinite variation. The essay instruction, then, while uniform, will enable students to work in the constructivist spirit of the general teaching approach.

My first job is to think of a topic for definition that the students will find accessible and interesting. As often is the case, my mind turns to music. I have met few people who do not like music of any kind, and I've especially met few teenagers who are not downright passionate about some kind of music. The idea of defining what makes excellent music of some kind appears to be a good way to scaffold students' thinking about how to write an extended definition, which they will later apply to an area of discrimination.

Further, by having students define excellence in a particular kind of music, I am also supporting students' ability to work on one of the course's final exam projects, an extended definition of quality literature, assuming some relation between the two. The instruction, then, meets a number of my goals for the unit and course as a whole.

Day 16 (Monday)

3 minutes: Attendance, housekeeping.

45 minutes: Before giving the students the actual assignment, I want to immerse them in the task itself. I'll start by presenting them with a slew of possibilities for kinds of music to think about, using the following handout:

What Is Good Music?

Just about everyone likes music. But not everyone likes the same kind of music. And even within a musical genre, there's disagreement about what sounds good. Our task in this activity is to work in small groups of three to five students to select a particular kind of music and decide what music within this genre is good and what is not so good. It's OK for more than one group to choose the same kind of music. Identify a musical genre, and begin working out a set of rules or criteria for what makes music within this genre high quality, considering real musicians with whom you are familiar. This process will be similar to the one with which we started the unit, in which we developed some rules or criteria for defining particular kinds of discrimination that you researched through your webquests.

2 minutes: Return the desks to their original positions; exeunt.

Day 17 (Tuesday)

On the second day of the extended-definition instruction, I'll help students take their initial ideas and provide a structure for them to work within. I've designed an activity based on my experience as a member of a jury in a Chicago street gang murder trial (see Smagorinsky 1994; http://www.petersmagorinsky.net/About/PDF/SS/SS1994.pdf) in which I've provided extended definitions for three kinds of killing: murder, voluntary manslaughter, and self-defense. You are welcome to use those examples to illustrate how criteria and examples are used to define a specific type of crime.

3 minutes: Attendance, housekeeping.

25 minutes: Pass out and review the following handout:

In the small groups you established yesterday, you will produce an extended definition of high-quality music of a particular genre. An extended definition includes the following four primary traits:

1. *Criteria*, or rules that state a standard that something must meet for inclusion in the category;

2. *Examples* that illustrate each criterion;

3. *Contrasting examples* that provide an illustration of something that superficially appears to meet the criterion but falls short in some critical way; and

4. *Warrants* that explain how the examples illustrate the criteria and how the contrasting examples fall short.

20 minutes: The students begin to formulate their extended definitions of quality music using this template. In an extended definition of quality music or quality literature, it's likely that the text in question would need to meet all of the criteria.

2 minutes: Return the desks to their original positions; exeunt.

Day 18 (Wednesday)

3 minutes: Attendance, housekeeping.

45 minutes: Students continue working in small groups on their extended definitions of a particular kind of music.

2 minutes: Return the desks to their original positions; exeunt.

Day 19 (Thursday)

I'll assume that things wrapped up nicely and neatly on Wednesday and that we can move into the feedback stage today. Here's an opportunity for students to give one another feedback on their efforts from the previous three days.

3 minutes: Attendance, housekeeping.

25 minutes: Students provide one another with peer feedback on the first draft of their extended definitions of a particular kind of music. I'll provide them with the following prompt:

> Exchange your criteria, examples, contrasting examples, and warrants for your extended definition of a particular kind of music with another group (or set up a three-way exchange). Read the definition carefully and provide feedback in response to the following questions. Your feedback should be written in the margins of the paper you are evaluating; you may also discuss your evaluation with the group whose paper you critique.
>
> ● Is each criterion clearly worded so that you understand what is and is not included in the definition?

- Is each criterion illustrated by an example that is clearly explained and convincingly tied to the criterion by means of a warrant?

- Is each criterion illustrated by a contrasting example that is clearly explained and convincingly tied to the criterion by means of a warrant?

20 minutes: Students receive their feedback and begin to revise their extended definition. In addition, they should write a brief introduction and conclusion. To do so, they should respond to the following prompt:

Use the feedback from your fellow students to revise your criteria, examples, contrasting examples, and warrants.

Finally, provide a brief introductory paragraph in which you explain what type of music you are defining and which qualities you expect to find in such music. These qualities should correspond to your criteria.

After explaining the criteria and supporting illustrations, provide a concluding paragraph in which you summarize your beliefs about this kind of music and what makes for a high-quality performance of it.

2 minutes: Return the desks to their original positions; exeunt.

Day 20 (Friday)

I anticipate that the students will need more time to complete a revision that they can turn in for a grade. Today's class, then, will provide some time to complete their group essays before presenting them to the class. If my forecast for time allotment is off, I can always fall back on a vocabulary game for today. But in all likelihood, the students will need time to sharpen their work before turning it in.

I need to develop a rubric that will help the students anticipate my grading decisions and help me be consistent as I work my way through their essays. I might plan the class, then, as follows.

3 minutes: Attendance, housekeeping.

15 minutes: Pass out and review the following rubric for evaluating extended definitions.

30 minutes: Students work on their revisions, using the rubric and peer feedback as guides.

2 minutes: Students submit the extended definitions; return the desks to their original positions; exeunt.

WEEK 5

One thing that might raise concerns is that all of our attention to learning processes has resulted in relatively little reading. Rather than having reading assignments every day and lots of quizzes, study guides, and worksheets on them, we are spending more time thinking about how to read and how to write in relation to reading. We thus have the old *breadth versus depth* conflict. Obviously, my bias is toward doing more with less—that is, having fewer assignments but thinking about them in greater detail. I believe strongly that valuing depth of analysis over breadth of coverage both engages students more with the curriculum and produces more long-lasting memories and understanding of what we do cover.

In the fifth week, we will turn our attention to the unit's main text, *Black Boy*. My goal is to have small groups of students lead their own discussions on the novel. Because they are inexperienced in leading discussions, I'll have to teach them how to pose different kinds of questions, following which they'll lead the class's consideration of the story.

Day 21 (Monday)

3 minutes: Attendance, housekeeping.

10 minutes: Pass out and review responsibilities for student-led discussions.

To discuss *Black Boy*, the class will organize into five small groups, with each group being responsible for leading a discussion of four chapters of the novel. Each group will be responsible for conducting a class discussion on its chapters for one full class period. To lead your class, you may adopt any format you wish: regular English class, talk show format, town hall meeting, courtroom, or other mode of your choice. Your discussion should involve all of the following:

- Each group member should take a roughly equal part in leading the discussion.

- You should make an effort to include each other class member in your discussion.

- The questions you pose should not ask for factual information from the story, unless those facts serve to help explore open-ended questions (i.e., those without a single correct answer).

Category	A	B
Introductory paragraph	The writer clearly identifies the topic of the paper and summarizes the criteria in the definition.	The writer identifies the topic and summarizes the criteria, but one or the other lacks clarity.
Criteria	Each criterion is worded so that the reader clearly understands what is and is not included in the definition.	Most, but not all, of the criteria are worded so that the reader clearly understands what is and is not included in the definition.
Examples	Each example is explained in sufficient detail so that the reader clearly sees how it supports the criterion.	Most, but not all, examples are explained in sufficient detail so that the reader clearly sees how they support the criteria.
Contrasting examples	Each contrasting example is explained in sufficient detail so that the reader clearly sees how it supports the criterion.	Most, but not all, contrasting examples are explained in sufficient detail so that the reader clearly sees how they support the criteria.
Warrants	The writer clearly explains how each example and contrasting example illustrates the criterion to which it is related.	The writer explains how most examples and contrasting examples illustrate the criteria to which they are related.
Conclusion	The conclusion both summarizes the definition and extends it to provide a new insight based on the thinking that has gone into the definition.	The conclusion summarizes the definition but does little to extend it to provide a new insight based on the thinking that has gone into the definition.
Form	The writer's introduction, each criterion, and conclusion are separated into different paragraphs.	The writers' introduction, each criterion, and conclusion are separated into different paragraphs.
Mechanics, spelling, grammar, usage	For the most part, the writing is clear and free from problems.	For the most part, the writing is clear and free from problems.

Extended Definition

C	D	F
The writer identifies the topic and summarizes the criteria, but both explanations are sketchy and/or worded unclearly.	The writer includes an opening paragraph but does not clearly explain the topic or the criteria.	There is no introduction.
Some, but not all, of the criteria are worded so that the reader clearly understands what is and is not included in the definition.	The writer makes an effort at writing criteria, but the wording makes it difficult to understand what is included in the definition and what is not.	There are few or no criteria.
Some, but not all, examples are explained in sufficient detail so that the reader clearly sees how they support the criteria.	The writer provides examples, but it's not clear how they are related to the criteria.	There are few or no examples.
Some, but not all, contrasting examples are explained in sufficient detail so that the reader clearly sees how they support the criteria.	The writer provides contrasting examples, but it's not clear how they are related to the criteria.	There are few or no examples.
The writer explains how some examples and contrasting examples illustrate the criteria to which they are related.	The writer makes an effort to relate the examples and contrasting examples to the criteria, but this relation is not clear to the reader.	There are few or no warrants.
The conclusion summarizes the definition but does not extend it to provide a new insight based on thinking that has gone into the definition.	The conclusion does not clearly summarize or extend the definition.	There is no conclusion.
The writers' introduction, each criterion, and conclusion are separated into different paragraphs.	The writing is all in one paragraph, or the paragraph divisions appear arbitrary.	The writing is all in one paragraph, or the paragraph divisions appear arbitrary.
The writing includes some problems that impede the reader's effort to understand what the writer is saying.	The writing includes many problems that impede the reader's effort to understand what the writer is saying.	The writing includes many problems that impede the reader's effort to understand what the writer is saying.

- The questions you pose should include at least one of each of the following categories:

  ▶ *Inferences* about characters or events within the text (e.g., how does joining a gang affect Richard's life?)

  ▶ *Generalizations* from the text to society at large (e.g., in what ways is Wright's story from the first half of the twentieth century relevant to today's society?)

  ▶ The *effects of literary form or technique* (e.g., do you think that Richard's presentation of his experiences is realistic?)

  ▶ The *purpose of a particular event* in terms of the text's meaning (e.g., how does Richard's life in the orphanage shape his perspective on life in the United States?)

  ▶ *Evaluations* of the literature (e.g., what parts of the story do you like best and least? Why?)

  ▶ *Emotions* that students have in response to the story (e.g., how did you feel when Richard burned down his grandparents' house?)

  ▶ *Personal connections* to the story (e.g., what connections do you feel with Richard during his employment at the optical company?)

5 minutes: Explain that they'll need to organize into five groups of roughly even size. Have students pick their groups and organize into them.

2 minutes: Explain that you will give them practice in generating the seven types of questions they should ask, using a story from the ones they have studied to this point (e.g., "Tony's Story"). The procedure will be for you to define each type of question and give an example and for each group then to come up with a similar type of example from the same story.

15 minutes: Define what an inference is (to make an educated guess about something that's not literally stated). Provide an illustration of an inferential question about "Tony's Story" (e.g., what is the difference between Tony's and Leon's feelings toward the power of the arrowhead necklace?), and explain clearly why it requires an inference. Have each group generate an inferential question about the story, and invite groups to share theirs with the class. Clarify how each question generated by students meets the expectations for this question type.

13 minutes: Define what a generalization to larger society is (to state what the story is saying about life in general). Provide an illustration of an inferential question about "Tony's Story" (e.g., why are Native American men who come back from the army "troublemakers on the reservation"? How does Leon believe that war veterans should be treated?), and explain clearly why it requires a generalization. Have each group develop a generalization question about the story, and invite groups to share theirs with the class. Clarify how each question generated by students meets the expectations for this question type.

2 minutes: Return the desks to their original positions; exeunt.

Day 22 (Tuesday)

3 minutes: Attendance, housekeeping.

9 minutes: Define what literary form and technique are (e.g., irony, figurative language, etc.). Provide an illustration of a question about technique for "Tony's Story" (e.g., what does Tony's dream symbolize?), and explain clearly why the question requires an understanding of technique or form. Have each group generate a question about the story's form or technique and invite groups to share theirs with the class. Clarify how each question created by students meets the expectations for this question type.

9 minutes: Define what a significant event is (an event that causes substantive changes in the lives of the characters). Provide an illustration of a question about significant events for "Tony's Story" (e.g., what role reversal do Tony and Leon engage in? How do you explain it?), and explain clearly why this question is centered on the significance of an event. Have each group generate a question about the story's significant events, and invite groups to share theirs with the class. Clarify how each question created by students meets the expectations for this question type.

9 minutes: Define what an evaluation is (to judge the quality of the literary work or parts thereof). Provide an illustration of an evaluative question about "Tony's Story" (e.g., did you feel that the three main characters were realistically portrayed? Would your answer change if you knew that the story is based on a real event?), and explain clearly why it requires an evaluation. Have each group generate an evaluative question about the story, and invite groups to share theirs with the class. Clarify how each question created by students meets the expectations for this question type.

9 minutes: Define what an emotional response to a story is (how the story made them feel). Provide an illustration of an emotional question about "Tony's Story" (e.g., how did your feelings about the three main characters change during the course of the story?), and explain clearly why it involves an emotional response. Have each group generate a different emotional question about the story, and invite groups to share theirs with the class. Clarify how each question created by students meets the expectations for this question type.

9 minutes: Define what a personal connection to a story is (a link between the reader's personal experiences and those of literary characters). Provide an illustration of a question requiring a personal connection for "Tony's Story" (e.g., what would you have done if you'd been in Tony's or Leon's situation in the final section of the story?), and explain clearly why it requires a personal connection. Have each group generate a personal connection question about the story, and invite groups to share theirs with the class. Clarify how each question created by students meets the expectations for this question type.

2 minutes: Return the desks to their original positions; exeunt.

Day 23 (Wednesday)

3 minutes: Attendance, housekeeping.

25 minutes: Have different groups take responsibility for different sections of *Black Boy*. You could do this through voluntary assignment or through a lottery of some sort. It's possible that students who do not want to read the whole book will lobby heavily for early chapters. A lottery system would take the pressure off you about which groups lead which discussions and add incentive for all students to complete the book.

After the discussion-leading responsibilities are distributed, remind students that the format of the discussion is up to them. Successfully led student discussions have come in all manner of formats. Encourage them to play with the assignment, though not at the expense of their discussion-leading responsibilities, and not out of proportion with the seriousness of the issues raised in the book. They should plan to lead their discussion for a full class period and so should make sure that their planning, while including a minimum set of questions from the types prescribed, also poses other questions for students to discuss. They might look to their reading logs to see what other kinds of questions they could pose for their discussions.

You might distribute your grading rubric prior to the small-group preparations. The following is one way to differentiate the grades for student performances:

Rubric for Grading Student-Led Discussions

A discussion receiving an A will be characterized by the following:

- Each group member takes a roughly equal part in leading the discussion.

- The discussion includes at least 75 percent of other students in the class.

- The questions posed ask for factual information only when those facts serve to help explore open-ended questions (i.e., those without a single correct answer).

- The questions include at least one from each of the following categories:

    ▶ Inferences about characters or events within the text

    ▶ Generalizations from the text to society at large

    ▶ The effects of literary form or technique

    ▶ The purpose of a particular event in terms of the text's meaning

    ▶ Evaluations of the literature

    ▶ Emotions that students had in response to the story

    ▶ Personal connections to the story

- The discussion occupies the entire class period.

A discussion receiving a B will be characterized by the following:

- Each group member takes a roughly equal part in leading the discussion, although some students speak noticeably more than others.

- The discussion includes at least 50 percent of other students in the class.

- The questions posed ask for factual information only when those facts serve to help explore open-ended questions (i.e., those without a single correct answer).

- The questions include at least one from most of the following categories:

  ▶ Inferences about characters or events within the text

  ▶ Generalizations from the text to society at large

  ▶ The effects of literary form or technique

  ▶ The purpose of a particular event in terms of the text's meaning

  ▶ Evaluations of the literature

  ▶ Emotions that students had in response to the story

  ▶ Personal connections to the story

- The discussion occupies the entire class period.

A discussion receiving a C will be characterized by the following:

- Some group members speak substantially more than others.

- The discussion includes fewer than half of other students in the class.

- The questions posed occasionally ask for factual information that does not serve to help explore open-ended questions (i.e., those without a single correct answer).

- The questions include at least one from at least four of the following categories:

  ▶ Inferences about characters or events within the text

  ▶ Generalizations from the text to society at large

  ▶ The effects of literary form or technique

  ▶ The purpose of a particular event in terms of the text's meaning

  ▶ Evaluations of the literature

- ◗ Emotions that students had in response to the story

- ◗ Personal connections to the story

- The discussion occupies most of the class period.

A discussion receiving a D will be characterized by the following:

- Some group members do most of the talking.

- The discussion includes no more than 25 percent of other students in the class.

- The questions frequently request factual information.

- The questions include less than half of the following categories:

  - ◗ Inferences about characters or events within the text

  - ◗ Generalizations from the text to society at large

  - ◗ The effects of literary form or technique

  - ◗ The purpose of a particular event in terms of the text's meaning

  - ◗ Evaluations of the literature

  - ◗ Emotions that students had in response to the story

  - ◗ Personal connections to the story

- The discussion ends well before the class period ends.

A discussion receiving an F will be characterized by the following:

- The discussion leaders give little evidence of having read the book.

- The discussion leaders give little evidence of having prepared questions of any kind.

- The discussion ends well before the class period ends.

20 minutes: Students begin working on their preparations for leading their set of chapters.

2 minutes: Return the desks to their original positions; exeunt.

Day 24 (Thursday)

3 minutes: Attendance, housekeeping.

45 minutes: Students work in small groups preparing their questions and formats.

2 minutes: Return the desks to their original positions; exeunt.

Day 25 (Friday)

3 minutes: Attendance, housekeeping.

47 minutes: Student group leads discussion of Chapters 1–4.

WEEK 6

Day 26 (Monday)

3 minutes: Attendance, housekeeping.

47 minutes: Student group leads discussion of Chapters 5–8.

Day 27 (Tuesday)

3 minutes: Attendance, housekeeping.

47 minutes: Student group leads discussion of Chapters 9–12.

Day 28 (Wednesday)

3 minutes: Attendance, housekeeping.

47 minutes: Student group leads discussion of Chapters 13–16.

Day 29 (Thursday)

3 minutes: Attendance, housekeeping.

47 minutes: Student group leads discussion of Chapters 17–20.

Day 30 (Friday)

With all the attention to process, this unit has stretched a little longer than I'd originally anticipated. It appears that we'll have to take an extra week to complete the extended definitions on a particular kind of discrimination. And we need to spend some time working on the multimedia assignments and portfolio exhibits. Because I want continuity in the extended-definition assignment, Friday appears to be a good day to work on the multimedia projects.

3 minutes: Attendance, housekeeping.

45 minutes: Provide the students the following assignment. I may also wish to bring in art supplies or be prepared to release students to other parts of the building where resources are available to work on their projects.

You have read a number of literary works and other texts that concern the theme of discrimination. To show what you have learned through your engagement with this literature, create an interpretive text in any form of your choice: collage, painting, poetry, music, drama, sculpture, performance art, or other textual form. You are also welcome to combine forms to produce your text. Keep the following in mind when designing your text:

- It should in some way depict your understanding of experiences with discrimination.

- It should make some kind of reference to at least one work of literature studied during the unit.

- You may produce your text individually or in a group of any size up to three.

- You will have one class period in which to work on your text and must do all additional work outside class.

- You must prepare a three- to five-minute presentation of your text to the class in which you explain its significance and what it shows about your understanding of discrimination and/or literature.

Students have the remainder of the period to work on the projects, which are due the following Wednesday.

2 minutes: Return the desks to their original positions; exeunt.

WEEK 7

Day 31 (Monday)

3 minutes: Attendance, housekeeping.

10 minutes: Introduce the extended-definition assignment with the following handout:

Throughout the unit we have considered the effects of discrimination. We have looked at questions of discrimination in a variety of situations, using examples from current events, from your personal experiences and observations, and from literature. In some cases, there has been disagreement on what counts as discrimination.

   Your task is to write an essay in which you provide an extended definition of discrimination of a particular kind, for example, gender discrimination in the workplace, racial discrimination in housing, religious discrimination in school, age discrimination in hiring, or any other sort that interests you. I encourage you to use the topic and information that you used for your webquest as the basis for this paper. To do so, provide the following:

- A general *introduction* in which you include an overview for your definition;

- A set of *criteria*, or rules that state clearly what discrimination is and is not;

- For each criterion, an *example* from literature, current events, or your personal experiences that illustrates the rule at work; at least half of your examples must come from the literature studied in class;

- For each criterion, a *contrasting example* from literature, current events, or your personal experiences that appears to meet the conditions of the rule yet lacks some essential ingredient; at least half of your contrasting examples must come from the literature studied in class;

- For each example and contrasting example, a *warrant* that clearly explains why the rule is or is not being met;

- For your whole argument, a *counterargument* expressing the viewpoint of someone who might disagree with you;

- Conventional grammar, spelling, punctuation, and usage throughout your essay; and

- Evidence of having written at least one rough draft that has been submitted for peer evaluation.

35 minutes: Students have the remainder of the class to work in small groups preparing outlines and rough drafts for their papers. Although they will do their preparation in small groups, they will each write their papers individually.

2 minutes: Return the desks to their original positions; exeunt.

Day 32 (Tuesday)

3 minutes: Attendance, housekeeping.

47 minutes: Students have the remainder of the period to work individually on their essays. They will bring completed drafts to class on Wednesday for peer feedback.

Day 33 (Wednesday)

On Day 33 the students will work in peer-response groups to provide one another with feedback. You can take different approaches to peer feedback. The most open-ended approach is to have students read their papers aloud to the group and then get feedback. I have found that, particularly early in the year, students benefit from having a particular set of feedback responsibilities. In my experience, students don't spontaneously know how to provide feedback, because for many of them it's a new experience.

My approach, then, is to organize students into groups of about four. I will provide a copy of the following set of three proofreading responsibilities, all derived from the assignment they are working on:

1. Read the whole paper carefully. For your feedback, focus your attention on the writer's *use of criteria*. Is each criterion clearly worded? Does it outline a rule that you could apply to any kind of discrimina-

tion within the topic? In the margins of the paper, make comments about how clearly the writer has written each criterion. Then, at the end of the paper, write a brief summary of your recommendations for how to improve the paper in this regard.

2. Read the whole paper carefully. For your feedback, focus your attention on the writer's *use of examples and warrants that clearly explain how the example illustrates the criterion*. In the margins of the paper, make comments about how effectively the writer has used examples, and explained their relation to the criteria with warrants. Then, at the end of the paper, write a brief summary of your recommendations for how to improve the paper in this regard.

3. Read the whole paper carefully. For your feedback, focus your attention on the writer's *use of contrasting examples and warrants that clearly explain how each contrasting example illustrates the criterion*. In the margins of the paper, make comments about how effectively the writer has used contrasting examples and explained their relation to the criteria with warrants. Then, at the end of the paper, write a brief summary of your recommendations for how to improve the paper in this regard.

Each student reads the paper of each other student in the group. The system works as follows:

1. For Round 1, the students pass their papers to the left. Students then critique the paper they receive according to the first responsibility identified above (use of criteria).

2. When students finish with this round, they again pass papers to the left for Round 2 so that they are reading a new paper, taking on the second responsibility (use of examples and warrants).

3. When finished, they again pass papers to the left for Round 3 (use of contrasting examples and warrants).

4. Following Round 3, the papers are passed once more to the left, returning to their authors. Each author now has three separate sets of feedback, each with a different focus. This feedback, along with the first draft, will get handed in along with the final copy of the paper.

This approach to critiquing, while somewhat methodical, worked quite well for my students, particularly after they'd done it a few times and understood the procedure and purpose of the activity.

You could either have students writing on the same topic critique one another's papers or make sure that each group is composed of students from different webquest groups. Each approach has its own advantages. For my lesson, I'll try the more heterogeneous approach as a way to help each student get exposure to different topics.

The day's class, then, might proceed as follows.

3 minutes: Attendance, housekeeping.

45 minutes: Distribute the peer-feedback tasks outlined previously, and explain the peer-response procedures. Remind the students that the papers will be evaluated according to the same rubric through which their music definitions were assessed. The students have the class period to work on their peer critiques, discuss one another's papers, and begin working on their revisions. The finished papers will be due on Friday.

2 minutes: Return the desks to their original positions; exeunt.

Day 34 (Thursday)

3 minutes: Attendance, housekeeping.

5 minutes: Tell students that they will devote the day to selecting good portfolio exhibits. Remind them that a good exhibit is not necessarily a good product but a source of important learning. It could be an individually produced exhibit or something generated in groups.

10 minutes: Have students freewrite about the most important things they've learned during the class so far. Remind them that their learning could be about themselves, the topic of discrimination, their learning process, particular stories, how to read literature in satisfying ways, how to write well, or anything else that they consider to be significant learning. Have them link the learning to some artifact that they could use as an exhibit.

12 minutes: Have students volunteer to share their learning experiences. The teacher's role is to classify the experience, write a brief statement about what the student learned, and catalog the relevant exhibit.

5 minutes: Demonstrate what an exhibit would look like in a portfolio: Include the artifact, followed by a page or so of reflection on how it contributed to significant learning. Distinguish between a *summary* of how it was produced and a *reflection* on how it contributed to learning. Their freewrites could serve as the basis of their reflections for particular exhibits.

15 minutes: Provide time for students to work on their portfolio exhibits.

Day 35 (Friday)

Today we'll conclude the unit. A few final activities would work well on a Friday afternoon after a lengthy unit of study. One is for the students to present their multimedia texts to the class and briefly explain them. The other is for the students to have an opportunity to evaluate the unit. Throughout this book I've advocated for the idea that you should always be assessing both your students and your own teaching. If the students have performed consistently well on their writing and discussion leading, then it's likely that your instruction was effective. If they didn't, then you need to think back on how you taught the class and consider ways that you could teach differently for the learning you seek. If it worked better for some groups of students than others, then you might need to give some thought to the question of why this differentiation occurred.

Another way to evaluate your teaching is to ask the students how they experienced the unit. We'll work today on an opinionnaire that will allow the students to share their experiences with the unit and provide suggestions on how to improve it. The day's plan, then, would go as follows.

3 minutes: Attendance, housekeeping.

27 minutes: Student presentations of multimedia projects, with time for questions and answers.

20 minutes: Students respond to the following unit evaluation opinionnaire:

Please answer each question that follows. Your comments will strongly influence my efforts to revise the unit for the next group of students, so I'd appreciate your complete honesty in responding. Keep in mind that I'm much more likely to act on thoughtful answers than those that are glib or sarcastic. *You do not need to identify yourself, though you are welcome to if you wish.*

- We read the following literature during the unit. Please write your honest opinion of each work of literature and recommend whether or not I should use it next year.

Songs

The Weavers: "Sixteen Tons"

Vanessa Williams: "Colors of the Wind"

Dave Matthews Band: "Cry Freedom"

Bob Marley and the Wailers: "War"

Johnny Clegg and Savuka: "Inevitable Consequence of Progress"

Randy Newman: "Short People"

The Crüxshadows: "Leave Me Alone"

Neil Young: "Southern Man"

Creedence Clearwater Revival: "Fortunate Son"

Song of your choice

Poems

Peter Blue Cloud: "The Old Man's Lazy"

Short Stories

Leslie Marmon Silko: "Tony's Story"

José Antonio Burciaga: "Romantic Nightmare"

Autobiography

Richard Wright: *Black Boy*

- What did you learn from keeping your reading log? Did you feel that you were adequately taught how to keep one? Please explain. Do you think that keeping a reading log would be a good idea for units that we do later this year? Why or why not?

- What did you learn from conducting your webquest? Did you feel that this was a good way to introduce the unit on discrimination? Please explain. Would you recommend using webquests in the future? Why or why not?

- What did you learn from writing your two extended-definition essays? Did you feel that you were adequately taught how to write an extended definition? Please explain. How would you recommend that I do this next year?

- What did you learn from leading your discussion? Did you feel that you were adequately taught how to conduct it? Please explain. How would you recommend that I do this next year?

- What did you learn from doing your multimedia project? Would you recommend including this assignment when I teach the unit next year? Why or why not?

- What would you recommend that I do the same if I taught this unit again to other students?

- What would you recommend that I do differently?

- What suggestions can you make for the way in which we learn about language, literature, and writing for the rest of this year?

With this evaluation, students can let you know what they found positive and negative about the unit. I found their feedback to be particularly useful the first time I taught a unit, because the first time you teach it you're likely to make the most errors in judgment. Your students can be good informants about the strengths and weaknesses of your unit design, the materials you selected, the adequacy of your instruction, and so on.

The Unit as a Whole

I have demonstrated one possible way to design a unit on discrimination. You could do it quite differently, particularly if you taught this unit to other students, with other texts available, with a different emphasis, or at a later point in the year. My intention has been to show how a unit of instruction fits in with an overall curricular context, is responsive to a variety of constraints, and is designed to meet its own stated goals.

14

Teaching Stressed Students Under Stressful Circumstances

Setting the Stage

Chapter 15 presents a unit set in a school enrolling low-socioeconomic-status (SES) students who are behind their peers in academic literacies or who rely on limited resources. In this modern age of accountability, schools whose students do poorly on standardized tests may be threatened by closure, takeover, or consolidation, and so the environmental realities of teaching cannot be ignored. To policymakers, these schools are just making excuses for their students' performances on tests, because in their reasoning, outside factors, particularly poverty, are irrelevant to school success.

This policy axiom that all students begin from the same starting point is part of the challenge of teaching in poorly funded schools that enroll low-SES students. The assumption from the centralized powers is that they are competing on an even field with students whose schools and communities are far more affluent. (See Kozol 1992 for a savage contrast between rich and poor school systems; and don't dismiss it because it's from the prior century. It's probably worse today.) As a result, they assume, students' performance is always and solely a consequence of the quality of the teaching.

Teaching in schools in which students have a difficult time engaging with the curriculum, however, can be challenging, because poverty, as Berliner (2014) and others have argued, in fact *does* affect school engagement and performance. The students might be very intelligent and competent in many areas of life, including their uses of language in the social world outside school. But the requirements and expectations for them in school do not build on those capabilities, instead suppressing them in favor of other norms, while also providing school environments that are so unsanitary that some fail building code inspections, and more probably should.

Schools that enroll students whose life experiences do not map onto school expectations do not always accommodate the progressive, constructivist ideas popular in colleges of education and routinely recommended in this book and many others on the educational market. The students might need more structure, scaffolding, and guidance; the school's bureaucratic demands might require heavily scripted teaching; and the curriculum might be geared toward "remediation" of presumed literacy deficits more than on building on the students' prior knowledge and language usage conventions.

As a result, entering a public school in which students live under challenging circumstances may require adaptations to the ideas I've presented in this book. One beginning teacher from UNC-Charlotte wrote me, saying that her school was hard to see represented in the first edition of this book:

> It would be encouraging to see [low-income, low-performing] students (and their teachers) included in introductory textbooks. How does a constructivist philosophy extend to an environment that is so restricted? How can we design units, reach students, justify our teaching choices, and become good teachers when the circumstances aren't just less-than-ideal, but actually hostile to learning? . . . I rarely saw my own classrooms in these pages. I work in an impoverished urban school. . . . Most [students] do not perform on grade level. Further, we do not have the resources to execute many of the activities suggested in this and other texts. We have few books, no computers, and teachers often can't assign homework because students have such volatile home lives (as well as jobs and children of their own, in some cases). As the struggle in the American public school system seems to worsen, I imagine that more and more classrooms will begin to look like mine.

Some might think that the writer is pathologizing the students and blaming them for her struggles in the classroom. I see instead a beginning teacher wanting to do right by her kids but not knowing the full extent of the barriers and not having sufficient experience to articulate the difficulties that produce conditions of this sort. That's the developmental psychologist in me talking: Just as I see kids' education as a long and unfolding process, I see teachers' development of an approach to teaching—a conception of how to teach effectively—as a work in progress. Learning to teach is informed over time by knowledge and experience. This learning pathway is hardly straight and narrow but instead twists and turns and may be headed toward multiple destinations at once because of conflicting values in the educational environment (Smagorinsky 2013; Smagorinsky, Cook, and Johnson 2003).

In the next chapter I collaborate with Darren Rhym, an African American man from an urban background who currently teaches in a Georgia public high school that primarily serves African American students of limited resources. Here I contextualize that unit with issues often faced by teachers working in highly stressed schools, a task that Darren helped with as well.

Adaptations

The first thing I would need to do is adjust some of the assumptions that I make. Schools that enroll large numbers of highly stressed students can't always assume that school readiness is available for many students. What must I take into account in planning instruction, then? I next review aspects of context that require attention in adapting instruction to specific classroom settings.

The Curriculum

Many curricula, especially those that are imposed from without on a teacher, are positioned as teaching scripts to follow. The students must adapt to the curriculum and the ways in which it is taught lest they become viewed as bad students or behavior problems, or both. In contrast, many teachers believe that it is their obligation to *adapt school to kids* by teaching in ways that build on their strengths and interests, rather than in ways that fill the gaps of their presumed deficiencies. I am going to take that second perspective, even though I recognize that if you teach within a rigid policy environment in which teachers have little authority to make decisions, then you will have to think within the requirements established by people who don't know your students.

The Policy Context

The policy context in which I am writing this book is currently committed to making kids conform to the curriculum. This phenomenon is not new. Schools have tended toward cultural reproduction throughout the history of US schooling (Doob 2013), in spite of earnest slogans dedicated to diversity. The push toward conformity is becoming more explicit now, with the twenty-first-century development of efforts such as the Common Core State Standards, No Child Left Behind, Race to the Top, and whatever awaits us in the years ahead. These curricula and assessment programs have made it difficult for teachers to critique the whole concept of standardization, because it is the overriding force in school management and evaluation.

With job protections eroding nationwide, critiquing the established power can prompt a quick exit from the teaching profession. In my state, for instance, there is no job protection, no union representative, no collective bargaining for work conditions or salary, no due-process procedure to protect dissidents from retaliation. If the principal doesn't want you, you're gone, and probably gone that day. So know your political and policy environment well. Your job may depend on it.

Students and Their Circumstances

The sort of school featured in this chapter is difficult to describe in satisfactory ways. Students living in poverty have often learned to distrust social institutions like schools, are situated in communities with poor tax bases, have far greater challenges than distinguishing *its* from *it's*, and are out of step with school and public institutions in a myriad of ways (Smagorinsky 2017). The challenges faced in these communities are laid at the doorstep of the kids and their families, along with their teachers. These students and families are characterized pathologically, and are typically blamed for their own circumstances, no matter how unfairly, inhumanely, or erroneously this perspective is imposed (see, e.g., Bomer, Dworin, May, and Semingson's [2009] critique of poverty guru Ruby Payne; see also http://rubypayneiswrong.blogspot.com/p/scholarship-de bunking-payne.html). My account of the contexts of students' lives is not designed to construct them and their families as dysfunctional or irresponsible. Rather, I describe some of the consequences of living an unstable life due to the absence of dependable income, food, health care, and shelter, in turn producing lives that are precarious and in need of support.

Shelter

Imagine living every day without confidence that you will have a bed to sleep in for the short or long term. Would reading your homework assignment of two chapters of *The Scarlet Letter* be at the forefront of your mind? Unfortunately, millions of US students are homeless (Goldberg 2015) or move frequently (Cushman 1999), making life a daily challenge and school an afterthought to survival. The uncertainty of living life without a stable residence that is safe from predators and material hazards, not to mention weather, creates immense challenges for youth. Teaching kids who don't know where they're going to sleep that night, contrary to what policymakers like to believe, requires attention to their most immediate needs for health and safety. Assuming that housing stability is available may easily lead to the sort of deficit conceptions that many teachers hold of their low-SES students, further penalizing them in their effort to lead a happy life that is advanced through success in school.

Food

Food costs money. Imagine not having any. (Food or money.) But also, consider the diets of people in urban "food deserts": large areas in which grocery stores will not establish locations, leaving residents (without cars) to eat what is available in convenience stores: overpriced junk food. Imagine living your life on potato chips and sugary soft drinks. (OK, rich kids do that too, but at least they have choices.) Imagine if you are born to a parent whose diet during pregnancy was limited to junk food and other unhealthy comestibles. Imagine sitting in a class with thirty-five other students with a throbbing toothache and having to take a quiz on whether a literary work exhibits first-degree or second-degree dramatic irony.

Kids who eat nutritionally vacant food are not firing on all cylinders, and may be firing on cylinders that point them in a different direction from that which you prefer. Teaching them under these circumstances requires a lot of attention to understand why they act as they do, and not simply to assume that their lack of attention in class is a character flaw, lack of personal motivation, or a consequence of living in a dysfunctional home.

Attendance

Attendance in low-SES schools can be spotty—for both teachers and students. LeCompte and Dworkin (1991) described the interwoven problem of teacher and student burnout. In this phenomenon, exhausted teachers give up hope and convey to students that school is fruitless; and disaffected students lead teachers to abandon optimism about the possibility of school producing an education. As a result, there is poor attendance by students, which leads to difficulty in establishing continuity; and poor attendance by teachers, whose absence conveys to students a lack of commitment and leaves gaps in instructional possibilities. When the attendance of both is spotty, finding days where everyone is present is rare, and teaching through Applebee's (1996) extended, thematic curricular conversations is unlikely to be possible.

It's very difficult to establish four to six weeks of continuity when the students and their teachers do not attend regularly. There is a tendency among people who've never been poor themselves to view traits like erratic attendance as a problem of character defects (Smagorinsky and Taxel 2005). If only the kids were more responsible, they assume, they'd be in school where they belong. If people are poor, they say, it's a consequence of making bad choices. The poor are the agents of their own poverty, according to this thinking, and helping them out only rewards their innate laziness and bad habits. Character education programs that hold this belief will address the issue by having a "character trait of the week" announced over the loudspeaker, thus presumably motivating students to be more responsible, punctual, obedient, and other traits following from the Protestant work ethic.

If the world were that simple—if it were just a matter of making good choices—then poverty might not be a systemic social challenge that recurs over generations. I will not pretend that I have any answers on what contributes to systemic, generational poverty. I think, however, that I can provide some context surrounding kids who are born into poverty and who carry its burdens into school on a daily basis. It's important to understand the circumstances that make it hard for them to view school as the best place to advance their station in life, or even to show up to periodically, unless it's to get a free meal or two during the day.

Home Models and Resources

An academic orientation is often modeled at home, where parents read to kids, help them with their homework, demonstrate their own education in a variety of ways, and in general assume that schoolwork is an important aspect of development toward a happy adulthood. But not all homes have books, or computers, or quiet time for reading and homework, or routines that provide opportunities for academic learning, or rooms to go to for homework. Not all homes include adults who view college as a desirable or worthwhile destination for themselves or their children. Some kids don't have homes at all. Kids without reliable places to sleep and meals to eat are especially prone to living amid turbulence that makes schoolwork a low priority. Now, don't get me wrong: Many exceptional people have been raised in such environments and have thrived in school and on the job. But they are exceptional. Is it fair to hold kids with less resilience and fewer resources to the same standard as the most remarkable of people?

Health

Both physical and mental health can be affected by the conditions of poverty. Some kids are born into tremendous disadvantages through the conduct of their parents before they are born (e.g., a mother's substance abuse) or through unhealthy environments created by people who benefit from their poverty (Kozol 1991). One risk factor is low birth weight, which can follow from a mother's young age, multiple pregnancies, previous low-birth-weight infants, poor nutrition, heart disease, hypertension, drug addiction, alcohol abuse, poor prenatal care, smoking, lead exposure, environmental pollution, and other factors (Clark et al. 2013). The case of the Flint, Michigan, water supply's government-engineered pollution scandal in 2016 demonstrates the ways in which people living in low-SES circumstances can be unconscious victims of other people's maliciousness and duplicity.

As I've reviewed, diet and shelter are compromised by poverty, and each affects health. But living and attending school in unsanitary conditions; feeling immense stress from all directions; having limited access to doctors, medications, and health guidance due to location and the lack of insurance; and other factors can contribute to the poor health and well-being of children and youth such that academic conduct is more difficult to undertake or aspire to. Have you tried to study when debilitatingly sick? What would you do if sickness were your typical state of body and mind?

Take a school full of kids who have eaten few healthy meals in their lives, put them in chaotic surroundings in and out of school, surround them with threatening environments, make academic literacies remote from their daily worlds, have them change residences routinely, and it's a wonder that they get to school at all. Of course, some people, through remarkable fortune and clarity of vision, do manage to succeed academically and enter the mainstream economy. These examples suggest to people born into affluence that it's possible to escape poverty through good decisions and high character. But the typical person is not so self-sufficient and resourceful, and filled with conviction. And typical people are what teachers find in their classrooms.

Self-Esteem

People living in poverty tend to get blamed for lacking money, and people with money tend to have little sympathy for them. Figueroa (2015), for instance, asserts that "Poor is a mentality. Just as rich is. People have the ability to be whatever they want to be, rich, poor, happy, unhappy, free, unfree, smart, stupid, etc. These are all choices that people have control over." Indeed, he continues, "It's really easy to not be poor: 1. Don't have children until you're ready; 2. Finish high school; 3. Don't quit your job." Because it's so easy to avoid poverty in this fashion, he claims, it's a choice, not a consequence of how other people structure your environment.

With many people believing that poor people choose to be poor, and that only a loser would make such a choice, kids living in poverty often are surrounded by the assumption that they are defective and of lesser value than people with money, who presumably have simply made better choices in life. This debilitating perspective on people in poverty has surrounded the low-SES population for many generations. Kids who have internalized this perspective inevitably find school frustrating, as much as through the assumptions that others make of them as through whatever difficulties they may have with academic work.

Schools and Their Circumstances

If you believe that schools have the responsibility to adapt to students, then attention to school structures is important to see how school itself may complicate the learning of youth who do not come from the sorts of homes that they are designed to support. The circumstances shaping students' lives outside school become exacerbated by inflexible schools that do not accommodate their needs (e.g., Milner 2015; Rodríguez 2014). I next review a series of factors that appear endemic to the institution of school and are especially common in poor urban and rural communities. These conditions often make school an inhospitable place for youth who exhibit the traits I have reviewed earlier.

Fixed, Externally Developed Curriculum

The early twenty-first century has experienced a move toward "accountability" in education. In the business world, where this model originated, accountability means meeting bottom line financial goals, typically represented in numbers. When numbers become the means of measurement in schools, and when there are few ways of comparing things like grades across schools of diverse makeup, the imposition of a standardized curriculum and assessment program is often the solution (Smagorinsky 2018d). This logic assumes that when all students take the same test based on the same curriculum, the playing field will be even, and a "true" measure of achievement will be available.

One must accept a standardized test, based on a standardized curriculum, as valid in order to embrace this sense of educational accountability. I don't buy this assumption, because for many decades, these tests have been found to represent the values of middle-class people, leaving students from other backgrounds handicapped in terms of the presumed knowledge base drawn on to perform well (FairTest 2012).

Ironically, in a field that is focused on making room for diversity and seeking to be inclusive and equitable, the policy world surrounding schools is obsessed with uniformity, standardization, and centralized curriculum development. Such a curriculum, and its teaching materials, are oriented to the world as experienced by people who are already positioned to do well within its contours: white students from middle- and upper-class backgrounds (Berchini 2016, 2017). As a result, the people most likely to be poor are served most poorly by a curriculum developed in a distant room by people who have no understanding of how low-SES people experience the world.

Out-of-Field and Uncertified Teachers

The Education Trust (2008) has reported that "In America's secondary schools, low-income students and students of color are about twice as likely as other students to be enrolled in core academic classes taught by out-of-field teachers . . . who possess neither certification in the subject they have been assigned to teach nor an academic major in that subject" (n. p.). Other sources (du Plessis, Carroll, and Gillies 2014) have found that the problem is international: Poor kids tend to get the teachers willing to take jobs in highly stressed schools, whether or not they are qualified for their assignments. Urban schools are also much more likely to employ uncertified teachers to fill faculty positions (Foster 2004). Funding shortages inevitably hit low-SES communities the hardest, because their constituents are scrambling to feed, clothe, and shelter themselves instead of hosting bake sales and other fundraisers to upgrade their bandwidth infrastructure or buy new uniforms for their athletic teams. Funding shortfalls further provide low salaries that do not attract in-field, certified teachers. As a consequence, students in underfunded schools often have had a lifetime of instruction taught by too many people who have few qualifications to teach the classes they are assigned.

Invisible Institutional Norms and Students Who Don't Fit Them

You have probably heard a set of terms that describe how US public institutions inscribe and normalize the values of the white middle and upper class: white privilege (amplified in males as male privilege), institutional racism, and others. These terms have caused quite a controversy among many white Americans who have a hard time viewing their lives as especially privileged. They might see their own circumstances as deeply oppressed, and justifiably so if they are working in industries with relaxed regulations that allow for unsafe work conditions, that pay the smallest salaries possible, that rig hours to reduce benefits, and that pay CEOs extravagant salaries with generous benefits. They might be unemployed themselves, or have limited work potential due to illness and injury, or live in poverty for many other reasons. Seeing people of color being awarded scholarships (https://www.unigo.com/scholarships/minority), being granted hiring advantages through such programs as Affirmative Action (Singh 2012), and being given other incentives for advancement can create conflict between low-SES groups that cause long-term, race-based resentments.

I won't try to persuade you in this short space that I have the correct answer to leveling the racial playing field, which many people appear to believe is slanted to favor everyone but themselves, no matter what race, color, creed, gender, or other disadvantage they feel they have. Rather, I'll make a few short points that are germane to teaching English in schools.

First, racial classifications based on skin color and related physical features often sort the world's many people into five distinct races (or six; see Korte 2016), a highly problematic way to classify the human race, especially when it produces rankings of inherent racial superiority (Smagorinsky, 2014b). But whiteness, like blackness or any other racial or ethnic category, is not so simple. White people may have little in common with one another, because of within-race diversity in terms of gender identification, socioeconomic class, neurodiversity, and many other factors (Jupp, Berry, and Lensmire 2016). The name for embodying multiple demographic categories that complicate any one identity is "intersectionality."

Four Arrows (2013) argues that the Eurocentric emphasis on competition (evidenced in the ways in which standardized test scores produce hierarchies) is at odds with Native people's value on building cooperative societies. Moll (2000) has argued that Mexican immigrants in the US Southwest lead lives oriented to collective achievement more than individual achievement, and so find school's competitive nature to create deficit perspectives on children of Mexican heritage. Many African American scholars (e.g., Majors 2015) have noted the discrepancies between African

American conversational practices and the norms expected for participation in classrooms. And to round out the Big Five racial categories, Asian Americans are far more complex than the "model minority" stereotype would suggest, with some Asian nationalities fitting US schooling patterns much better than others, having stronger familial models than others for school success, and immigrating with greater resources with which to undertake life in a Western nation. This within-race diversity disrupts the notion that Asians represent a stable, homogeneous racial group ready-made for school success (Le 2012).

When talking about whiteness as an institutional value, I am not necessarily talking about white people, and surely not all of them. Rather, I refer to the manner in which values that principally favor white people produce a form of investment in those values that result in discriminatory practices for other cultural and racial groups (Lipsitz 2006). This phenomenon involves the institution of school following European educational models founded on competition, individualism, and the aggregation of power at the top of hierarchical social structures; the colonial value on the conversion of outsiders into status quo beliefs and belief that nonconformists are barbarians—originally meaning outside threats—who must be kept from the gates; the reification of masculinity as the optimal stance; the dismissal of femininity as soft and relativist rather than strong, certain, and absolute; and the general belief that departure from established norms is a sign of cultural inferiority. These values tend to be "invisible" because they are so deeply embedded in practice and policy that, like the water surrounding a fish, it seems normal to its inhabitants. Even as schools claim to value diversity, they typically are more exclusive than inclusive when it comes to people whose home lives do not prepare them for the expectations for conduct in school.

The challenging circumstances that surround teaching in low-SES areas often involve trying to impose these historical, institutional values on students for whom school can be an intimidating, unwelcoming place to begin with, because these values stand outside their cultural repertoires. These students often engage in a wide variety of literacy practices outside school that they find culturally appropriate, socially significant, and personally fulfilling. Yet they don't find their literate lives reflected in either the curriculum and its canonical literary requirements or the sorts of student-produced texts recognized as academic and thus worthy of school assessment (Kirkland 2011). In this sense, a specific set of cultural norms is valued and rewarded above others, leading students from other cultures to feel that school is not a place that fits their style or meets their needs (Kinloch and Dixon 2018; Ladson-Billings 1998; Matias 2013; Stovall 2006; Young 2011). This consequence is most likely to befall students of color, often enrolled in underfunded schools. I next review the sorts of gaps that typically follow between instruction and students as a consequence of the institutionalization of the dominant culture's ways of navigating social life, coupled with the view that other cultures are inferior and in need of remediation, as are the people who follow their practices.

Gaps Between Instruction and Students

Centrally developed curricula that fit well within the conventions of Western society tend to represent the home and family lives of the people developing them, who tend to be relatively affluent white people. Indeed, many of the architects of national curricula and assessment programs, such as billionaire Bill Gates, are products of exclusive private-school educations. The gap between the life experiences of curriculum designers and low-SES children, often from urban or rural backgrounds, is vast and produces deficit conceptions of the kids, who often lack exposure to the assumptions behind curricular choices and instructional materials.

Kirkland (2011), for instance, reviews how African American males are often viewed as lazy because they don't do school reading assignments. These students find the assignment of *Beowulf* and other canonical texts to represent a white curriculum that they reject, even as they engage enthusiastically with cultural texts outside school. To Kirkland, this repudiation of school reading is not simply a matter of different tastes but a matter of ideological resistance to the imposition of a colonizing curriculum as the measure of intelligence and achievement. It actually takes a good bit of energy to face down discrimination, in contrast to the assumption that refusal to work always represents sloth.

In a curriculum of this sort, the experiences of nonwhite cultural, racial, and ethnic groups are often depicted through the lens of white authors who make symbolic use of the characters to make points about white society, such as Mark Twain's construction of Jim to symbolize societal hypocrisy and cruelty (Morrison 1992). To those who feel that their people are depicted simply as symbols manipulated by others to make points about themselves, such reading can be quite alienating (Emdid 2016; Hartlep and Porfilio 2015; Rodríguez 2016; Tall Bull 2007). From this perspective it's critically important to understand cultural perspectives from the standpoint of those who feel marginalized from mainstream education. In other words, they would see it as more appropriate to learn about racism from Toni Morrison than from Mark Twain.

Most typically, however, the canonical status of the literature curriculum leads teachers to depict race from the curriculum's dominant cultural perspective. With the teaching force largely white, and with a Eurocentric curriculum structuring how people and morality are represented in fundamental ways, those on the fringes—including people of color and the other sorts of students who are enrolled in schools presented with challenging circumstances—tend to be viewed as inferior sorts of people because of how they perform on tasks designed to suit European rational dispositions.

Administrative Smoke and Mirrors

People who administer organizations are often charged with maintaining appearances. In school, this need for good public relations often obscures real problems in the school and, instead of addressing them, shifts attention to a shiny new toy or other distraction. In my region, for instance, a school district got national attention for its one-to-one laptop computer initiative. The public campaign emphasized the potential for enhanced learning available through the laptops, especially for those students from homes where technology is not affordable.

What it overlooked was the problem that many students had no Internet access at home, that in short order many of the computers were broken or stolen, that the computers were being used for entertainment at least as much as for academics (and served as a classroom distraction when academics were the focus), and that a computer initiative would not, in and of itself, be a panacea for the kids. As Kim (2012) has argued, providing technological tools without accompanying *psychological tools* for using them squanders time and resources. Teachers in turn wondered if the money might have been invested in something less shiny and trendy but more likely to help kids with their learning.

Antagonistic Environment Toward School

My first steady teaching assignment was during student teaching at Martin Luther King, Jr. HS on the South Side of Chicago. I assigned homework, and the kids told me they'd get beaten up if they left school carrying books. Discussions with others confirmed that yes, carrying books in some neighborhoods can be hazardous to your health.

My impressions have been amply described by African American scholars doing research in urban areas. Lee (1993), for instance, describes how her teaching was challenged by the whole of the environment, particularly violence. Lee's account is not designed to further pathologize urban neighborhoods but to provide a realistic portrait of what you might find teaching in an urban school. Lee acknowledges that the school made an effort to maintain order with guards and other measures, yet the environment remained threatening to many.

You might be heartened to learn that Lee's teaching produced significant gains for the students in their ability to interpret complex literary texts, and her account is worth reading if you are assigned to an impoverished urban school in a dangerous neighborhood. Yet she had to adapt her teaching to account for the problems experienced by the students, often from well out of their control, all arising from challenges in the home, community, and school environments that increased the demands on her patience and instructional ability.

Adaptations and Adjustments

Rather than viewing such students as inherently deficient, view them as products of their surroundings in and out of school and the possibilities that their settings afford. This suggestion does not mean that you should view your students pathologically, as people beyond hope. Instead, like everyone else, they are in a long-term process of growth toward adulthood. Teachers are among the adults who cultivate that growth in appropriate and useful ways. Is it easy? Hardly; there will be obstacles that seem impossible to overcome. But if you're going to be a teacher, then I think that finding effective ways to teach kids who generally are not school-ready due to the impact of diminished environments should be a primary concern. In other words, it's important that you accept kids where they are and build on what they bring, rather than hold them to a set of expectations developed for kids who live in stable, comfortable environments.

With these matters of context now outlined, I'll turn to how Darren designed instruction that responded to conditions faced by his students. Darren himself had grown up in the urban environment of Trenton, NJ, and so speaks from experience both from his youth and from his teaching in Georgia. In our conversations surrounding how to write this chapter, he was clear on one fundamental point: the issue of *trust*. Kids have learned that the adults in their lives, including teachers, can leave them feeling abandoned. This revolving door of adults, as Darren called it, causes kids to build emotional barriers so that they do not become overly attached to people who might betray them by disappearing on them.

Building trust with such students can be a long-term project, often lasting into the second semester of an academic year. Kids, he said:

> need to develop trust that you are still there and trying and pushing, not quitting their jobs or on the kids. Students can take pride in running off teachers. Without trust it is hard to engage the students. Students

learn when they allow you to teach them. They must be receptive to your information. They give you their attention as a gift. Teaching, certainly in Title I schools, is a calling that not all are called upon to do.

Teaching is not simply an array of methods and techniques. Rather, teachers need to *develop relationships with their students* so that students trust that classrooms are being conducted in their best interests. Many teachers adopt a "savior complex" through which they hope to redeem students from hardship. Taking on the savior role popularized in films like *Freedom Writers* and *Dangerous Minds* might seem enticing, but it also involves a form of condescension and egotism that can produce questionable effects. Look to the kids to help you find a direction, rather than assuming that you know what is best for them.

It's important to have their interests at heart, but that effort begins with knowing who they are, how they live, what impedes their engagement with school, and what motivates them to become literate. Part of that commitment means not bailing out on them, either by quitting or disengaging through absenteeism and dependence on the scripts of the curriculum, which rarely are designed with their lives in mind.

Nobody said this job would be easy. Well, actually, too many people do think it's easy. But not many of them are teachers.

Adapting Design Principles to Challenging Circumstances

Taking all these factors into account requires a number of adaptations of the teaching approach available in this book to make instruction more accessible and engaging for students living in stressed circumstances. Here I'll switch to a plural voice as Darren joins the chapter to talk about how to make the sorts of adjustments we'd require to apply these design principles to low-SES schools and their students.

Adjusting to the Attendance Challenge

The erratic attendance of both teachers and students can make it difficult to pursue a single topic in unit-length style, because such an approach requires reasonable continuity from day to day. The first adaptation we would make, then, would be to teach in much shorter conceptual units and to have fewer expectations for homework. As a result, the unit featured in this chapter will have a duration of a few weeks rather than four to six.

Adjustments to the Community Setting

As with the previous chapter designed for a suburban sort of community, we'll start with a characterization of the community environment, constructed as a composite of the sorts of communities that the student teacher from UNC-Charlotte found herself in. It doesn't describe Darren's school setting specifically but has much in common with it. The School is a "Title 1" school, that is, it is classified among those public schools with the highest percentages of children from low-income families. Unemployment among adults is 15 percent, and half of the adults rely on some form of public assistance, such as welfare. The racial makeup of the students is African American, 75 percent; Latin American, 15 percent; white, 5 percent; Asian American, 3 percent; multiracial, 1 percent; Pacific Islander, 0.7 percent; Native American/Alaskan, 0.3 percent. Most of the students qualify for a program that provides them with free and reduced-price meals or free milk during the school day. The meals are more nourishing than convenience store food, yet by nutritional standards are more filling than healthy (e.g., pancake breakfasts made with refined white flour, sugar, salt, and many chemicals).

The students have grown up in an environment of systemic and institutional racism that depresses their opportunities to break out of these generational cycles. Because they have become alienated from public institutions—from school to police to the workforce—many students do not look to school as a vehicle for changing their life prospects. Their experiences in Title 1 schools where programs must use instructional strategies based on "scientifically based research" conducted in relatively affluent suburban schools have led them to see school as a place that is distant from their experiences and needs.

These feelings of estrangement can create distance between students and the school's academic programs, while also being part of a paradox: In Darren's experience, students often feel that school is the one place where they are safe, loved, cared for, fed, and so on. The emotional connection to teachers, peers, and counselors is separate from the academic frustrations. Building trust with students, then, would seem paramount so that they see teachers as reliable people who care for their welfare. As prerequisite to teaching well-planned lessons, then, teachers need to pay careful attention to students' emotional states, which may be negatively affected by what goes on outside school, and often within it. Within the more ordered school environment—an order that may take a bit of adjustment for students to feel comfortable within—teachers need to be *attuned to how kids feel* and adapt their methods and demeanor so that kids' threat alarms are not unnecessarily raised.

In reviewing the difficulties presented by their environment to young people who grow up in poverty, we have tried to avoid pathologizing them as the agents of their own circumstances. Often, students who are disengaged from school are said by adults to lack motivation, to be handicapped by personal character flaws. If only these kids were motivated to learn, and if they would just make better choices, they say, these kids would do well in school, go to college, get jobs, and become part of the middle class. This perspective ignores the real factors that lead them to appear unmotivated for schoolwork, such as the priority on getting a meal, or finding clean clothes, or fighting through poor health, or getting through the day in one piece; and such as the problem that they find classes in school to be boring and irrelevant. Those are the challenges they face, much more than a choice between studying or goofing off.

When they attend class, what might motivate them to participate in the day's activities? That question—rather than, why aren't these kids motivated to learn?— seems the right one to ask. Given the students' life circumstances, immediate needs, and points in literacy development, how can we structure class so that students grow in fluency through the topics we explore and the texts that they construct? Should we rely on canonical works like *The Great Gatsby* and *Romeo and Juliet,* or should we teach through more current texts from popular culture to engage their interests? Should we rely on the support provided by instructional manuals, on websites, in the curriculum, and other established teaching approaches—a common fallback for new teachers—or think completely outside the box and come up with new approaches to helping students mature as literate citizens as a result of our teaching? Should we even be thinking about teaching techniques when they might be irrelevant if the kids think we don't care about them and might desert them at any moment, like so many other adults in their lives?

Different readers might come to different conclusions in response to these questions. Darren, for instance, maintains a belief in the power of canonical literature and its enduring themes, similar to Lee (1993) and other African American educators who find that the classics have lasted because of their relevance to each new generation in terms of universal themes, regardless of their cultures and other demographic factors. Others argue more for the inclusion of pop culture texts and home speech practices that are closer to students' immediate experiences (e.g., Emdin 2016). Perhaps if trust is established, either approach might work. In some cases, the curriculum might leave you with little flexibility. But considering these questions seems to be central to making appropriate choices for the students you teach.

Assumptions

The sort of school we are describing is undoubtedly subject to a very different set of assumptions than you might enter the setting with, based on your own education. To teach effectively, you might take into account the following possibilities to undergird your planning:

+ The students may not have access to technology outside school; and the school itself may have insufficient bandwidth to accommodate instructional needs, which are often displaced by online testing when Internet access is limited. Many of the students have cell phones, which can be distracting during class. But they often lack WiFi and computers at home.

+ Students themselves may be parents, which especially for the girls becomes their primary focus instead of homework.

+ The students' home situations may be itinerant. They may move frequently among family members, may live homelessly on their own, and may live with unstable adults. They may be restricted to owning what they can carry with them, and so having them take books home would mean leaving something else behind.

+ Attendance may be affected by health, transportation, caregiving roles, parenting responsibilities, and other factors. In addition, school may not advance them toward the roles they see for themselves in life, and so missing class does not set them back in their minds. This problem gets worse when what happens in classrooms is preparation for a test that is irrelevant to the young person's needs.

+ Students may be undocumented and therefore might be subject to deportation if they get in trouble, or simply if they are in the wrong place at the wrong time. In all such cases, families may live with the constant fear that their families may be torn apart at any minute, leading to uncertainty that may make a long-term investment in school a difficult commitment to undertake.

+ Students might hold jobs after school to feed their families, pay for transportation, buy clothing, and take care of other basic human needs. These jobs may or may not be a part of the mainstream economy.

+ The school itself may have no technology infrastructure or connectivity and may have only a limited number of outdated computers running ancient versions of software whose primary purpose to administrators is online testing, not entering a dazzling world of technological literacy.

- The students may be socialized to participate in school in ways that are different from those provided by your own experiences and from the way the curriculum assumes they will participate. They may speak out of turn and in louder voices than you are accustomed to, with a different vocabulary and syntax, and these practices may result in their being constructed as trouble-making, unruly behavior problems.

- For most of the day, and for most of their lives, your students may have not been surrounded by, and may not have communicated extensively with, people who speak textbook English. Don't assume, then, that you can provide them with a whole new way of speaking in your relatively isolated class. Expect hybrid speech, think developmentally, and don't expect your hour or so a day with them will change how they speak the rest of the day. Indeed, don't assume that learning to speak like a middle-class person is in their best interests in much of their social lives.

- Some students are more likely to seek affiliation in groups outside school than inside school, making it possible that you will have gang members, and members of rival gangs, in your class.

- Students of color are likely to have been disciplined more often and more severely than white students, and so may require a lot of trust-building in order to believe that school works to their advantage (US Department of Education Office for Civil Rights 2016).

This list of factors might alarm the beginning teacher and suggest that a job in the suburbs might provide a less intimidating, less stressful work environment. It's not my goal to tell you where to look for work, only to alert you to the serious challenges that await the teacher in low-SES communities. For those who undertake teaching in low-SES circumstances, a romanticized view of teaching based on movies like *Dangerous Minds* and *Freedom Writers*, where a teacher's simple apology can immediately turn a class of hostile, distrustful students into dedicated writers, can lead to a crushing sense of failure when real students with real-life problems are not so malleable. Understanding the conditions of teaching in such settings would provide for a more sober, realistic approach that would allow for reasonable goals to be attempted. In outlining the challenges that a teacher in such environments can expect, my intention is to prepare you, not scare the heck out of you or make you feel inadequate before you begin. In the next chapter, we outline a way of teaching that might be appropriate should your teaching assignment land you in a school in which high school graduation, more than college attendance, is the mark of great achievement.

Down and Dirty 2

Planning Instruction for Stressed Students Under Stressful Circumstances: A Unit on Power and Race

with Darren Rhym

With the factors reviewed in the previous chapter in mind, what might a teacher design for ninth-grade students living in stressful circumstances? What do these kids face on a consistent basis that they need to understand, and how can instruction provide them with tools for not only literacy development but the generation of a framework for thinking about how to change their surroundings to benefit themselves and others? In this sense, to return to Chapter 3, instruction could work with the realm of *critical pedagogy*, one that makes explicit how power works in and across social groups.

This approach is at times undertaken with religious zeal by teachers who aim to radicalize their students with revolutionary ideas and intentions. The approach we're taking is less bold and revolutionary, at least at the outset, and involves teachers in the role of modeling investigative processes and deconstructive modes of inquiry, rather than playing the role of revolutionary preacher or perhaps savior. The purpose is to heighten the students' awareness of their surroundings and to enhance their ability to identify and articulate problems and solutions to the problems they perceive around them. Through this process, the instructional motive is to help the students develop agency in improving their lives and those of the people in their communities. Literacy thus does not serve as the solitary key to a better life. Rather, it works in service of a frame of mind, as a medium of understanding and expression so that students develop the tools to try to change obstacles to living life in fulfilling ways, as daunting and perhaps elusive a possibility as that might be.

Overarching Theme: Power and Society

Toward that end, we would design a unit within the overarching theme of *power*, a topic that fits well within the critical theory framework grounded in the work of Freire (1970). Power, as an overarching theme, could be broken into a series of short units. We're identifying eight possible units, each being three to four weeks, assuming about five hours of class a week. We're also assuming that a lot of instructional time will be spent on test preparation and test taking, which typically are viewed as important ways, at least to policymakers, of ensuring that no child gets left behind or that everyone is equipped to run a race to the top (of something). It's possible, then, that this plan would provide all that you could manage to teach while also meeting the demands of the rest of the curriculum.

Subtopics within the overarching theme of power might include the following, which are accompanied by the sort of "essential questions" that Darren's school requires for lesson plans:

Power and Race: In your experience, which racial groups hold power in society? How is a person's "race" constructed by individual people and those who surround them? How have the dominant racial groups accumulated power, whereas others have less? What conditions keep race-based power relationships from becoming more equitable? What happens when people from a particular racial group are denied the possibility of reaching their potential?

Power and School: What social hierarchies exist in the school? How did they come into being? Who benefits most, and who benefits least, from the social order of the school? How might it be restructured to produce more a democratic environment?

Power and Money: Who controls money in society? What does money enable and disable in people? What is gained and lost in the pursuit of wealth? What opportunities exist for people to become wealthier, and what must one do to pursue them? Do some people have greater access to wealth than others, and if so, how and why?

Power and Community: In our community, who is in control, and who has little power? How did these roles become established? Is there an opportunity to move up in the community power structure? How is power wielded by those who have it, and how is it responded to by those who don't?

Power Within Social Groups: What social groups exist in my school and community? Within the social group or groups I occupy, do members have equal status, or are some people more powerful than others? What makes a person powerful within a social group? How might power be more equally distributed?

Power Between Social Groups: In my school and community, do some social groups have more power and its tools—money, authority, access, and so on—than others? If so, how do they achieve power when other groups achieve less? How do conflicts between social groups get carried out, and what determines their relative success when they clash?

Power and the Media: What news gets reported in the media? Why do various media outlets report news and opinion differently from what others provide? What news does not get reported? What do the topics, themes, and people who become news reveal about the power structure of society, as revealed in the news media? Whose perspective is favored in media reports? How can groups not considered newsworthy produce public texts that report and reveal their perspective on society?

Power and Age: What power is available to teens in society? How do they gain it? How can teens assert their perspective in a society in which authority often follows from seniority? What sorts of authority are available to younger people in society, how do they attain it, and what consequences follow for younger people who lack authority?

For this chapter, we will base instruction on a unit that Darren has recently taught on The Harlem Renaissance, adapted for the topic of Power and Race. We frame the unit on the positive—*power*—rather than the negative—*oppression* or *poverty*—to emphasize the goal of working toward a more authoritative, agentive role in society. A focus solely on oppression would be insufficient for generating tools for agency, in that it often stops at identifying the oppressors and finding them to be oppressive.

Instead, we try to engage students in discussions that potentially introduce meaningful ideas and actions through which they engage their surroundings. Will this approach produce a whole-school turnaround and a societal revolution designed to produce societal equity? Will an expanded sense of equity based on the US founding documents (which restricted power to white landowning men) become possible for all? Probably not. However, helping students to recognize how society is structured can help them find ways to think about undertaking local change, which is a reasonable goal for a high school English class, even as school shootings at the time I am writing this sentence have prompted young people to seek change at the national level.

As teachers, we must also accept that, even as school may well be a refuge for many students, other students may harbor intense and deep psychological traumas that produce intense disdain, distrust, and hatred for school and authority. We might have to live with the fact that our inclusion of attention to power in the classroom may not engage all of our students, due to their profound alienation from the institution of school. On the other hand, it's possible that by making their own experiences and cultural orientation the central texts in the class, students might find reason to participate that otherwise might elude them.

A Critical Pedagogy Approach

Our rationale for the unit, then, would find grounding in work in critical pedagogy, the issues in human development that are specific to urban or impoverished populations, the manner in which schematic knowledge helps to frame new learning (and thus the emphasis on students' prior knowledge rather than remote curricular knowledge), the need for cultural significance as a relevant issue, and the civic awareness that might follow from considering the issue of power in social life. Building classroom inquiries on their experiences, social positioning, personal goals, and social group goals may provide some motivation for them to participate in these units.

We next outline a unit on power and race, using canonical texts from the Harlem Renaissance, a variety of rap and hip-hop texts from more recent African American social commentators, and texts either located or produced by the students based on their cultural experiences in society. We borrow from Jones (2006) to introduce a set of critical moves that help the students examine their surroundings with an idea toward positive change. These moves include the following:

> *Gathering information*: the process of inquiry through which one learns about a problem in sufficient reliable detail to take an informed perspective on it.

> *Deconstruction*: the process of carefully breaking down and examining texts and other aspects of the environment that potentially limit their opportunities. In the process of deconstruction, participants take an idea apart to examine its features, processes, impacts, and other components. This act requires a close, hard reading of people, places, texts, actions, and other objects of interrogation so that their implications are clearly revealed.

Reconstruction: the process of reimagining how the surroundings would be more equitable and less oppressive to social groups with little power in society. This act could be achieved through conversation and the generation of new visions of how things might be.

Social action: the process of working to change the power structure to some degree by working actively and deliberately toward the sorts of goals imagined during the process of reconstruction. This step, as argued by Johnson and Smagorinsky (in press), moves beyond conventional writing process stage theories that end with publication, instead making *social action* the ultimate step of greatest impact because of its intention to produce positive change.

To engage in this process, students need to consider how the meaning of a "text"—a set of related words, an image, a social reality, a set of laws, or any other societal structure or sign—is a function of one's perspective based on personal experiences, one's positioning relative to the nexus of social power, and one's degree of power in effecting social change.

Attention to Contexts

Next, we locate our teaching approach in a critical perspective while also attending to the ways in which stressed schools limit the decisions that a teacher can make. This attention to a different context—the policy and regulation structure of present-day teaching—is an unavoidable constraint for teachers who have little job security.

The plans that follow implement the Freirean (1970) approach of urging teachers to develop academic environments that inspire students to become social activists who critique their surroundings as a first step toward changing them for the better. Teachers who adopt his principles position students as active, engaged participants. Critical pedagogy is an excellent vehicle through which to teach students to critique cultural politics in texts they read. Critical pedagogy is fundamentally committed to the development and enactment of a culture of schooling that supports the empowerment of culturally marginalized and economically disenfranchised learners to create more democratic classrooms (Darder, Boltodano, and Torres 2009). This ideal is easier to state in journal articles and professional books than to create in a real school, because it requires both students and teachers to understand that their surroundings are not fixed but rather are open to interpretation, critique, and reformation.

In Darren's school, the department, grade level, district, state, and country each impose a constraint on teachers' decision-making. From a Freirean perspective, these rules and regulations need to allow for students to create additional possibilities for their learning. Ultimately, finding the balance between what is possible and what is necessary is a local question subject to teachers' ability to navigate the complex political environment of schooling in relation to what they believe is best for their students.

Darren's experiences teaching in various schools in Georgia suggest that if the students aren't happy with what they are being taught, then they will find a way to make teaching and learning difficult. They will not cooperate unless they are engaged. In an impoverished rural school like the one that provides the site for the teaching we describe in this chapter, *student participation often has to be earned by teachers.*

So how do we plan to get students involved—and *engaged*—within all this structure? How can students play a role in their learning? In what follows, we use instructional design principles to work within the bureaucratic and administrative structure of a small, rural school in an economically depressed county to both respect the requirements and obligations of the teaching contract and to serve students in their growth toward full rights of citizenship.

Requirements and Forms

Darren's high school requires a template for teachers to follow in constructing lesson plans. Although it is time-consuming and limiting to work within, its use is non-negotiable and cannot be ignored. Lesson plans based on this format must address three stages.

Stage one requires teachers to list the goals of each lesson and to state an *essential question* for the lesson, which leads students toward the instructional goals. Stage two involves demonstrating a plan for assessing students and their learning for each class, which assumes that a day's work has a neat and tidy ending. This second stage requires teachers to list *assessments*—formal or informal, formative or summative—at least three times each week. The teaching must also involve instruction in *daily life skills*, under the administrative assumption that kids are not necessarily learning life skills at home. The teaching also must further keep an eye on the state-mandated end-of-course tests (EOCT) covering state-mandated content standards, an assessment with high-stakes consequences for students to pass the course, and for teachers whose job evaluation may be tied to their students' performance.

Stage three requires the explicit listing of *Standards covered* in the day's instruction, with key words underlined to demonstrate that the teacher is conversant with the language that the state will focus on in the high-stakes testing. Lesson plans must include a *warm-up* at the beginning of class and a clear sense of *closure* at the end. For example, Darren might begin class with some aspect of the lesson's essential question so that students come into the classroom and immediately get settled and get to work during the taking of attendance and end with what his school calls a *closer*, such as a formative assessment designed to assess how the students have done with the day's lesson.

Stage three must be broken down into *warm-up*, *minilesson*, and *work session*. The *warm-up* is an extension of the opener. The *minilesson* is an instructional period in which students get background or information about the academic topic or focus for the day and lay the groundwork for the practice on the day's standard. The minilesson should help them eventually demonstrate "mastery"—a term I use with scare quotes because I think that mastery is a chimera when it comes to complex literacy practices—of that day's standard during a summative assessment and on the EOCT. In the *work session*, students are working on concepts and lessons discussed in the minilesson and demonstrating their attempts at "mastery" of the standards. During the work session, students can also create texts for assessment.

School, State, and National Standards

Darren's lesson plans help students learn how to collect and cite textual evidence when writing in response to literary and informational texts, including poems, song lyrics, lectures, and documentaries. Students are required to take extensive notes on each of these texts and are expected to cite them as sources when writing about them. The state-mandated standards also require students to know how to identify an author's central ideas or themes and to determine word meaning.

Vocabulary instruction can be instructive for students and teachers alike, especially when their own knowledge is tapped to provide the foundation for new learning. In Darren's classes, students often introduce new terms when presenting and critiquing their music, and in so doing must define terms and teach their meanings of these terms to the class. Their texts should include figurative language and other rhetorical devices that help introduce students to traditional texts that rely on the same sorts of figurative language (Lee 1993). Whenever possible, Darren uses student-chosen texts to discuss or to make connections to conventions of textbook English and other aspects of language use in context.

Under the state-mandated Speaking and Listening standards, students need to engage in comprehension, collaboration, and persuasive discourse, working on these skills when they respond to questionnaires and discuss their beliefs. During formal assessments students will deliver presentations that include PowerPoint, Prezi, posters, papers, museum boxes, and other vehicles to demonstrate what they have learned through the unit.

The students' musicians represent many genres and are included at appropriate points in the instruction. Musical tastes become quickly dated, so these listings should be viewed as if they came from a time capsule and should not be assumed to appeal to later generations, or possibly the next year's students. Michael Jackson's "Man in the Mirror" has been used in discussions of social justice; Queen Latifah's "U.N.I.T.Y." for women's issues; Migos's "Rich Then Famous (Intro)" for success; T. I.'s "Prayin' for Help" for community responsibility; and others. Drawing on the students' interests provides them an opportunity to see meaning and purpose in their studies and helps them feel whole and more knowledgeable about themselves, their society and environment, their fit with the world, and their ability to make better sense of it.

In Darren's own doctoral research (Rhym 2018), he is finding that one reason that rappers gravitate to the medium is that it allows them a way to *tell their own stories*, which they rarely have found possible during their education, given how little of African American culture they find built into their school studies. By including students' own texts—both those they consume from pop culture and those they produce to embody their own experiences—teachers can give students who are often disengaged from school a reason to participate and grow through their educational process.

Using hip-hop music is not to be undertaken lightly, given the preponderance of profanity, sexuality, misogyny, antiestablishment sentiments, and other uses of language discouraged in schools. Teachers can either line-edit lyrics taken from Internet resources, or rely on musical websites that provide "clean" radio-edit versions of hip-hop material. Pop culture is often viewed as vulgar and not worthy of curricular status, as a lower art form not lofty enough for academic study. Yet to students, it's often the key motivator to find a reason to find school worth attending and the curriculum worth engaging in.

Goals

Keeping in mind the process of *information gathering, deconstruction, reconstruction, and social change*, we have structured this unit to work toward a single goal in which the students investigate a social inequity and use this four-stage process to engage in critique. Their task is to learn about a type of inequity that concerns them, produce a text that identifies how it represents systemic injustice, and consider social action to produce positive change. The following assignment would detail their task to them.

Assignment

Either by yourself or in a group of up to four students, produce a research report on a social inequity that you believe must be addressed through social action.

+ Your report may be prepared using a medium of your choice. It may be written, performed, produced through computer images, produced through an art form, presented as a written research report, or prepared through any other medium that I approve of.

+ You should provide *information about the inequity* that you gather either from firsthand accounts (interviews, observations, etc.) or secondhand accounts (the media, source books, etc.) whose reliability you account for; that is, you should show that the source is not "fake news" or other bogus authority.

+ You should *deconstruct* the inequity by detailing how power imbalances have given some an unfair advantage and some a difficult disadvantage to overcome.

+ You should *reconstruct* the inequity by imagining what would need to change in order for equity to become possible.

+ You should detail *social action* that could address the problem and produce a better world.

Rubric

Before suggesting a rubric, we will provide a brief rationale for our categories. Without lowering our expectations excessively, we construct this rubric so that it takes into account students' developmental places and needs. One reason that we allow for collaboration is that this sort of project might be new, and doing it for the first time might benefit from having a collaborator to stimulate thinking and provide feedback on both emerging and final draft ideas.

Assuming that the students might be behind grade level, might have a difficult time doing work outside class, might be trying out a new way of thinking and composing that would be set back by punitive grading, and might be developing new competencies that should be encouraged rather than corrected, our rubric does not impose a myriad of detailed requirements. Rather, it is relatively streamlined and flexible so that students do not fear making errors but instead see errors as part of the process of thinking through new ideas. With those guidelines in mind, we have developed the following rubric through which to evaluate the students' work:

Grand	A	B
Topic	The topic clearly fits the unit theme of power and race and is explained clearly through examples from research.	The topic fits the unit theme of power and race and is explained through examples from research.
Deconstruction	The material covered clearly depicts how the topic involves inequity based on power and race.	The material covered depicts how the topic involves inequity based on power and race.
Reconstruction	The project offers a vision of how alternative structures might produce greater equity.	The project offers a limited vision of how alternative structures might produce greater equity.
Social Change	The project concludes with a plan for social action that is appropriate to the problem and has a reasonable chance of contributing to positive social change.	The project concludes with a plan for social action that is reasonably appropriate to the problem and has a possibility of contributing to positive social change.
Form	The form of the text produced allows for an audience to understand clearly the ideas conveyed through the project.	The form of the text produced allows for an audience to understand the ideas conveyed through the project.

Rubric to evaluate students' work

C	D	F
The topic is about power or race, but not necessarily both, and may include examples without those illustrations clearly representing the inequity.	The topic has only a marginal relation to the unit theme of power and race and may have little or no grounding in research.	The topic in no way fits the unit theme of power and race and has no research support.
The material covered depicts how the topic involves inequity based on power or race but does not establish the relationship.	The material covered only marginally relates to inequity based on power and/or race.	The material covered in no way relates to inequity based on power and race.
The project offers a vision of how alternative structures might produce greater equity, but that vision might be contradictory, unrealistic, or otherwise difficult to realize.	The project offers a cursory vision of how alternative structures might produce greater equity.	The project offers no vision of how alternative structures might produce greater equity.
The project concludes with a plan for social action, but that plan may be unrealistic to implement or have little chance of producing change.	The project concludes with a plan for social action that has little chance of producing social change.	The project does not provide a plan for social action.
The form of the text produced may cause confusion in the reader's ability to grasp the concepts presented.	The form of the text produced only marginally allows for an audience to understand the ideas conveyed through the project.	The form of the text produced allows for no understanding of the ideas conveyed through the project.

Materials

The following are texts that might be used in this unit. Versions of most can be found through Internet searches. The students' interest inventories may yield other artists that you would add to this list or use for replacements. Flexibility is a critical aspect of your role as instructional unit designer and teacher.

Classic Popular Music

"Strange Fruit" (versions by Billie Holiday, Jill Scott, Nina Simone)

Sample Literature from the Harlem Renaissance

Langston Hughes, "Harlem," "I Too Sing America," "The Negro Speaks of Rivers"

Paul Laurence Dunbar, "We Wear the Mask"

Arna Bontemps, "A Black Man Talks of Reaping"

Georgia Douglas Johnson, "The Heart of a Woman"

Sample Nonfiction on Civil Rights

Langston Hughes, "The Negro and the Racial Mountain"

W. E. B. DuBois, *Souls of Black Folk* (excerpt)

Malcolm X, "The Ballot or the Bullet," "Message to the Grassroots" (excerpts)

Martin Luther King, "Letter from Birmingham Jail"

C. C. J. Carpenter, Joseph A. Durick, Rabbi Hilton L. Grafman, Bishop Paul Hardin, Bishop Nolan B. Harmon, George M. Murray, Edward V. Ramage, Earl Stallings, "Public Statement by Eight Alabama Clergymen"

Video

"Langston Hughes & the Harlem Renaissance: Crash Course Literature 215" available at https://www.youtube.com/watch?v=ir0URpI9nKQ&t=25s

Sample of Rap and Hip-Hop Artists

Biggie Smalls (the Notorious B.I.G.)

Blackstarr (Mos Def and Talib Kweli)

Brother Ali

Dead Prez

Eminem

Eve

Grand Master Flash and the Furious Five

Ice Cube

Immortal Technique

Jay-Z

KRS-One

N.W.A.

Nas

Public Enemy

T.I.

Tupac

Interest Inventories

Interest inventories are designed to help a teacher learn about who students are and what they spend their time on, helping a teacher generate essential questions in light of kids' perspectives, and choose relevant authors and texts that match their interests and needs. Although the unit design here might appear to have been constructed in advance of reading students' interest inventories, the materials are offered provisionally based on Darren's experience teaching students of this demographic and might require local adaptation to your school and students. Some materials are standard curricular choices designed to complement students' selections, allowing this unit to be grounded in literary texts that colleagues and administrators would consider appropriate to the level being taught.

At intervals at the beginning of the year, you could distribute a pair of interest inventories to get a sense of the students' interests broadly speaking, and their interests in contemporary music. Their responses can provide a lot of information about who the students are and what they are interested in. The questions also give students the opportunity to state the names they prefer to be called and to provide contact information for connecting with parents or guardians.

General Interest Inventory

Last/first name _____

What do you want me to call you? _____

What are your goals for this semester? _____

Parent/foster parent/legal guardian name(s) _____

Parent/foster parent/legal guardian occupations(s) _____

Your cell phone _____ home phone _____

email: _____

Parent cell phone _____ home phone _____

work phone _____ email: _____

What expectations do your family members have of you in and out of school?

_____

What expectations do you have of yourself in and out of school?"

_____

Describe your personality from your point of view. _____

_____

Describe your personality as other people see you. _____

_____

What makes you happy? _____

_____

What do you do when you are happy? _____

_____

What makes you angry? _____

_____

What do you do when you are angry? _____

_____

Do you practice or have knowledge of anger-management techniques?

_____

What is your greatest quality? _____

Complete this statement: "I am an expert on _____."

What is one thing people don't know about you? _____

_____

What would your teachers from last year tell me about you? _____

_____

What do you have trouble dealing with? _____

_____

Who is the most influential person in your life, and why? _____

_____

Complete this statement: "It is difficult for me to learn _____

_____."

Complete this statement: "It is easy for me to learn _____

_____."

Complete this statement: "I want to know more about _____

_____."

Is there anything you would like me to know about you that may affect your success in this class? _____

_____

_____

What has been your greatest strength in your previous classes? _____

_____

In what area do you need the most improvement? _____

_____

If you had to choose, would you rather read or write? _____

What is your favorite book? _____

What are some of the reasons you enjoy this book? _____

_____

_____

What do you plan to do this year to succeed in this class? _____

_____

_____

What can I do to help you be successful in this class? _____

_____

What types of things do you read on your own? _____

_____

For the purposes of this chapter, let's assume that the first unit in the year's exploration of the overarching theme of *power* is the unit on *power and race*. This topic has been a staple of rap and hip-hop music since the genre first appeared in the 1970s and has helped shape the political consciousness of several generations of youth. Because music has long been central to adolescent culture, knowing students' tastes and interests will help you target instruction to meet their passions. The following Musical Interest Inventory will provide information about their musical knowledge and prime them for linking literature to contemporary music.

Musical Interest Inventory

Name _____ Date _____

How many hours a week do you think you spend listening to music? _____

How much time do you spend making music yourself? _____

How much time do you spend hearing live music? _____

Of the recorded music you listen to, what types of technology do you use to listen to it? How might this compare to how your grandparents listened to music in their youth? What inventions of the twentieth century most affected the listening public? _____

_____

_____

_____

If none of these technologies was available to you, how do you think your life would be different? _____

_____

Who are the recording artists you like and listen to the most? _____

_____

What, specifically, do you like about these artists? Be as specific as you can; try to write at least five sentences about each artist. _____

_____

_____

_____

_____

_____

_____

Have any of these artists made you aware of a problem or issue in our society?

_____

If so, what problems or issues has the music brought to your attention?

_____

_____

_____

How does the song or music make you feel about the issue? What role do the lyrics play? What role does the music itself play? _____

_____

_____

_____

_____

_____

_____

Can you think of a time in history when protest music was especially important (e.g., the Vietnam War era, the Black Lives Matter movement)? What issues was the music designed to address? _____

_____

_____

_____

_____

Can you think a recording artist you know who has been considered "daring" for bringing a social issue to public attention via music? What might still be a taboo (something that people don't talk about) issue today? _____

_____

_____

_____

_____

The purpose of the inventory is to give students the opportunity to introduce their music to the class's analysis and discussion. The inventory cues students to focus on music they listen to that speaks to the theme of social justice. Over the course of the year, the class can build a large catalogue of music that explores the role of power and race in society that allows students to have a stake in their learning, and perhaps develop a website about music and social justice.

Introductory Activity

For the specific introduction to the unit on power and race, you could begin with an opinionnaire designed to provoke discussion. Many of the statements in the following opinionnaire are taken almost verbatim from media reports of what people say when discussing poverty, race, character education, motivation, and other topics in relation to school. Ideally, there will be a range of response to the items, although some might be inflammatory enough to generate vociferous, yet unified, disagreement. The point is to get the kids engaged with the topic by relying on what they already know and making it relevant in class. The opinionnaire might be constructed as follows.

Opinionnaire

Read each of the next ten statements carefully. Rate each on a scale of 1–5. If you disagree strongly, rate it a 1. If you agree completely, rate it a 5. If you have mixed feelings, rate it somewhere in between.

1. People are poor because they make bad choices. If they made better choices, they would not be poor. Some people just make better decisions than others, which is why they have jobs, money, and success.

2. Success is based on the content of your character, not the color of your skin or the size of your bank account.

3. Only white people can be racists.

4. The National Basketball Association in 2015 was 74 percent black, 23 percent white, 2 percent Latin, and less than 1 percent Asian. This is unfair to white people, so there should be a rule that says that every team must have at least five white players.

5. The best way to be successful is to study hard in school, get good grades, and go to college.

6. People who say that poverty holds people back in life are just making excuses. Anyone can become wealthy if they just make good decisions.

7. Police officers are committed to upholding the law, no matter who breaks it or what they look like.

8. People who are elected to political offices are committed to helping all people, not just those who voted for them.

9. You need to speak proper English to get ahead in this world.

10. Schools do a great job of making all students feel at home, feel valued, and feel that their lives are reflected in their textbooks.

To participate, the only knowledge the students need is what they already know. At this point, they are not required to read texts written by others or produce written responses. They needn't be fluent or committed writers. Rather, they simply have the opportunity to chime in when they have something to say. It's possible that the issues on the opinionnaire could take more time to discuss than the time allotted in the Day 1 plans that follow, so you might need to decide to extend the opinionnaire into the next day, depending on students' interest and investment in the topics they raise.

The lessons that follow assume daily 60-minute class sessions. Other forms of scheduling would call for a different distribution of time. For the "out the door" informal assessment at the end of each class, each serving as an informal assessment, we have borrowed ideas from Edutopia (2016). Each day's plans include both the lesson itself and some accompanying commentary on our thinking about how to design for this setting.

WEEK 1

Day 1 (Monday)

The first day of the unit relies on the opinionnaire we have just presented as a way to open discussion that will be sustained across the weeks of the unit. We provide charts of the sort that Darren is required to develop as a model for how you might keep records if your school has a similar system. We have based the phrasing on what we have seen in Georgia curriculum documents, not to endorse them but to recognize their role in schooling and show how you might maintain records in schools with similar requirements.

Essential question	Does everyone have equal opportunity to succeed in society?
Assessment	Informal formative assessment of students' understanding of social inequity
Daily life skills instruction	Respectful turn taking in group discussions
Standards covered	• Participate in a range of discussions on topics, texts, and issues so as to contribute personal ideas and learn from the perspectives of others. • Evaluate a text's speaker's point of view, reasoning, use of evidence, and rhetorical style; and identify and critique weak reasoning practices.

Record keeping, 10SL1 and 10SL3

5 minutes: (attendance, other business) *Warm-up*: In a journal write in response to the question: Where in life do you feel powerful, and where in life do you feel powerless?

10 minutes: *Minilesson*: Distribute the opinionnaire, and give the students 10 minutes or so to respond to the items.

35 minutes: *Work session*: Ask the students to respond to the items in a whole-class discussion; or, if the class can work maturely in small groups, start in small groups and then shift to a whole-class follow-up. The whole-class discussion needn't go in the order in which the items are presented; you could allow the students to start with the items they feel most passionate about.

10 minutes: *Closure, aka "ticket out the door":* Give students time to write about any issue that has come up that they want to discuss more as the unit unfolds. Collect their writing and read their responses to assess their current writing levels, their perspectives, and their potential interests to develop as the unit unfolds.

Day 2 (Tuesday)

Unless the Day 1 opinionnaire discussion extends to another day (or two), the class follows up the opening discussion with a look back to the Harlem Renaissance. The poem selected for this lesson, Langston Hughes's "Harlem," works well here because it consists of a series of analogies that can be initially modeled and then turned over to students for analysis. This approach illustrates the scaffolding techniques emphasized throughout this book. The poem is available in many places, such as https://www .poetryfoundation.org/poems/46548/harlem. Copyright laws prevent quoting directly from it, so in what follows, we identify lines from the poem and refer readers to online versions for specific quotes.

In this unit, we are greatly reducing the amount of reading compared to the unit in Chapter 13 (which itself involves less reading than many curricula require), shifting instructional time to teaching students how to engage in the analysis of texts. This concession recognizes the difficulty that many students have in completing homework for a variety of reasons and directs classroom time to learning analytic procedures that could be applied to texts read outside class. The emphasis is then less on covering vast amounts of material and more on how to engage with the material read.

Essential question	How can literary writers change society for the better?
Assessment	Informal formative assessment of students' writing skills via their journal entries
Daily life skills instruction	Understanding historical knowledge that shapes today's actions
Standards covered	• Construct arguments that include valid claims, evidence, and interpretations, and present them such that listeners can follow the line of reasoning and the organization and determine their appropriateness to the rhetorical situation. • Use digital media to enhance the presentation of persuasive thinking and texts.

Record keeping, 10SL4 and 10SL5

5 minutes: (attendance, other business) *Warm-up:* In a journal, write in response to the following prompt: How can a poet or performer change society for the better?

15 minutes: *Minilesson:* Allowing for time to set up the technology, show "Langston Hughes & the Harlem Renaissance: Crash Course Literature 215" available at https://www.youtube.com/watch?v=ir0URpI9nKQ&t=25s.

15 minutes: *Work session:* Ask: Do you see any connections between the issues discussed in response to the opinionnaire and the role of the Harlem Renaissance in fighting bigotry for earlier generations of African Americans? If students see none, prompt for such connections as:

- Compare and contrast racial prejudice of today with racial prejudice of Langston Hughes's time.

- In what ways are poetry and arts good ways to fight bigotry today? How did they help fight bigotry back then?

- Who are today's artists fighting back against racism?

- What are their messages and methods?

- Do these artists produce any changes, or do things always remain the same? Or do they make things worse?

- What might young people do to fight back against prejudice, either against themselves or other social groups?

- What risks do artists take when protesting injustice?

5 minutes: Introduce Billie Holiday's version of "Strange Fruit" by saying that it was a song of protest; play the song. See https://www.youtube.com/watch?v=h4ZyuULy9zs for a performance, and http://www.azlyrics.com/lyrics/billieholiday/strangefruit.html for lyrics. Distribute or display the lyrics for students to consult as they watch the performance.

Optionally, play versions by Jill Scott (https://www.youtube.com/watch?v=OkXAxpzE6Gk) or Nina Simone (https://www.youtube.com/watch?v=P8Lq_yasEgo, which includes graphic images of lynchings), or other artists.

10 minutes: *Discussion*: How does this song protest social injustice? How did the song make you feel? What did the song make you want to do? Is violence an appropriate response to violence? Is singing an appropriate response to violence? Do law enforcement and the court system provide better ways of fighting prejudice than art? How, and how not?

10 minutes: *Closure, aka "ticket out the door"*: Depending on the length of the discussion, either have the discussion conclude the class, or again have students write their impressions, feelings, thoughts, or other responses to the unit thus far. Perhaps use the following prompt:

Explain the main idea of the discussion using an analogy, such as, "Fighting injustice with music is like _____."

If time allows, have students volunteer their analogies and use their ideas to generate further discussion, either on this day or the next.

Day 3 (Wednesday)

The first two days have introduced to students the idea that societal inequity exists, has existed for many years, and has been protested by artists for generations. Now the class may begin to learn procedures for undergoing the process of critical inquiry through the deconstruction of texts, reconstruction of possibilities, and undertaking of social action.

Essential question	How does one conduct a critical analysis that includes the processes of deconstruction, reconstruction, and positive change?
Assessment	Formative assessment of students' understanding of the processes of deconstruction, reconstruction, and positive change
Daily life skills instruction	Learning critical skills to critique inequity
Standards covered	• Analyze how the same story may be told in different sorts of texts of varying modes (e.g., writing, graphic images) and which features are best expressed through which symbol systems. • Determine how an author argues points and assess the validity of the reasoning and evidentiary quality of the examples. • Analyze historical documents for content and persuasive style.

Record keeping, 10R17–19

5 minutes: (attendance, other business) *Warm-up*: Explain in a letter to a friend what you think is most in need of change in society.

10 minutes: *Minilesson on Deconstruction*: Distribute Langston Hughes's poem "Harlem." Lead students through the process of how to read the poem's answer to the question, posed in the poem's first line in which the speaker asks about the consequence of deferring a dream. The first interrogative in response to this question appears in the second and third lines of the poem, which were later taken up by Lorraine Hansberry for the title to her black family drama *A Raisin in the Sun*. Students may or may not be familiar with interpreting analogies, so it would be useful to pair the two items for comparison, using whatever means of presentation or projection is available (whiteboard, projector, etc.).

[Poem's initial question]	[First analogy in poem's second and third lines]

How are the two similar? How are they different? Why would Hughes make an analogy between the opening abstraction and the simile in lines 2–3? The teacher could lead an investigation into this question, using the space beneath each item to record students' suggestions. Depending on how the students manage this task, the next stage of this scaffold could have the teacher either continue leading a discussion of the next analogy or begin to turn over the task to students working in pairs. The next analogy for a dream deferred appears in lines 4–5 and compares a deferred dream to an open wound. If students work in pairs, have them offer their interpretations after several minutes of discussion.

20 minutes: *Work session*: The next analogy appears in line 6 and compares deferred dreams to decaying, stench-emitting flesh. Students could undertake the analysis in pairs, assuming that this scaffolding process is effective in helping students work with Hughes's series of analogies. The class could work in this fashion over the remaining analogies.

Lines 7–8 provide an image of deceptive sweetness.

Lines 9–10 suggest a burden.

One possibility would be to have students write individually on the last, explosive analogy of the poem in line 11. This writing could then serve as the basis for a discussion of the whole poem in a whole-class setting.

15 minutes: *Minilesson on Reconstruction*: In response to the inequities revealed by Hughes, what vision is available to change society for the better? Have students work in pairs to come up with alternatives that help to address these societal challenges, saving a whole-class exploration for the next day.

10 minutes: *Closure, aka "ticket out the door"*: Depending on the length of the discussion, either have the discussion conclude the class or again have students write their impressions, feelings, thoughts, or other responses to the unit thus far. Perhaps use the following prompt:

> Explain the main idea using an analogy, such as, "Fighting injustice with poetry is like _____."

If time allows, have students volunteer their responses and discuss them.

Day 4 (Thursday)

This class extends the previous day's discussion, with students given agency in deconstructing texts, reconstructing possibilities, and identifying means of social action in relation to "Harlem."

Essential question	How can critique become social action?
Assessment	Informal formative assessment of students' ability to make sense of a text that engages in social critique and to make inferences about social change
Daily life skills instruction	Generating ideas for constructive social action
Standards covered	• Identify the main theme of a text and how it is developed, and summarize the text's contents.

Record keeping, 10RL1–2

10 minutes: (attendance, other business) *Warm-up*: Compare and contrast Langston Hughes's poem "Harlem" to a modern song or poem that critiques society's inequities. For follow-up, ask students to volunteer their contemporary examples and why they chose them.

40 minutes: *Minilesson on Reconstruction and Social Action and Work session*: Have groups share their ideas from the previous day's reconstruction of Hughes's social critique. What problems is he addressing, and how can students use their imaginations and knowledge to address them? What solutions do they see available to themselves as youths to make society more equitable and to reduce the effects of racism? The teacher's role in this segment will be to act as a recorder of the students' ideas, using the best available medium for making their views public.

10 minutes: *Closure, aka "ticket out the door"*: Have the students write in response to one of the following question stems, discussing them as time allows:

"I believe _____, because _____."

"I am confused by _____."

Day 5 (Friday)

The next class provides an opportunity to link Hughes's poetry to contemporary music and poetry. Hughes himself was once a pop culture artist whose work was of such quality that it became part of the national culture. Every generation produces enduring artists and a preponderance of passing fads. What qualities make a contemporary artist stand up over time? The students begin to explore that question with today's activities.

Essential question	What are the consequences of an artist's social critique?
Assessment	Informal assessment of students' learning through their discussions and conclusions
Daily life skills instruction	Understanding popular culture through critical thinking
Standards covered	• Analyze word usage in terms of rhetorical impact and figurative effects, both at the local and global textual levels. • Analyze a text's structure, order, and pacing and how they potentially produce specific effects on a reader. • Identify the perspective taken by the author of a verbal text. • Interpret figures of speech and analyze their role in a text.

Record keeping, 10RL4–6 and 10L5

10 minutes: (attendance, other business) *Warm-up*: In a journal write in response to the following prompt: "'Popular culture' refers to what is currently happening in a society, often in terms of entertainment. As time moves ahead and new things come along, some works of popular culture remain part of historical culture, whereas others are forgotten. Which works of popular culture from today do you think will become part of historical culture over time? Why will they endure when others are forgotten?"

15 minutes: *Minilesson*: This writing could then become the basis for a class discussion. Ask students to suggest works from current pop culture that they believe will become part of historical culture, perhaps using a projector or whiteboard to record their responses as follows:

Popular culture song, video, performance, etc.	Reasons it will last when other works fade away

Pop culture chart

15 minutes: *Work session*: In small groups, have students identify the traits that enable a work of popular culture to become, like Hughes's "Harlem" and the song "Strange Fruit," part of historical culture.

15 minutes: *Follow-up*: Whole-class discussion in which students share their emerging definitions of "enduring work of popular culture."

5 minutes: *Closure, aka "ticket out the door"*: Compare and contrast: Briefly, write about a work from current pop culture that will outlast its current popularity with one that you believe will not. What is the difference between them?

Day 6 (Monday)

This session will focus on two rap performances from the 1990s, one of which has become canonical, the other of which has not. Using music that the students may be familiar with through older family members, this day's activities will extend the students' inquiry into what products of popular culture have the potential to help change society.

Essential question	What works of popular culture become part of historical culture, and why?
Assessment	Informal formative assessment of students' writing skills via their discussions
Daily life skills instruction	Judging the quality of popular culture songs
Standards covered	• Determine the figurative, connotative, and technical meanings of words and phrases as they are used in different sorts of texts written in specific communities of practice. • Analyze the quality of an author's claims and supporting evidence. • Determine an author's point of view, and analyze how the author advances it.

Record keeping, 10R14–16

10 minutes: (attendance, other business) *Warm-up*: In a journal, write in response to the following prompt: "Think of popular music from previous generations that you believe still has value, either political, musical, or through other features. Why has this music remained relevant long after its own time?"

10 minutes: *Minilesson*: Follow up the journal writing with a discussion on which works of pop culture survive their own time and are relevant to later generations. Referring back to the previous day's discussion, see if the students would change anything about the definition of "enduring work of popular culture."

10 minutes: *Work session*: Play a sanitized version of a rap song from the 1990s that has had enduring value, and one that has long been forgotten. These songs might include the following:

Enduring: Public Enemy, "Fight the Power" (radio edit at https://www.musixmatch.com/lyrics/Public-Enemy/Fight-the-Power-radio-edit)

Forgotten: A selection from any of the "worst hip-hop songs of the '90s" websites such as http://www.mademan.com/mm/10-worst-rap-songs-90s.html. For purposes of illustration, we will use "Take Me There" by Mya featuring Blackstreet, Mase, and Blinky Blink (radio edit at https://www.youtube.com/watch?v=4_TyO0PEwpo).

10 minutes: Have students work in small groups to discuss these two songs. Which do they think has endured? Which is in history's dustbin? Why would one survive as significant, but not the other (even as it might survive as camp or curiosity because the Internet archives everything)?

15 minutes: Ask each group to explain their decision and to provide reasons for their conclusion.

5 minutes: *Closure, aka "ticket out the door"*: "The Minute Paper"—Have the students write briefly on the most meaningful thing they've learned so far during this unit.

Day 7 (Tuesday)

Day 7 will continue to look at canonical and contemporary, socially oriented poems and music, using more feminist work from both the Harlem Renaissance and contemporary hip-hop. Both of these periods have produced both male and female artists, yet males have gotten most of the attention. This class specifically looks at the concerns of women writing about inequities they experience in society.

Essential question	What do authors of Harlem Renaissance texts and current hip-hop artists deconstruct in society?
Assessment	Informal formative assessment of students' writing skills via their journal entries
Daily life skills instruction	Understanding historical discrimination and its relation to the present

Standards covered	• Analyze different accounts of the same subject told in different mediums, and determine which details are emphasized in each account. • Construct arguments that include valid claims, evidence, and interpretations, and present them such that listeners can follow the line of reasoning and the organization and determine their appropriateness to the rhetorical situation. • Analyze historical documents for content and persuasive style.

Record keeping, 10R17–19

5 minutes: (attendance, other business) *Warm-up*: Have the students write a Twitter post in less than 140 characters that sums up their view of what they have discussed so far.

20 minutes: *Minilesson*: Using both a classic poetic work from the Harlem Renaissance and a contemporary work from the hip-hop genre, engage in a process of deconstruction, reconstruction, and social action. These two texts might include the following:

> Harlem Renaissance: Georgia Douglas Johnson: "The Heart of a Woman" (https://www.poetryfoundation.org/poems-and-poets/poems /detail/52494)

> Hip-Hop Genre: Eve: "Who's That Girl?" (radio edit at https://www .amazon.co.uk/Whos-That-Girl-Main-Radio/dp/B002WQVOBO)

Begin with the relatively short Johnson's "The Heart of a Woman." Lead the class through the following process:

Deconstruction: What is the artist criticizing about society?
Reconstruction: What would the artist imagine to be a better society?
Social Action: What does the artist either state or suggest would change society for the better?

"Heart of a Woman" discussion

30 minutes: *Work session*: Using the same chart, play the radio-edit version of Eve's "Who's That Girl?" and have the students work in groups to go through the process of critical inquiry to analyze Eve's view of what is wrong with society and how to change it. Follow up with a whole-class discussion of their small-group conclusions.

5 minutes: *Closure, aka "ticket out the door"*: Debrief: Have students reflect in writing on the messages behind the poem and rap song, and on the author's message in terms of their own lives.

Day 8 (Wednesday)

At this point, the analysis of social inequity shifts from art to reality. After having studied inequity in song and poetry, the students are urged to think of inequities that they see in their own lives and how to address them through social action.

Essential question	Which societal inequities can be addressed through informed social action?
Assessment	Informal formative assessment of students' critical faculties through their class contributions
Daily life skills instruction	Critiquing one's surroundings
Standards covered	• Read and comprehend appropriate grade-level literary nonfiction.

Record keeping, 10RI10

10 minutes: (attendance, other business) *Warm-up*: Quick-write: Have students write in response to the following prompt: "Without stopping, write about what most confuses you about deconstruction, reconstruction, and social action."

Have students volunteer their points of confusion and help the class come up with ways to address them.

20 minutes: *Minilesson*: Lead students through a process of identifying a social problem that is not so great that it cannot be easily solved (e.g., racism) or so small that it does not amount to a significant social problem (e.g., a panhandler bothers people on a street corner). You might exercise caution in selecting this topic that you model. For instance, if you were to say "police brutality," you might invite the criticism that you are against the police force in general, even as there are both good and bad police officers. More safely, you could say that "redlining" is a social problem that needs addressing. This term refers to the documented practice of mortgage lenders who draw red lines around neighborhoods on maps, cordoning off areas where they do not want to make loans, often excluding people on the basis of race, which is illegal.

If you were to select redlining, you could introduce and define the term, providing them with copies of the Fair Housing Act (https://www.federal reserve.gov/boarddocs/supmanual/cch/fair_lend_fhact.pdf) that makes redlining illegal. Either by explaining or leading a discussion, go through the process of deconstructing the problems of redlining, reconstructing possibilities for fairer housing practices, and imagining social action that could produce positive social change. But redlining is only one of many possibilities; choose a form of discrimination that fits your circumstances well. Ideally, the minilesson would not involve a lecture but would provide as many opportunities for students to construct the critique as possible.

30 minutes: *Work session*: Have students work in small groups to identify a social inequity, deconstruct it, reconstruct it, and generate ideas for positive social change. In this segment, if *students* were to identify police brutality as a societal problem, it is less politically volatile than it would be for the *teacher* to introduce it as a model topic. If you think it would be beneficial to the students, provide them with charts of the sort introduced earlier that include space for Problem, Deconstruction, Reconstruction, and Social Change.

0 minutes: *Closure, aka "ticket out the door"*: Today's class ends without formal closure.

Day 9 (Thursday)

This class provides an extension of the previous day's discussion, with students sharing their ideas with their classmates and getting feedback on their initial thoughts.

Essential question	How can literary writers change society for the better?
Assessment	Informal formative assessment of students' writing skills via their journal entries
Daily life skills instruction	Understanding historical knowledge that shapes today's actions
Standards covered	• Construct arguments that include valid claims, evidence, and interpretations, and present them such that listeners can follow the line of reasoning and the organization and determine their appropriateness to the rhetorical situation. • Use digital media to enhance the presentation of persuasive thinking and texts. • To enhance understanding of informational texts, use context clues to determine word meaning, draw on secondary sources to inform reading, and corroborate understandings with multiple sources.

Record keeping, 10SL4–5, and 10L4

13 minutes: (attendance, other business) *Warm-up*: Top-Ten List—Have students write in response to the following prompt: "What are the ten worst things about society (written with humor if possible)." Follow up by having students volunteer ideas from their writing to the whole class.

2 minutes: *Minilesson*: Explain that today's work builds directly off Day 9.

20 minutes: *Work session*: Have each group report back on its topic for the previous day. What is the social problem they have identified? How have they deconstructed it, reconstructed a better way, and identified social action that potentially brings about change? Include opportunities for each group's presentation to serve as a springboard for additional discussion.

15 minutes: Have each group return to their small-group setting. Have each identify every new vocabulary word they have learned so far during the unit (profanity excluded). Each group then reports back to class their new words and their definitions, with examples.

10 minutes: *Closure, aka "ticket out the door"*: Write a short reflection that includes at least three new non-profane words that the class has learned during the course of the unit. Ask for volunteers to read their thoughts.

Day 10 (Friday)

With considerable discussion and exploration already undertaken, we now point the students directly to the task of the unit assignment.

Essential question	What research topics are available to study social inequity?
Assessment	Informal formative assessment of students' narrowing of topics to investigate
Daily life skills instruction	Knowing how to investigate a topic and explain it to other people
Standards covered	• Write clearly, coherently, and appropriately in relation to a variety of writing situations. • Use technology to produce, revise, and publish texts.

Record keeping, 10W4–6

5 minutes: (attendance, other business) *Warm-up*: Illustration—Have the students draw a picture that illustrates a social inequity they have discussed during the unit. Allow them to share theirs with classmates.

15 minutes: *Minilesson*: Distribute to the students the assignment and rubric detailed in the first goal for this unit, for which students deconstruct, reconstruct, and propose social action for an inequity they see in society.

10 minutes: *Work session*: Students return to their work groups with the assignment and rubric. They are tasked with making final decisions on whether any of them wish to work together on a topic, whether they would all work together on one topic, or whether they should go their separate ways. They should also use these discussions to refine their topic to something manageable within the terms of the time available and resources. Their topics might be

- Local to their immediate environment of school, neighborhood, and community (e.g., a specific inequity with which they are personally familiar); and/or

- More distant and requiring consulting secondary sources (e.g., a specific incident from the news that represents a broader problem such as the events that resulted in the Black Lives Matter movement).

The sort of topic they select needs to be available for research using handy sources. Given the declining resources available in many schools—as I write this, schools in Oklahoma are so poorly funded that many can afford only four days of school each week (Brown 2017)—the sorts of digital searching and composing often prized by educational writers may simply not be possible. Following this session, each student should have an understanding of the expectations for their next stage in investigating race and power in society.

20 minutes: At this point, how you proceed would depend on how well resourced your school is. Sadly, schools that enroll impoverished students tend to have the fewest resources to support their learning. A school's Internet bandwidth, for instance, might allow for only online testing to be available for much of the time, making online searches impossible (Johnson, Sieben, and Buxton 2018). Even in the absence of the Internet, students can learn such investigative skills as interviewing people that require only a recording device or good note-taking skills. For the remainder of the class, review possible ways for them to investigate and share their research with their classmates.

Means of Investigation

Learning from published sources (print or online)

Learning from primary sources (people, observations)

Means of Presentation

Slideshow with accompanying spoken or written text

Written research report

Creative/artistic depiction

Written narrative

10 minutes: *Closure, aka "ticket out the door"*: Have students write how they intend to investigate their topic, and turn their proposal in for review.

WEEK 3

Day 11 (Monday)

The next few classes will help students learn procedures for investigating a social problem. Today they will learn how to conduct interviews. Later classes will take them to the media center to learn research skills, although as we will note, we cannot make assumptions about the sorts of resources that schools serving students living under stress will provide for them.

Essential question	How can social inequity be investigated, deconstructed, reconstructed, and subject to social action?
Assessment	Informal formative assessment of students' writing skills via their journal entries
Daily life skills instruction	Learning how to evaluate knowledge sources
Standards covered	• Conduct research to answer a question or solve a problem, drawing on multiple sources and assessing each source's verity; integrate information into texts without plagiarism and in ways that work within the flow of the report.

Record keeping, 10W7–8

5 minutes: (attendance, other business) *Warm-up*: Tagxedo (http://www.tagxedo.com/)—Have the students write down key words that they associate with their topic.

25 minutes: *Minilesson*: Gathering information—Students will learn how to learn from primary sources. This segment will involve the teacher conducting an interview with a student about a possible topic on which the student may have personal knowledge. This interview might involve a set of common question types, adapted here for modeling an interview on a possible local situation: African American youth being treated suspiciously in local businesses. The teacher should also model either recording (possibly with a cell phone recorder or a downloadable computer software recorder such as Audacity) or taking notes from the interview. The following template could be reproduced for students to draw on when they conduct their own interviews:

- **Behaviors**: Please describe for me a situation in which you or someone you know got treated suspiciously in a local business. What was the business, what was the person doing in there, and what did the people in the business do to suggest that you were acting suspiciously?

- **Opinions/values**: What is your opinion of the situation that you either experienced, observed, or were told about? Why do you think that the treatment was unfair?

- **Feelings**: How did you feel about the ways in which you were treated?

- **Knowledge**: What information about the situation would help you to convince other people that you were being treated unfairly?

- **Sensory**: Did this experience involve any physical sensations—such as being touched, or beginning to sweat, or feeling your heartbeat increase—that contributed to how you felt about the experience?

- **Background/demographics**: In what ways do you think that your personal characteristics were part of the reason that you were treated unfairly?

20 minutes: *Work session*: At the conclusion of the interview, the teacher could model how to take this information and present it as a social inequity to be deconstructed. Using the student's interview data, the class as a group could deconstruct the events, reconstruct a more equitable possibility, and discuss social action through which they could address the problem. The teacher could model how to organize the information from the interview into an account that is amenable to the process of deconstruction.

10 minutes: *Closure, aka "ticket out the door"*: Explain your solution—Have students write the steps they could take to interview someone and undertake a process of deconstruction, reconstruction, and social action.

Day 12 (Tuesday)

Essential question	How can primary sources inform an understanding of social problems?
Assessment	Informal formative assessment of students' interviewing and data-collection skills via their in-class interviews
Daily life skills instruction	Learning how to listen carefully to make sense of other people's experiences
Standards covered	• Participate in a range of discussions on topics, texts, and issues so as to contribute personal ideas and learn from the perspectives of others.

Record keeping, 10SL1

10 minutes: (attendance, other business) *Warm-up*: Have students write in response to the following prompt: "How has the topic you are investigating been portrayed in popular culture?"

Follow up with volunteers from the class who explain their responses.

15 minutes: *Minilesson*: Distribute the question set from the previous day's interview demonstration. Have students work with their project partners to prepare interview questions for their own interviews. Students who choose to work independently may partner for this segment with other independent workers or other students they recruit for feedback.

15 minutes: *Work session*: Have students identify an interviewee from within the class. Each project group should announce to the class the focus of its inquiry and seek volunteers who will provide them with an interview. This activity structure assumes that the class will include someone who has either directly experienced this inequity or can relate an observation or secondhand experience to provide material for the interviews.

20 minutes: Students will use the remaining time to conduct interviews with classmates, recording and/or taking notes to provide them with material for their projects.

Closure, aka "ticket out the door": The interviews' conclusions will provide closure for today's class.

Day 13 (Wednesday)

Essential question	What secondary sources can provide additional information about a topic?
Assessment	Informal formative assessment of students' investigative skills
Daily life skills instruction	Learning how to use secondary sources to learn about a social problem
Standards covered	• Use digital media to enhance the presentation of persuasive thinking and texts. • Provide evidence to support analysis, reflection, and research.

Record keeping 10W8–9

5 minutes: (attendance, other business) *Warm-up*: The warm-up will consist of walking to the school's media center to consult with secondary sources.

15 minutes: *Minilesson*: What will happen will depend on the richness and variety of the school's print and online resources. If Internet is available, students will be taught how to conduct searches for relevant material and how to distinguish a reputable source from a disreputable source, real news from fake news. If only print resources are available, students will learn how to locate information in a library.

30 minutes: *Work session*: Students search for sources that could advance their knowledge on their research topic.

10 minutes: *Closure, aka "ticket out the door"*: As students leave the media center, briefly check in with each group to assess their progress.

Day 14 (Thursday)

Essential question	How can information from a variety of sources be assembled into a coherent whole for presentation?
Assessment	Informal formative assessment of students' investigative and integrative skills
Daily life skills instruction	Working collaboratively to produce a robust group project
Standards covered	• Integrate multiple sources of information presented in diverse media or formats after evaluating the credibility of each source. • Evaluate a text's speaker's point of view, reasoning, use of evidence, and rhetorical style; and identify and critique weak reasoning practices.

Record keeping 10SL2–3

5 minutes: (attendance, other business) *Warm-up*: The warm-up will consist of walking to the school's media center to consult with secondary sources.

50 minutes: *Minilesson and Work session*: The students will continue looking into secondary sources and record the information they intend to use in their research reports.

5 minutes: *Closure, aka "ticket out the door"*: As students leave the media center, briefly check in with each group to assess their progress.

Day 15 (Friday)

Essential question	What is an appropriate response to an inequitable situation?
Assessment	Informal formative assessment of students' investigative and integrative skills
Daily life skills instruction	How does a news consumer draw clear conclusions from conflicting sources?
Standards covered	• Construct arguments that include valid claims, evidence, and interpretations, and present them such that listeners can follow the line of reasoning and the organization and determine their appropriateness to the rhetorical situation.

Record keeping, 10SL4

5 minutes: (attendance, other business) *Warm-up*: The warm-up will consist of walking to the school's media center to consult with secondary sources.

50 minutes: *Minilesson and Work session*: The students will continue looking into secondary sources and record the information they intend to use in their research reports.

5 minutes: *Closure, aka "ticket out the door"*: As students leave the media center, briefly check in with each group to assess their progress.

WEEK 4

Day 16 (Monday)

The classes of the last week or so have focused on teaching students how to gather information. They now return to the process of critical inquiry to make sense of the social problem they are investigating.

Essential question	How can information from a variety of sources be assembled into a coherent whole for presentation?
Assessment	Informal formative assessment of students' investigative and integrative skills
Daily life skills instruction	Working collaboratively to produce a robust group project
Standards covered	• Use digital media to enhance the presentation of persuasive thinking and texts.

Record keeping, 10SL5

10 minutes: (attendance, other business) *Warm-up*: Interview you—Have students respond to the following prompt: "You're the guest expert on a TV news show. How would you answer the following questions: What are you an expert on when it comes to societal inequity? Why should other people care about this topic?"

Allow time for students to share responses if they wish.

20 minutes: *Minilesson*: Using one project group as a model, have them go through a process of

- Presenting the information they have researched;
- Identifying the social inequity involved;
- Deconstructing the problem as they see it;
- Reconstructing a possible way for society to function more equitably; and
- Identifying ways of producing positive social change.

25 minutes: *Work session*: Provide time for each group to go through this process.

5 minutes: *Closure, aka "ticket out the door"*: Simile—Have students write, using the following prompt: "What we learned today is like learning how to
_____."

Day 17 (Tuesday)

Assuming that the students are making progress on understanding how to engage in social critique, we can now turn our attention to the means by which the students develop a textual product to share with their classmates. For this segment of the instruction, we are offering a wide range of possibilities so that students can learn new information and strategies without the additional burden of learning a new textual genre, such as the formal research report. The purpose of the instruction at this point in the year is for them to feel confident in their critical abilities. As the year goes on, specific instruction in how to write in particular genres may become appropriate. Here, however, we are concerned with supporting their existing skills as they put them in service of solving new problems.

This unit is possibly longer than what we might have originally conceived of. Note, however, that it has required the reading of only a few texts in the classroom setting. Rather than covering a large body of material, our goal is to focus on a smaller number of texts through which we teach students how to do a particular type of reading, how to engage in a particular sort of conversation, and how to convey to their classmates the nature of a problem and the possibilities for addressing it. Like other instruction recommended in this book, it attends heavily to learning how to do things and less so to reading many texts quickly and superficially. We move deliberately and in accordance with students' needs, rather than in step with the pacing guide of a curriculum designed by people who have no knowledge of the contexts of students' lives. We have designed a curriculum that is a mile deep and an inch wide, rather than an inch deep and a mile wide.

Essential question	What is the process of moving from social critique to social action?
Assessment	Informal formative assessment of students' investigative and integrative skills
Daily life skills instruction	Negotiating difference when working toward group goals
Standards covered	• Adapt speech conventions to meet the expectations of tasks and contexts.

Record keeping, 10SL6

15 minutes: (attendance, other business) *Warm-up*: Define—Have the students write in response to the following prompt: "What is the difference between an appropriate, effective social action and an inappropriate, ineffective social action? Give examples of each."

30 minutes: *Minilesson*: Using one group's topic and research as a model, provide a menu of ways for students to take their information and ideas and present them to the class. Using, for instance, the inequity of youth being treated suspiciously in local businesses, the lesson might review the following:

> *Slideshow with accompanying spoken or written text*: What presentation software would best enable students to share their information? How can information, deconstruction, reconstruction, and social action be depicted through images available in the software?

> *Written research report*: Again using the four-part structure of information, deconstruction, reconstruction, and social action, provide a model for what a written report would look like and how to include their research in this presentation.

> *Creative depiction*: Using a medium such as drama, visual art, rap, ballad, or other textual means, present the problem and its possible solutions through a creative performance or product.

> *Written narrative*: Rather than telling the story through art or performance, tell the story as a narrative.

15 minutes: *Work session*: Provide time for each group to begin planning how they will present their ideas to their classmates.

Closure, aka "ticket out the door": Check with each group informally as time expires on their plans for their presentation.

Day 18 (Wednesday)

From here on out, the students are given class time to work on their presentations, in accordance with the unit and rubric. We are assuming that many students will not have opportunities to do schoolwork outside class, making class time the primary workshop site. Students may be encouraged to work outside class but should not be penalized if that time is not available to them.

Essential question	What is the process of moving from social critique to social action?
Assessment	Informal formative assessment of students' investigative and integrative skills
Daily life skills instruction	Negotiating difference when working toward group goals
Standards covered	• Adapt speech conventions to meet the expectations of tasks and contexts.

Record keeping, 10SL6

10 minutes: (attendance, other business) *Warm-up*: 3–2–1—Have students list three things they have learned, two things they find interesting, and one thing about which they remain uncertain. Allow time for students to share their responses.

50 minutes: *Minilesson and Work session*: Provide the students time to work on their presentations.

Closure, aka "ticket out the door": Check with each group informally as time expires on their plans for their presentation.

Day 19 (Thursday)

Essential question	What is the process of moving from social critique to social action?
Assessment	Informal formative assessment of students' investigative and integrative skills
Daily life skills instruction	Negotiating difference when working toward group goals
Standards covered	• Adapt speech conventions to meet the expectations of tasks and contexts.

Record keeping, 10SL6

10 minutes: (attendance, other business) *Warm-up*: None. Students get right to work.

50 minutes: *Minilesson and Work session*: Provide the students time to work on their presentations.

Closure, aka "ticket out the door": Check with each group informally as time expires on their plans for their presentation.

Day 20 (Friday)

Essential question	What is wrong in society, and how can it be changed for the better?
Assessment	Formal assessment, based on the rubric, of the students' projects
Daily life skills instruction	Paying attention respectfully to other people's views
Standards covered	• Adapt speech conventions to meet the expectations of tasks and contexts.

Record keeping, 10SL6

10 minutes: (attendance, other business) *Warm-up*: Have the students write in response to the following prompt: "What is the most controversial thing you've learned during this unit?"

50 minutes: *Minilesson and Work session*: Student presentations.

Closure, aka "ticket out the door": High fives, fist bumps, or other affirmational gesture as students exit the classroom.

The student presentations conclude the unit. One way to grade the presentations is to provide each student with a copy of the rubric and have the students grade each other, with the teacher taking their evaluations into account in determining grades.

Note that the unit does not require the students to proceed to take social action. We backed off from that idea because the unit may achieve its ends by teaching the process of critique, and may already be replete with activities and responsibilities. Students could be given the option of taking social action for extra credit, although extra credit often provides advantages to students with leisure time that is not available to students with jobs, family care, school activities, and other obligations.

The projects that the students undertake in this unit do not have the specific genre orientation of instruction recommended for other units in this book. Rather, as a way to invite students to present their thinking in the most comfortable ways possible, for this initial unit of the long-term exploration of power in society, the students have flexibility in how they produce their findings. Other units might include more specific instruction in how to write particular types of papers. After the unit on power and race, for instance, the remaining units in the year's exploration of power could include instruction in the following writing genres (for specific instruction in each, see Smagorinsky, Johannessen, Kahn, and McCann 2010):

Power and School: *Classification paper*: Which social groups populate the school, how are they organized, how do they relate to one another, and by what means do some establish and exert control over others?

Power and Money: *Extended definition*: Define and illustrate "success" as it relates to financial power.

Power and Community: *Personal narrative*: What stories can students tell that illustrate a power differential they have experienced in their community?

Power Within Social Groups: *Fable*: What moral tale could illustrate the ways in which power within groups can produce inequitable, harmful relationships?

Power Between Social Groups: *Argument*: Which social groups within the school have the greatest authority, and how do they hold it? How might that authority be more broadly distributed across social groups?

Power and the Media: *Research report*: What news that is important to youth social groups is not reported in the media, and what sort of media report would share that news and experience more broadly?

Power and Age: *Fictional narrative*: How might youth create fictional visions of their own role in using power wisely as they accrue it with age? How might young people create stories that illustrate the forms of power that they do have?

Will this unit solve all the world's problems? Hardly. But it will tie the curriculum to students' interests, give them tools to challenge inequity, and provide them with possible avenues for social action that they may not have seen as possible for them. From what we can tell, that's a lot more than they are getting out of school as presently conducted, and that's reason enough to give it a try.

16

Linking Reflective Practice to Beginning Teacher Performance Assessment

I f you are reading this book in a university teacher education program, it's likely that you are required to meet the standards of a *performance assessment*. As I write this book, the most widely used assessment for beginning teachers is called edTPA. But many states have developed their own versions: the Washington Teacher Performance Assessment, the California Teaching Performance Assessment, the Virginia Teacher Performance Evaluation System, and others. Although they vary, the general approach appears to be similar. This chapter is designed to show you how to navigate these exams by helping you to understand what they are looking for, how they are constructed, and how they will be assessed. These evaluations might provide occasions for reflecting on the sort of teacher you are becoming, although that reflection might not be included in what you submit for evaluation.

These assessments are controversial and have been the subject of many criticisms. *My purpose here is not to endorse them.* I was not involved in any aspect of the development of any beginning teacher assessment program, although I have proposed one for practicing English teachers (Smagorinsky 2014c). Many people have identified what they see as problems in these assessments (e.g., Gorlewski

2013; Meuwissen, Choppin, Cloonan, and Shang-Butler 2016). Rather than hashing through their beefs, I'll leave it to your Internet search skills to become informed on their benefits and hazards. I imagine that you'll be able to articulate a few of your own before you are done getting assessed.

Performance assessment requires you to perform a set of prescribed tasks, document your experiences with them, and demonstrate that you are a capable teacher through the means of evidence prescribed in the assessment. Because the documentation also involves explanation, you have the opportunity to think about your teaching and why you have adopted your particular approach. Conceivably, while proving to a stranger—one who uses a rubric designed by yet more strangers—that you can teach well, you might also be able, through systematic reflection, to articulate for yourself why you teach as you do.

I have long believed that teaching and research have much in common (Smagorinsky 1995). In particular, good teaching requires reflection, and systematic reflection may serve as a form of research. Having beginning teachers take on this disposition can be beneficial, then, in allowing for focused, intentional reflection on the consequences of teaching practices. But this potential is available only if the regimen that is required is viewed as authentic and informative by those on whom it is imposed and if the people going through the assessment process embrace it as a way to use reflective analysis of their performance as a means of professional growth.

Performance Assessment for Beginning Teachers

I've created some hypothetical tasks and rubrics based on some of the current national assessments as a way to analyze how they function. I intend to lay bare the assumptions and outline the educational traditions that I find embedded in common assessments and to identify what they suggest about how to demonstrate your teaching competence. This way, when you prepare your portfolio, you will understand what the assessors are looking for. I hope that my thought process will help you to break down the assessment required of you and approach it with confidence and ideally with an eye toward benefitting yourself as you satisfy the expectations of others.

There's a distinction between preparing for a performance assessment and preparing for a career in the classroom. Even though the exam serves as a gatekeeping mechanism, it should not determine how you teach outside the bounds of the assessment. Rather, it imposes the values of one tradition out of many on your teaching. Understanding this focus of the assessment may enable you to reflect on how you align your teaching with prior traditions and how traditions of teaching are built into the assumptions of any curriculum and all instruction. Just keep in mind that how you perform for the assessment should not determine how you teach when you have your own classroom.

The Assessment Process

The general question posed by assessors of beginning teachers is something along the lines of, "How can you show us that you are ready to do this job?" Your response to this question will be evaluated by hourly employees who are confined by the ticking of the clock so that they can complete their batch of dossiers within their pay period. Knowing this limitation should help you to respond appropriately to the prompts you are given. Let's say, hypothetically, that the prompt you are given includes a statement like the following: "In no more than nine single-spaced pages for each of the following prompts, respond in the spaces provided. If you exceed this page maximum, these pages in excess will not be scored."

This last part is important. If you describe the greatest teaching of all time, and if it takes you fifteen pages, and if you have been forewarned that only nine pages will be evaluated, then you have written six pages that nobody will ever read and that will not be considered in your assessment. Also, it's likely that if you write fewer than nine pages, it will work against you, because filling nine pages is part of the instructions.

So, as inappropriate as it might seem in an assessment built on the foundation of authenticity, when they say nine pages, write nine pages, no more and no less. That assessor going through a giant stack of dossiers submitted by strangers won't have the time or the investment in your future to assess you in ways that go outside the scope of what was stressed in the assessment training session. It's important to distinguish between the professors who know you and the assessors who don't. Your assessors will grade you without the sympathy you might get from someone who works directly with you, someone who knows you and cares about you as a person. This "objective" stance of assessors is considered to be a virtue of high-stakes standardized assessments administered across a large population, because your charming personality won't be a factor in your score. Just the evidence, thank you very much.

Tasks and Rubrics

Current performance assessments tend to be rubric-driven to provide consistency in evaluation and clear criteria for teacher candidates to align their work with. In performance assessment, they may be both rigid to the candidate and useful to the evaluator. Either way, they will always be part of the system, because they standardize the evaluation process.

Assessment categories tend to follow fairly uniform protocols. You'll probably be assessed on your demonstration of your skills in *instructional planning*. You'll then probably be assessed on your *instruction*, that is, your implementation of those teaching plans with students. Finally, you will likely be required to demonstrate the fairness and appropriateness of your *assessment* of student work.

Rubrics tend to work according to categories of performance, often settling on three or so levels. There will be a low, nonpassing category; a middle, passing-but-not-with-honors category; and a high performance category that shows that you really rock. If there are additional categories, they'll define performances somewhere in between. Your task is to align your portfolio with the categories that enable you to pass the assessment.

The tasks may require that you used cited scholarship to support your ideas. In other words, you can't just say that you are using a jigsaw discussion method because it's cool and it works well. You would need to say, "My use of jigsaw discussions is based on Clarke's (1994) method which, he argues, provides students an opportunity to actively help each other build comprehension." Note that 1994 was probably before you were born, and it's not a good idea to rely heavily on ancient citations. "Currency" should be a factor in your referencing. You might consider the wisdom of using as many citations as possible from recent years and not to rely too heavily on one source, even a totally awesome one like this book.

You also probably shouldn't reference your current teaching solely to ideas developed long ago, no matter how effective you find them. So, if you claim, "I relied on Kilpatrick's (1918) project method to provide my students with a constructivist task and active learning environment," be sure to add something contemporary at the end, such as (cf. Knoll 2014) so that you don't appear to be a century behind the times, even if old-school methods still work well. It's a good idea to keep a running list of sources on which you base your teaching throughout your teacher education program, so that you can have a nice catalogue to draw on as you assemble your portfolio.

A Breakdown of One Assessment Category

I will next break down one hypothetical *instructional planning* category that will resemble what you'll find in these performance assessments. I will borrow the general setup from current assessments that, in the prompt, provide a *focus* for each category, *sources of evidence* that you should provide in relation to this focus, *a guiding question* to keep in mind when preparing your documentation, *criteria* that the rubric provides for each level of performance, and an idea of *what the assessors look for* when seeing if you meet these criteria.

Focus, Sources of Evidence, and Guiding Question

I'll use a hypothetical task that is presented in accordance with the components I've seen on current performance assessments for beginning teachers. I intentionally borrow not only the tasks, but common assumptions I've seen built into the phrasing. These assumptions point to what an assessor will be taught to look for during training sessions and do not necessarily represent the views of your guide (*moi*).

> **Focus**: *Planning for understanding*
>
> **Sources of evidence**: You will find evidence for the implied claim of your response: "I know how to plan for students' understanding of the material." The evidence will likely come from lesson plans that you present and explain, along with those citations from instructional scholarship that suggested these methods to you.
>
> **Guiding question**: You might be provided with something like the following: "How do your plans build students' abilities to *understand* the material they are studying? In particular, how have you taught your students how to use *textual references* to construct meaning from, interpret, or *respond to complex texts*?"

I've italicized a few words because I think that they embody a whole belief system about what counts as knowledge. It's worth posing some questions about its assumptions, values, and purpose so that I know how the task is constraining what I should prepare in my documentation. Here's what I'd ask.

+ What is a "complex text," and how is it determined to be complex?

+ Must the text be written, or would another sign system's texts—paintings, music, architecture, computer images, and so on—be appropriate for this demonstration?

✦ Might the same text be "complex" to one reader (especially an assessor) and not complex to another? Or is complexity a property of the text itself?

✦ If the prompt locates meaning solely in the text, is it possible for me to refer to readers' personal constructions of meaning and still get a passing score on this item? Or is their understanding limited to their ability to break a text down technically such that their evidence comes from textual clues only?

✦ What if my students are in eleventh grade and struggle to read anything assigned in school, much less Faulkner's *Go Down, Moses*? Am I still required to teach my students texts that are complex to literate adults to meet this standard?

✦ To demonstrate my competency, should I teach to appropriate developmental levels of the students in front of me or to a standard that has been set outside my classroom, given that this is a standardized performance assessment?

✦ What does it mean to "understand" a text? And how do I know when a student has understood one?

✦ When the prompt says that I need to demonstrate how my students "respond to *complex texts*," how do I know what "respond to" allows in this assessment? What if their response is "I hate this story"? Is that "response" a good one to feature in this assessment?

That's a lot of questions for what might appear on the surface to be a simple prompt. To me, the prompt itself is actually a very complex text embedded with innumerable questions and assumptions. Your future, or at least the beginning of it, might well depend on how you answer these questions and those in the other categories as you go through the same assessment. So it's important to know how to interrogate their rhetoric in order to know how to respond appropriately.

Some assessments embrace definitions of text complexity issued by the Common Core State Standards (Common Core State Standards Initiative 2017). Here's how they figure out a text's complexity via their "Three-Part Model for Measuring Text Complexity":

> The Standards' model of text complexity consists of three equally important parts. (1) Qualitative dimensions of text complexity. In the Standards, qualitative dimensions and qualitative factors refer to those aspects of text complexity best measured or only measurable by an

attentive human reader, such as levels of meaning or purpose; structure; language conventionality and clarity; and knowledge demands. (2) Quantitative dimensions of text complexity. The terms *quantitative dimensions* and *quantitative factors* refer to those aspects of text complexity, such as word length or frequency, sentence length, and text cohesion, that are difficult if not impossible for a human reader to evaluate efficiently, especially in long texts, and are thus today typically measured by computer software. (3) Reader and task considerations. While the prior two elements of the model focus on the inherent complexity of text, variables specific to particular readers (such as motivation, knowledge, and experiences) and to particular tasks (such as purpose and the complexity of the task assigned and the questions posed) must also be considered when determining whether a text is appropriate for a given student. Such assessments are best made by teachers employing their professional judgment, experience, and knowledge of their students and the subject. (p. 4)

My main caveat here is that you don't get to score your own portfolio. Rather, an hourly wage assessor, trained in how to use rubrics prepared elsewhere, will. Although the language of these definitions suggests that your own professional judgment helps determine a text's complexity, in fact, someone else will be judging your professional judgment. I suggest erring on the side of superficial complexity that an assessor can easily see, rather than one that requires a lot of explanation and persuasion on your part, based on your own more sophisticated grasp of textual complexity. Your rationale may convince you, your professor, and your classmates that you are choosing complex texts in relation to your students and their circumstances; but not the person determining your score.

The Rubric and Its Criteria

One way to interpret a prompt's intentions is to look at how it will be assessed. Next I present a hypothetical rubric for this task, presented in order from lowest performance level to highest. Ordinarily, I'd start from high and work downward to low, but the rubrics are additive: After the first (failing) level, increasing levels of performance are presented as "everything from the previous category, but better." So we need to build from the bottom up to see what they are not looking for and then to understand what they view as performances of increasing quality.

This assessment is both a performance evaluation and a rhetorical task. Some assessments include components in which a video segment of your teaching, running 5–10 minutes, will be watched and evaluated according to a rubric. Assessors will see these brief exhibitions (which you may film multiple times to get right) but not the extended teaching that produces learning, relationships, and development over time. Aside from these videos, however, much of the assessment is based on your ability to represent your teaching in writing. You could conduct the world's most provocative classes in history and get low scores if your rhetorical presentation is not determined by assessors to meet the criteria that they are trained to evaluate. The task, then, requires you to demonstrate good teaching, but your score ultimately will be a function of your *representation of your teaching* through writing fluency and your ability to present the kinds of evidence that the assessors are looking for.

When you demonstrate your readiness to teach through video evidence—something perhaps required in the *instruction* segment of the assessment—the teaching that you film does not have to be perfect, although I recommend that it be pretty good. In preparing this evidence, pay attention to what the evaluators are trained to look for. Perhaps they will look for classes in which students interpret texts by interacting with each other, as well as with you, in discussion. If so, don't film yourself up there conducting a monologue, no matter how hypnotic your amazing lecture might be. The evaluator may also look for how you recognize and reflect on the strengths and shortcomings of your lesson, and the ways in which you discuss what you would do to improve it.

If you search the Internet, you'll find lots of stories about how to prepare the videos, and it's worth knowing what works according to people who've been through the process. As with your written evidence, what matters is your ability to analyze your own teaching thoughtfully and with an idea toward improvement, as long as you are teaching in interactive ways, using "complex texts" and teaching for interpretation, analysis, and the vague notion of "response."

In what follows, I'll give the real role of each scoring category, rather than the euphemism that is provided by the assessors. If your portfolio is awarded a 1 as the lowest possible score, and if they call it "Emerging" or "Basic" or "Developing," what they really mean is "You Fail." So don't pay attention to the name, which has been softened to ease the fall. Pay attention to how many points are awarded relative to how many you need to be allowed to teach.

Lowest Score (Failing). Again, I'll borrow language from existing assessments to create the rubric's criteria for this category. To teach in an unacceptable way, you should

1. Document your teaching with instructional plans that focus solely on literal comprehension of text. You should provide little or no opportunity for students to construct meaning from their reading or to interpret or respond to a "complex text;"

2. Teach such that you present inaccurate information that leads to student misunderstandings;

3. Teach so that your standards, objectives, tasks, and materials do not align with one another; and

4. Plan instruction in which students' learning of content and processes is only vaguely, or not at all, related to the "complex texts" studied or to students' efforts to construct meaning from, interpret, or respond to these texts.

The first item emphasizes teaching so that students engage at a deep level with a *complex text*. For most people, *Moby-Dick* is a complex text. But as a teacher, I had classes where the kids struggled to read *Scope* magazine. It was a complex text to them but probably not to portfolio assessors. Teaching for literal comprehension struck me as a good idea with kids who needed to start somewhere. Once the class got a rhythm, I could really help the kids with their writing and reading. But to feature such a class for my performance assessment, I might be making a questionable decision, even if I taught reading skills thoughtfully and effectively. Teaching for summary, even though it's long been considered an essential comprehension skill (The Commission on Reading 1985), would not be viewed as good teaching in the assessment, especially if the summary does not yield an inference or interpretation.

Always keep in mind that an assessor may know nothing more about literary reading than what was presented in a training session. You cannot take for granted that the assessor will ever have been a teacher, much less one in English/language arts. You'd be wise to think like an assessor trained by an assessment corporation, not like a critical university student, when deciding which lessons to feature for assessment purposes. I would choose a class in which the texts used meet a safe standard for complexity, not your own good judgment about what is appropriate for your own students.

Often the performance assessment requires you to provide a description of the students in the class. They want to know the number of students with Individualized Education Programs and 504 plans, which serve special needs students with accommodations, modifications, and other services. You will also identify the number of students for whom English is not a first language, who are not reading at the same rate as their peers, and who are behind grade level in a variety of ways. Further, you are prompted to explain the students' strengths and needs. In other words, you must account for the kinds of students enrolled in your class in light of general expectations for students at that grade level.

Doing so may help you justify a particular text as "complex" in your teaching. You should explain your selection of texts in terms of their complexity relative to your students' readiness to read and make sense of them, erring on the safe side when it comes to agreeing on what counts as a complex text. How you phrase your decisions is important. You shouldn't say, "I chose this text because it is easy enough for my students to read." Rather, you would say something like, "I chose this text because it is appropriately challenging to my students' reading levels. I placed the text at this point in the instructional sequence to help scaffold my students' growth in engaging with complex texts." As you can see, I'm using the assessors' own language to justify my teaching, even though that's not how I'd explain it to a friend.

I'm recommending, then, that you be highly pragmatic in preparing your portfolio and attentive to the language of the prompts and their implications. Perhaps, in addition to what you submit for assessment, you could reflect on the notion of text complexity and what it means in your teaching with your students and further reflect on how policies designed for uniformity have consequences for how you teach and grade your diverse students.

Teaching English by Design should help you with the criteria that emphasize alignment. If your goals (i.e., objectives) are aligned with the learning tasks (i.e., activities) and materials (i.e., texts), as this book emphasizes, then you should avoid this pitfall. Whether or not you have inaccuracies is more in your hands. If you think that Moby-Dick was Alexander the Great's horse, then there's not much I can do for you.

This criterion also emphasizes the idea of substantiating interpretations with textual references. If you teach a lesson on the great green shark Moby-Dick, for instance, you'd better be able to find a place in the novel where it's stated as such. As I understand this criterion, a teacher's knowledge of literary technique drives the assessors' judgment. Indeed, it seems clear that the interpretive emphasis is largely analytic, rather than creative. As alluring and effective as it might be to construct activities that don't include a formal analytic dimension, you might consider the wisdom of documenting your teaching ability with lessons that more clearly respond to how the criteria direct assessors' attention in their evaluations.

Assessors are given target evidence to look for when evaluating your portfolio and are trained to look for particular things on which to determine your satisfaction of the rubric's measures. The document might say something like, "The evidence that an assessor looks for should not be used as a checklist." However, given the limitations that assessors have in terms of time and attention, I suspect that they might indeed use these items as a checklist, and so it's worth paying attention to what they are looking for.

So, what are they looking for? If you wish to fail the assessment, you might be told that scores of 1 are awarded to planning that

+ Is teacher-centered rather than student-centered;

+ Involves literal comprehension rather than interpretation or response;

+ Does not allow students to develop subject-specific understandings;

+ Includes errors in information; and

+ Is not aligned with the instructional goals

The takeaway for me here is that the text itself must be one that allows for teaching beyond the literal. I further infer that if your teaching load includes students who struggle with reading, and if you believe that it is appropriate to use such texts as pop culture media to provide them a reason for reading (Alvermann 2016), then this class might not provide the best evidence of good teaching on an assessment employing this phrasing.

Using texts from pop culture might be a great way to teach for engagement. Students might, for instance, compare the representation of the entertainment icon Beyoncé on Fox News and BET. This task, however, would require a careful justification to explain how these texts are complex and how you have promoted inferential thinking by using them. You could easily persuade me. What's not clear is whether or not an assessor would be convinced enough to give you a high score. Good teaching, from this perspective, might not pass this assessment, *because it might not be the right kind of good teaching according to the phrasing of the prompts and rubrics and according to the emphasis of the assessors' training sessions.*

The other point worth making here concerns the directive to avoid "teacher-centered" teaching, such as, I assume, lectures or didactic lessons. Rather, the instruction featured should show how students learn how to engage with a text under your instructional guidance. Simply avoiding lectures does not guarantee that you will circumvent teacher-centered instruction. You could probably pull off a rhetorical smoke-and-mirrors show to make yourself sound learner-centered, even if your "discussions" are directed to produce the interpretation that you favor as a literary critic (Marshall, Smagorinsky, and Smith 1995) or if they involve only your most engaged students. You might be able to appear student-centered even if, by following the guidelines of the teacher's manual, you are reinforcing *status quo*, authoritarian values (Berchini

2016). The main point is that you need to present, in the context of this assessment, documentation and accompanying text that demonstrate that you have taught the students how to defend interpretations by arguing from textual evidence.

From a reflective standpoint, you might consider what it means to be teacher-centered or student-centered, and whether the rubric does or does not correspond to the beliefs you associate with these conceptions. I would not include this reflection in the portfolio, because assessors are not trained to regard your personal perspective as a legitimate point to include. However, it might well be worth thinking about to make your own judgments about which educational and literary traditions are built into the rubric, where they come from, how you do and do not agree with them, and how you might use this reflection to generate new ideas on how you might teach once you are beyond the demands of this performance assessment.

Medium Score (You Pass, But Could Have Done Better). As I said earlier, the rubrics tend to be additive. The criteria typically follow the same organization from score to score, but the expectations are greater with each level. The first level of passing performance takes the failing level's negatives and requires that they be positive. The criteria for this level might be something like this:

+ Document your teaching with instructional plans that move beyond literal comprehension of text. The successful candidate provides opportunities for students to construct meaning from their reading or to interpret or respond to a "complex text;"

+ Teach such that you present accurate information that leads to student understandings;

+ Teach so that your standards, objectives, tasks, and materials are reasonably well aligned with one another; and

+ Plan instruction in which students' learning of facts and procedures is related to the "complex texts" studied or to students' efforts to construct meaning from, interpret, or respond to these texts.

The method of instructional planning and teaching that I recommend in this book would be very useful in meeting these criteria, although the "complex text" dilemma remains. I emphasize plans that build on each other so that targeted literacy skills grow over the course of a conceptual unit. The whole notion of a "conceptual" unit suggests that the instruction is all related to a focus such as a theme or strategy. You should be very safe with this part of the rubric if this book makes sense to you.

Portfolios getting a score of 2 are centered on what appear to me to be analytic values of making points and illustrating them with relevant examples from the text.

In this book, I argue that argumentation of this sort is an important aspect of the English/language arts curriculum but not the exclusive approach to making intelligent meaning from texts. Even if you had your students draw a picture to depict *The Picture of Dorian Gray*, the assessment would require you to show how your students are using textual evidence as the basis for their interpretation. So although you might be able to make a case that students' interpretations of a complex text may be realized in artistic forms, without formal attention to textual evidence, an assessor will probably not treat it as good teaching.

Assessors are trained to look for the presence of learning tasks that are aligned with materials, goals, and other aspects of the overall design. If you establish and articulate goals that build understandings of the discipline of English/language arts, you are in good shape for meeting this expectation.

High Score (You Are a Rock Star). The third level of performance requires a candidate do everything required of a score of 2 and then some. The criteria require that you

+ Document your teaching with instructional plans that move well beyond literal comprehension of text. Highest-scoring candidates engagingly and provocatively provide opportunities for students to construct meaning from their reading or to interpret or respond to a "complex text;"

+ Teach such that you present relevant and accurate information that leads to student understandings;

+ Teach so that your standards, objectives, tasks, and materials are immaculately aligned with one another; and

+ Plan instruction in which students' learning of facts and procedures is clearly and unambiguously related to the "complex texts" studied or to students' efforts to construct meaning from, interpret, or respond to these texts.

Your rhetorical task here is to demonstrate that your teaching is purposeful and aligned. The assessors expect you to explain clearly how your students build the skill sets necessary to make textual inferences from challenging reading that are supported by textual examples. There are plenty of other good ways to teach. *But this is the sort of teaching assessed here.* Perhaps it's a sample of all teaching approaches. Perhaps it's a way to make the training and performance of assessors less expensive by narrowing the possibilities. Either way, this is the way it is, so it's in your interest to figure out how to do it right, with "right" defined as aligned with the higher rubric scores that the assessors are trained to use.

Teaching English by Design, as my commentary might suggest, is not wholly aligned with my hypothetical, if reality-based, performance assessment task and rubrics. The requirement to teach your students to interpret or "respond to" a "complex text" by drawing on textual evidence means that the students study a text and make sense of it in a discussion or essay in which they support claims with textual examples. That sounds like "literary analysis" to me, even though my own approach to engaging with literature suggests the potential of having students create interpretations through other forms of expression that needn't be so wedded to and justified solely by the literary text.

Traditions Invoked in Performance Assessment

When I make inferences about the values embedded in the criteria, I can trace the discourse to historical traditions of the philosophy of education. In the criteria I have hypothetically developed, traditional analytic conventions, originating in the European Enlightenment's rationalism and the "essayist tradition" that has followed from it (Farr 1993), are reinforced through the emphasis on "deep subject-specific understandings." I don't make this point to critique rationalism. I like rational thought and wish there were more of it. But my reading of the question, which would not be deemed terribly complex according to a "readability" formula, suggests that the best way to approach this assessment is through a rationalist lens, rather than one focused on, say, your sense of students' affective experiences with school. Because that's what the readers of your dossier will be doing.

High-scoring candidates are teaching in ways aligned with those of university professors for whom literary analysis is a way of life. This value is required of all teacher candidates, including those whose students are not college bound or who teach struggling readers. The values behind the rubric therefore suggest that candidates hoping to get the highest scores should demonstrate their teaching chops with the sort of students who help you look good in the eyes of the assessors.

There's an implication to me, then, that high-scoring teacher candidates are teaching students who are in a college preparatory curriculum that positions secondary school English as a way to get kids ready for being students in college English classes, rather than reading for pleasure and social engagement, as advocated by Smith, Wilhelm, and Fransen (2016). If you're looking for something to reflect on in meeting these criteria, you might consider whether college English is the ideal blueprint for all secondary English students, including those who find school to be tedious and irrelevant to their futures. Is formal literary criticism the most appropriate sort of textual engagement for them, or might they benefit from becoming literate in other ways? What is the purpose of a general education for all students? Is argumentation the principal means of engaging with a text? What is the role of other sorts of engagement in an English/language arts curriculum? These questions are important to consider, in spite of how your approach to teaching English is structured by the assessment prompts and rubrics.

And In Conclusion

I've tried to achieve a few goals with this chapter. Strategically, I've tried to lay bare the essentials of a reality-based, hypothetical performance assessment for preservice teachers. This way, you see the sorts of tasks involved and how to approach them, both in terms of understanding their hidden messages and in terms of getting a passing score. I have tried to break down a sample of a performance assessment to give you a process for interrogating the particular educational traditions that are manifested in their values and emphases.

I will leave the remaining analysis of performance assessments and their implications for your preparation of your portfolio to you and your classmates. Regardless of which performance assessment you face, I hope that this chapter is useful to you in preparing for and passing whatever your program of study requires of you.

I introduced performance assessment as an occasion for more than just passing an exam. These occasions serve as high-stakes, gate-keeping evaluations of your teaching. Going through the tasks and producing your portfolio may provide you with an opportunity to reflect on how its values are built into the expectations for what you will document. In thinking about the values of the assessment, you might ruminate on the degree to which your own values, based on your experiences as a student, your learning in your courses, your experiences in schools, and other factors are and are not aligned with what the assessment views as optimal teaching.

One thing that my own recent studies of teacher education have emphasized is the way in which teachers are torn among many competing influences. Universities and schools tend to operate according to different values, and you may well be experiencing tensions between the more constructivist, often romantic assumptions of universities and the hard, practical realities of classrooms. But those are only two among many competing value systems. Barnes and Smagorinsky (2016) include the following portrait, drawn by Michelle Zoss, of a beginning teacher trying to navigate a host of influences on a twisting, multidirectional pathway toward an approach to teaching.

This figure shows a teacher candidate being pulled in many different directions by a host of influences. It depicts how universities, rather than being stable and

Figure 16–1 Teacher trying to navigate competing influences

unified sites, provide competing influences between English and education courses, which typically conceive of curriculum, instruction, teachers, and students in different ways (Addington 2001). Schools, too, provide no singular perspective but have competing values within and across departments. Parents, students, and communities also try to shape teaching values and practices, and policies and bureaucracies further impose educational traditions on teachers. Finding your way in this maze, or even getting a sense of where your pathway is headed, can be vexing. I hope to show that there is no consensus on which values should guide teaching. What is embedded in any performance assessment is one of many ways of teaching effectively. It's your task, then, both to recognize whose traditions are valued in the assessment portfolio that you are required to produce and to recognize that other traditions are available to you when the assessment is over.

This is where my book ends and yours begins. I hope that by offering this approach to designing units and understanding performance assessment, I've helped to stimulate your thinking as you consider how to go about the complex, challenging, and ultimately satisfying work of designing instruction.

REFERENCES

Addington, A. H. 2001. "Talking About Literature in University Book Club and Seminar Settings." *Research in the Teaching of English*, 36: 212–48.

Alvermann, D. E. 2016. *Adolescents' Online Literacies: Connecting Classrooms, Digital Media & Popular Culture* (Revised edition). New York: Peter Lang.

American Association of University Women. 1995. *The AAUW Report: How Schools Shortchange Girls*. New York: Marlowe.

American Psychological Association. 2001. *Publication Manual of the American Psychological Association*. Washington, DC: Author.

Applebee, A. N. 1993. *Literature in the Secondary School: Studies of Curriculum and Instruction in the United States*. NCTE Research Report No. 25. Urbana, IL: National Council of Teachers of English.

———. 1996. *Curriculum as Conversation: Transforming Traditions of Teaching and Learning*. Chicago: University of Chicago Press.

Barnes, D. R. 1992. *From Communication to Curriculum*. 2nd ed. Portsmouth, NH: Heinemann.

Barnes, D. R., J. N. Britton, and M. Torbe. 1971. *Language, the Learner and the School*. Harmondsworth, UK: Penguin.

Barnes, M. E., and P. Smagorinsky. 2016. "What English/Language Arts Teacher Candidates Learn During Coursework and Practica: A Study of Three Teacher Education Programs." *Journal of Teacher Education*, 67(4): 338–55.

Berchini, C. 2016. "Curriculum Matters: The Common Core, Authors of Color, and Inclusion for Inclusion's Sake." *Journal of Adolescent & Adult Literacy*, 60(1): 55–62.

———. 2017. "Critiquing Un/Critical Pedagogies to Move Toward a Pedagogy of Responsibility in Teacher Education." *Journal of Teacher Education,* 68: 1–13.

Berchini, C., and P. Smagorinsky. 2018. "Calling All Writers: Using Cell Phones to Teach Argumentation and Other Genres." *Journal of Teaching Writing*, 33(1): 23–42.

Berliner, D. C. 2014. "Exogenous Variables and Value-Added Assessments: A Fatal Flaw." *Teachers College Record*, 116(1): 1–31.

Bomer, R., and K. Bomer. 2001. *For a Better World: Reading and Writing for Social Action*. Portsmouth, NH: Heinemann.

Bomer, R., J. E. Dworin, L. May, and P. Semingson. 2009, June 3. "What's Wrong with a Deficit Perspective?" *Teachers College Record*. Retrieved March 12, 2018 from http://www.tcrecord.org

Bransford, J. 1979. *Human Cognition: Learning, Understanding, and Remembering*. Belmont, CA: Wadsworth.

Brown, E. 2017, May 17. "With State Budget in Crisis, Many Oklahoma Schools Hold Classes Four Days a Week." *Washington Post*. Retrieved May 28, 2017 from https://www.washingtonpost.com/local/education/with-state-budget-in-crisis-many-oklahoma-schools-hold-classes-four-days-a-week/2017/05/27/24f73288-3cb8-11e7-8854-21f359183e8c_storyhtml?utm_term=.6ec6bfefce57

Bruner, J. S. 1975. "The Ontogenesis of Speech Acts." *Journal of Child Language* 2: 1–40.

———. 1986. *Actual Minds, Possible Worlds*. Cambridge, MA: Harvard University Press.

Cahnmann-Taylor, M., and M. Souto-Manning. 2010. *Teachers Act Up: Creating Multicultural Learning Communities Through Theatre*. New York: Teachers College Press.

Clark, C. A. C., H. Fang, K. A. Espy, P. A. Filipek, J. Juranek, B. Bangert, M. Hack, and H. G. Taylor. 2013. "Relation of Neural Structure to Persistently Low Academic Achievement: A Longitudinal Study of Children with Differing Birth Weights." *Neuropsychology,* 27(3): 364–77.

Clarke, J. 1994. "Pieces of the Puzzle: The Jigsaw Method." In *Handbook of Cooperative Learning Methods*, ed. S. Sharan, 34–50. Westport CT: Greenwood Press.

Coleman, D., and S. Pimentel. 2012. *Revised Publishers' Criteria for the Common Core State Standards in English Language Arts and Literacy, Grades K–2*. Common Core State Standards. Available at http://www.corestandards.org/assets/Publishers_Criteria_for_K-2.pdf

The Commission on Reading. 1985. *Becoming a Nation of Readers*. Washington, D.C.: The National Institute of Education, The National Academy of Education. The Center for the Study of Reading.

Common Core State Standards Initiative. 2017. "Appendix A: Common Core State standards for English Language Arts & Literacy in History/Social Studies, Science, and Technical Subjects." Retrieved January 16, 2017 from http://www.corestandards.org/assets/Appendix_A.pdf

Connors, R. J., and A. A. Lunsford. 1988. "Frequency of Formal Errors in Current College Writing, or Ma and Pa Kettle Do Research." *College Composition and Communication* 39: 395–409.

Cotner, C. 1996. Untitled collage. *English Journal*, 85(5): 62.

Csikszentmihalyi, M. 1990. *Flow: The Psychology of Optimal Experience*. New York: Harper and Row.

Cushman, E. 1999. "Critical Literacy and Institutional Language." *Research in the Teaching of English,* 33(3): 245–74.

Darder, A., M. P. Boltodano, and R. D. Torres, eds. 2009. *The Critical Pedagogy Reader* (2nd ed.). New York: Routledge.

Delpit, L. D. 1995. *Other People's Children: Cultural Conflict in the Classroom.* New York: New Press.

Dewey, J. 1934. *Art as Experience.* New York: Berkeley.

Dixon, J. 1975. *Growth Through English: Set in the Perspective of the Seventies.* London: Oxford University Press for the National Association for the Teaching of English.

Doob, C. B. 2013. *Social Inequality and Social Stratification in US Society.* Upper Saddle River, NJ: Pearson.

Dreher, R. 2014, August 1. "When Poverty Is the Fault of the Poor." *The American Conservative*. Retrieved January 27, 2017 from http://www.theamericanconservative.com/dreher/poverty-the-fault-of-the-poor/

du Plessis, A. E., A. Carroll, and R. M. Gillies. 2014. "The Meaning of Out-of-Field Teaching for Educational Leadership." *International Journal of Leadership in Education, 17,* 87–112.

Dyson, A. H. 1990. "Weaving Possibilities: Rethinking Metaphors for Early Literacy Development." *The Reading Teacher, 44*: 202–213.

Edutopia. 2016. *53 Ways to Check for Understanding.* Retrieved May 25, 2017 from https://www.edutopia.org/sites/default/files/resources/edutopia-finley-53-ways-to-check-understanding-2016.pdf

Eisner, E., ed. 1985. *Learning and Teaching the Ways of Knowing*. Eighty-Fourth Yearbook of the National Society for the Study of Education, Part II. Chicago: University of Chicago Press.

Emdin, C. 2016. *For White Folks Who Teach in the Hood . . . And the Rest of Y'all Too*. Boston, MA: Beacon Press.

Enciso, P. (1992). Creating The Story World: A Case Study of a Young Reader's Engagement Strategies and Stances. In J. Many & C. Cox (Eds.), *Reader Stance and Literary Understanding: Exploring the Theories, Research, and Practice* (pp. 75–102). Norwood, NJ: Ablex.

FairTest. 2012, May 22. *What's Wrong with Standardized Tests?* Jamaica Plain, MA: Author. Retrieved January 27, 2017 from http://www.fairtest.org/facts/whatwron.htm

Farr, M. 1993. "Essayist Literacy and Other Verbal Performances." *Written Communication,* 10(1): 4-38.

Figueroa, Q. 2015, March 29. "Poor People Choose to be Poor." *Slayerment*. Retrieved January 24, 2017 from http://www.slayerment.com/poor-people-choose-be-poor

Foster, M. 2004. "An Innovative Professional Development Program for Urban Teachers." *Phi Delta Kappan*, 85(5): 401–406.

Four Arrows. 2013. *Teaching Truly: A Curriculum to Indigenize Mainstream Education*. New York: Peter Lang.

Freedman, S. W., E. R. Simons, J. S. Kalnin, A. Casareno, and the M-CLASS Teams. 1999. *Inside City Schools: Investigating Literacy in Multicultural Classrooms*. New York: Teachers College Press.

Freire, P. 1970. *Pedagogy of the Oppressed*. New York: Continuum.

Georgia Department of Education. 2015. *Georgia Milestones Assessment System*. Atlanta, GA: Author. Retrieved March 24, 2017 from http://www.gadoe.org/Curriculum-Instruction-and-Assessment/Assessment/Pages/Georgia-Milestones-Assessment-System.aspx

Goldberg, E. 2015, September 15. "Number of Homeless Public School Students Hits Record High. Here's Who's Helping." *The Huffington Post*. Retrieved February 1, 2017 from http://www.huffingtonpost.com/entry/homeless-public-school-students_us_55f997bce4b0b48f67018e4a

Gorlewski, J. 2013, June 3. "What Is edTPA and Why Do Critics Dislike It?" *Diane Ravitch's Blog*. Retrieved October 28, 2016 from https://dianeravitch .net/2013/06/03/what-is-edtpa-and-why-do-critics-dislike-it/

Haidt, J. 2012. *The Righteous Mind: Why Good People Are Divided by Politics and Religion*. New York: Vintage.

Hairston, M. 1981. "Not All Errors Are Created Equal: Nonacademic Readers in the Professions Respond to Lapses in Usage." *College English*, 43: 794–806.

Hartlep, N. D., and B. J. Porfilio, eds. 2015. *Killing the Model Minority Stereotype: Asian American Counterstories and Complicity*. Charlotte, NC: Information Age Press.

Hillocks, G. 1972. *Observing and Writing*. Urbana, IL: National Council of Teachers of English.

———. 1986. *Research on Written Composition: New Directions for Teaching*. Urbana, IL: ERIC Clearinghouse on Reading and Communications Skills and National Conference on Research in English.

———. 1995. *Teaching Writing as Reflective Practice*. New York: Teachers College Press.

———. 2002. *The Testing Trap: How State Writing Assessments Control Learning*. New York: Teachers College Press.

———. 2007. *Narrative Writing: Learning a New Model for Teaching*. Portsmouth, NH: Heinemann.

Hillocks, G., B. McCabe, and J. McCampbell. 1971. *The Dynamics of English Instruction, Grades 7–12*. New York: Random House.

Johnson, L. L., N. Sieben, and D. Buxton. 2018. "Collaborative Design as Mediated Praxis: Professional Development for Socially Just Pedagogies." *English Education*, 50(2): 172–98.

Johnson, L. L., and P. Smagorinsky. in press. "Beyond Publication: Social Action as the Ultimate Stage of a Writing Process." *L1-Educational Studies of Language and Literature*

Johnson, T. S., Smagorinsky, P., Thompson, L., & Fry, P. G. 2003. Learning to Teach the Five-Paragraph Theme. *Research in the Teaching of English, 38*: 136-176.

Jones, S. 2006. *Girls, Social Class, and Literacy: What Teachers Can Do to Make a Difference*. Portsmouth, NH: Heinemann.

Jupp, J. C., T. R. Berry, and T. J. Lensmire. 2016. "Second-Wave White Teacher Identity Studies: A Review of White Teacher Identity Literatures from 2004 through 2014." *Review of Educational Research*, 86(4): 1151–91.

Kilpatrick, W. H. 1918, September. "The Project Method." *Teachers College Record,* 19: 319–35.

Kim, M. S. 2012. Cultural-Historical Activity Theory Perspectives on the Construction of ICT-Mediated Teaching Metaphors. *European Journal of Teacher Education, 35*(4), 435-48.

Kinloch, V., and K. Dixon. 2018. "Professional Development as Publicly Engaged Scholarship in Urban Schools: Implications for Educational Justice, Equity, and Humanization." *English Education*, 50(2): 147–71.

Kirkland, D. E. 2011. "Books Like Clothes: Engaging Young Black Men with Reading." *Journal of Adult and Adolescent Literacy*, 55(3):199–208.

Knoll, M. 2014. Project Method. In *Encyclopedia of Educational Theory and Philosophy*, Vol. 2, ed. D. C. Phillips, 665–69. London, UK: Sage.

Kohn, A. 2006. "The Trouble with Rubrics." *English Journal, 95*(4): 12–15.

Korte, G. 2016, September 30. "White House Wants to Add New Racial Category for Middle Eastern People." *USA Today*. Retrieved January 29, 2017 from http://www.usatoday.com/news/

Kozol, J. 1992. *Savage Inequalities: Children in America's Schools*. New York: Harper Perennial.

Ladson-Billings, G. 1998. "Just What is Critical Race Theory and What's It Doing in a *Nice* Field Like Education?" *Qualitative Studies in Education*, 11(1): 7–24.

Langer, J. A., and A. N. Applebee. 1987. *How Writing Shapes Thinking: A Study of Teaching and Learning*. NCTE Research Report No. 22. Urbana, IL: National Council of Teachers of English.

Le, C. N. 2012. *A Closer Look at Asian Americans and Education*. Retrieved December 2, 2014, from http://education.jhu.edu/pd/newhorizons/strategies/topics/multicultural-education/a%20closer%20look%20at%20asian%20americans%20and%20education

LeCompte, M. D., and A. G. Dworkin. 1991. *Giving Up on School: Student Dropouts and Teacher Burnouts*. Thousand Oaks, CA: Corwin.

Lee, C. D. 1993. *Signifying as a Scaffold for Literary Interpretation: The Pedagogical Implications of an African American Discourse Genre*. Urbana, IL: National Council of Teachers of English.

———. 2000. "Signifying in the Zone of Proximal Development." In *Vygotskian Perspectives on Literacy Development: Constructing Meaning Through Collaborative Inquiry*, ed. C. D. Lee and P. Smagorinsky, 191–225. New York: Cambridge University Press.

Lipsitz, G. 2006. *The Possessive Investment in Whiteness: How White People Profit from Identity Politics*. Philadelphia, PA: Temple University Press.

Loewen, J. W. 1995. *Lies My Teacher Told Me: Everything Your American History Textbook Got Wrong*. New York: Touchstone.

Majors, Y. J. 2015. *Shoptalk: Lessons in Teaching from an African American Hair Salon*. New York: Teachers College Press.

Marshall, J. D., P. Smagorinsky, and M. W. Smith. 1995. *The Language of Interpretation: Patterns of Discourse in Discussions of Literature*. NCTE Research Report No. 27. Urbana, IL: National Council of Teachers of English.

Matias, C. E. 2013. "On the 'Flip' Side: A Teacher Educator of Color Unveiling the Dangerous Minds of White Teacher Candidates." *Teacher Education Quarterly*, 40(2): 53–73.

Meuwissen, K., J. Choppin, K. Cloonan, K., and H. Shang-Butler. 2016. *Teaching Candidates' Experiences with the edTPA as an Initial Certification Test in New York and Washington States: Survey Results from the Second Year of a Two-Year Study*. Rochester, NY: Warner School of Education, University of Rochester. Retrieved October 28, 2016 from https://www.warner.rochester.edu/files/research/files/2016edTPAreport.pdf

Milner, H. R. 2015. *Rac(e)ing to Class: Confronting Poverty and Race in Schools and Classrooms*. Cambridge, MA: Harvard Education Press.

Moll, L. C. 2000. "Inspired by Vygotsky: Ethnographic Experiments in Education." In *Vygotskian Perspectives on Literacy Development: Constructing Meaning Through Collaborative Inquiry*, ed. C. D. Lee and P. Smagorinsky, 256–68. New York: Cambridge University Press.

Morrison, T. 1992. *Playing in the Dark: Whiteness and the Literary Imagination*. Cambridge, MA: Harvard University Press.

Newman, D., P. Griffin, and M. Cole. 1989. *The Construction Zone: Working for Cognitive Change in School*. New York: Cambridge University Press.

Nystrand, M. 1986. *The Structure of Written Communication: Studies in Reciprocity Between Writers and Readers*. Orlando, FL: Academic.

O'Donnell-Allen, C. 2006. *The Book Club Companion: Fostering Strategic Readers in the Secondary Classroom*. Portsmouth, NH: Heinemann.

Pooley, R. C. 1954. "Grammar in the Schools of Today." *The English Journal*, 43(3): 142–46.

Reid, L. 2006. "From the Editor." *English Journal*, 95(5): 12–14.

Rhym, D. 2018. *Where Do Rappers Come From?: Hip-Hop as a Remixing of the African-American Oral Tradition and How It Engaged Three African-American Students*. Unpublished doctoral dissertation, The University of Georgia.

Rodríguez, L. F. 2014. *The Time Is Now: Understanding and Responding to the Black and Latina/o Dropout Crisis in the U.S.* New York: Peter Lang.

Rodríguez, R. J. 2016. *Enacting Adolescent Literacies Across Communities: Latino/A Scribes and Their Rites*. Lanham, MD: Rowman & Littlefield.

Rosenblatt, L. M. 1978. *The Reader, the Text, the Poem: The Transactional Theory of Literary Response*. Carbondale, IL: Southern Illinois University Press.

———. 1938/1996. *Literature as Exploration*. 5th ed. New York: Modern Language Association.

Searle, D. 1984. "Scaffolding: Who's Building Whose Building?" *Language Arts*, 61: 480–83.

Shaughnessy, M. P. 1977. *Errors and Expectations: A Guide for the Teacher of Basic Writing*. New York: Oxford University Press.

Singh, R. 2012, May 8. "Minority Report: The Role of Race in Hiring." *ERE Media*. Retrieved January 29, 2017 from https://www.eremedia.com/ere/minority -report-the-role-of-race-in-hiring/

Smagorinsky, P. 1994. "Bring the Court Room to the Classroom: Develop Civic Awareness with Simulation Activities." *The Social Studies, 85*: 174–80.

———. 1995. "The Social Construction of Data: Methodological Problems of Investigating Learning in the Zone of Proximal Development." *Review of Educational Research, 65*: 191–212.

———. 2013. "The Development of Social and Practical Concepts in Learning to Teach: A Synthesis and Extension of Vygotsky's Conception." *Learning, Culture, and Social Interaction, 2*(4): 238–48.

———. 2014a, July 17. "Viewing Every Black Student as At-Risk: Are We Pathologizing Children Rather Than Helping Them?" *Atlanta Journal-Constitution*. Retrieved March 9, 2018 from http://www.petersmagorinsky.net/About/PDF /Op-Ed/BlackAtrisk.html

————. 2014b, July 19. "The Ideal Head: Bizarre Racial Teachings from a 1906 Textbook." *The Atlantic*. Retrieved January 29, 2017 from http://www .theatlantic.com/education/archive/2014/07/the-ideal-head-bizarre -racial-teachings-from-a-100-year-old-textbook/374693/

————. 2014c. "Authentic Teacher Evaluation: A Two-Tiered Proposal for Formative and Summative Assessment." *English Education*, 46(2): 165–85.

————. 2016a. "Adaptation as Reciprocal Dynamic." In *Creativity and Community Among Autism-Spectrum Youth: Creating Positive Social Updrafts Through Play and Performance*, ed. P. Smagorinsky, 51–76. New York: Palgrave Macmillan.

————. 2016b. "Huck and Kim: Would Teachers Feel the Same If the Language Were Misogynist?" *English Journal,* 106(2): 75–80.

————. 2016c, November 29. "Common Core Turns Students into Literary Critics. Does It Turn Them into Lifelong Readers?" *Atlanta Journal-Constitution*. Available at http://getschooled.blog.myajc.com/2016/11/29/common-core -turns-students-into-literary-critics-does-it-turn-them-into-lifelong-readers/

————. 2017. "Misfits in School Literacy: Whom are U. S. Schools Designed to Serve?" In *Adolescent Literacy: A Handbook of Practice-Based Research*, eds. D. Appleman and K. Hinchman, 199–214. New York: Guilford.

————. 2018a. Literacy in Teacher Education: "It's the Context, Stupid." *Journal of Literacy Research, 50*(3): 281–303.

————. 2018b. "Deconflating The ZPD and Instructional Scaffolding: Retranslating and Reconceiving the Zone of Proximal Development as the Zone of Next Development." *Learning, Culture and Social Interaction.*

————. 2018c. "Emotion, Reason, and Argument: Teaching Persuasive Writing in Tense Times." *English Journal*, 107(5): 98–101.

————. 2018d, February 14. "When Schools Mine Data to Death, Teacher Spirit Also Dies." *Atlanta Journal-Constitution*. Retrieved March 3, 2018 from http://www.petersmagorinsky.net/About/PDF/Op-Ed/DataMining.html

Smagorinsky, P., L. S. Cook, and T. S. Johnson. 2003. "The Twisting Path of Concept Development in Learning to Teach." *Teachers College Record,* 105: 1399¬436.

Smagorinsky, P., L. R. Johannessen, E. A. Kahn, and T. M. McCann. 2010. *The Dynamics of Writing Instruction: A Structured Process Approach for Middle and High School*. Portsmouth, NH: Heinemann.

Smagorinsky, P., T. McCann, and S. Kern. 1987. *Explorations: Introductory Activities for Literature and Composition, Grades 7–12*. Urbana, IL: National Council of Teachers of English.

Smagorinsky, P., and J. Taxel. 2005. *The Discourse of Character Education: Culture Wars in the Classroom*. Mahwah, NJ: Erlbaum.

Smith, M. W. 1991. *Understanding Unreliable Narrators: Reading Between the Lines in the Literature Classroom*. Urbana, IL: National Council of Teachers of English.

Smith, M. W., J. D. Wilhelm, and S. Fransen. 2016. "The Power of Fostering Pleasure in Reading." In *Adolescent Literacy: A Handbook of Practice-Based Research*, eds. D. Appleman and K. Hinchman, 169–81. New York: Guilford.

Smitherman, G. 2006. *Word from the Mother: Language and African Americans*. New York: Routledge.

Sommers, C. H. 2000. *The War Against Boys: How Misguided Feminism Is Harming Our Young Men*. New York: Simon and Schuster.

Stovall, D. 2006. "Forging Community in Race and Class: Critical Race Theory and the Quest for Social Justice in Education." *Race, Ethnicity and Education*, 9(3): 243–59.

Strong, W. 1994. *Sentence Combining: A Composing Book*. 3rd ed. New York: Random House/McGraw-Hill.

Tall Bull, L. 2007. *Preserving Our Histories for Those Approaches to Literacy in Development, Ethnography, and Education*. New York: Longman.

The Education Trust. 2008, Nov. 25. "CORE PROBLEMS: Out-of-Field Teaching Persists in Key Academic Courses, Especially in America's High-Poverty and High-Minority Schools." Washington, DC: Author. Retrieved February 26, 2017 from https://edtrust.org/press_release/core-problems-out-of-field-teaching-persists-in-key-academic-courses-especially-in-americas-high-poverty-and-high-minority-schools/

US Department of Education Office for Civil Rights. (2016). *A First Look: Key Data Highlights on Equity and Opportunity Gaps in Our Nation's Public Schools*. Retrieved April 24, 2018 from https://www2.ed.gov/about/offices/list/ocr/docs/2013-14-first-look.pdf

Vygotsky, L. S. 1962. *Thought and Language*. Cambridge, MA: MIT Press.

———. 1987. Thinking and Speech. In L. S. Vygotsky, *Collected works* (Vol. 1, pp. 39–285) (R. Rieber and A. Carton, eds.; N. Minick, trans.). New York: Plenum.

Weaver, C. 1996. *Teaching Grammar in Context*. Portsmouth, NH: Heinemann.

Wilhelm, J. D. 1997. *You Gotta BE the Book: Teaching Engaged and Reflective Reading with Adolescents*. New York: Teachers College Press.

Young, E. Y. 2011. "The Four Personae of Racism: Educators' (Mis)Understanding of Individual Vs. Systemic Racism." *Urban Education*, 46(6): 1433–60.

Quiz: What is the name of the author's cat?

INDEX